THE VÖLSUNG BALLADS FROM THE FAROE ISLANDS IN ENGLISH TRANSLATION

FOUNDATIONS

Further Information and Publications

www.arc-humanities.org/series/book-series/

THE VÖLSUNG BALLADS FROM THE FAROE ISLANDS

IN ENGLISH TRANSLATION

Translated from Faroese by

HELEN F. LESLIE-JACOBSEN

and **MORTAN NOLSØE JACOBSEN**

ARC HUMANITIES PRESS

British Library Cataloguing in Publication Data
A catalogue record for this book is available from the British Library.

ISBN (Hardback): 9781802700428
ISBN (Paperback): 9781802703313
e-ISBN (PDF): 9781802703306
e-ISBN (EPUB): 9781802703290

www.arc-humanities.org

Printed and bound in the UK (by CPIGroup [UK] Ltd), USA (by Bookmasters), and elsewhere using print-on-demand technology.

Publisher (manufacturer) details: Arc Humanities Press, 14 Clifton Moor Business Village, James Nicolson Link, York YO30 4XG, United Kingdom.

EU Authorised Representative details (for GPSR purposes): Amsterdam University Press, Nieuwe Prinsengracht 89, 1018 VR Amsterdam, The Netherlands. www.aup.nl

CONTENTS

Abbreviations vii

Preface and Acknowledgements ix

HELEN F. LESLIE-JACOBSEN — Ballads on the Faroe Islands 1

Characteristics of the Faroese Ballads 3

The Medieval Origins of Faroese Ballads 8

Faroese Ballads in the Early Modern Period Onwards 10

Faroese Ballads Today 14

The Legend of Sigurd the Dragon-Slayer 16

Manuscripts of the Ballads 18

Scholarly Work on the Ballads 21

About the Translations in this Book 24

THE BALLADS

Regin the Smith (*Regin smiður*) 27

The Ballad of Brynhild (*Brynhildar táttur*) 46

The Ballad of Høgni (*Høgna táttur*) 85

The Second Ballad of Høgni or *The Ballad of Aldrias* (*Annar Høgna táttur* or *Aldrias táttur*) 108

The Ballad of Gestur or *The Ballad of Ásla* (*Gests ríma* or *Áslu ríma*) 115

The Ballad of Nornagestur (*Nornagests ríma*) 119

Ísmal the Brave Hero (*Ísmal fræga kempa*) 123

Sjúrður and the Dwarf Maiden or *Dwarf Maiden I* (*Sjúrður og Dvørgamoy* or *Dvørgamoy I*) 132

The Beautiful Dwarf Maiden or *Dwarf Maiden II* (*Dvørgamoyggin fagra* or *Dvørgamoy II*) 141

Ása the Dwarf Maiden or *Dwarf Maiden III*
(*Ása Dvørgamoy* or *Dvørgamoy III*) 149

The Ballad of Kvørfinn or *Dwarf Maiden V*
(*Kvørfinns táttur* or *Dvørgamoy V*) 158

The Giant of Hólmgarðar or *The Mound Ghost*
(*Risin í Hólmgørðum* or *Dysjadólgur*) 170

The Giant of Leittraberg (*Risin av Leittrabergi*) 176

HELEN F. LESLIE-JACOBSEN — Summaries of the Ballads

Regin the Smith (*Regin smiður*) 191

The Ballad of Brynhild (*Brynhildar táttur*) 192

The Ballad of Høgni (*Høgna táttur*) 195

The Second Ballad of Høgni or *The Ballad of Aldrias*
(*Annar Høgna táttur* or *Aldrias táttur*) 198

The Ballad of Gestur or *The Ballad of Ásla*
(*Gests ríma* or *Áslu ríma*) 198

The Ballad of Nornagestur (*Nornagests ríma*) 199

Ísmal the Brave Hero (*Ísmal fræga kempa*) 200

Sjúrður and the Dwarf Maiden or *Dwarf Maiden I*
(*Sjúrður og Dvørgamoy* or *Dvørgamoy I*) 201

The Beautiful Dwarf Maiden or *Dwarf Maiden II*
(*Dvørgamoyggin fagra* or *Dvørgamoy II*) 202

Ása the Dwarf Maiden or *Dwarf Maiden III*
(*Ása Dvørgamoy* or *Dvørgamoy III*) 203

The Ballad of Kvørfinn or *Dwarf Maiden V*
(*Kvørfinns táttur* or *Dvørgamoy V*) 204

The Giant of Hólmgarðar or *The Mound Ghost*
(*Risin í Hólmgørðum* or *Dysjadólgur*) 206

The Giant of Leittraberg (*Risin av Leittrabergi*) 206

Bibliography 209

ABBREVIATIONS

CCF	CCF numbers refer to the number of the ballad in Svend Grundtvig and Jørgen Bloch, eds. *Føroya kvæði: Corpus Carminum Færoensium*. Vols. 1–6. Copenhagen: Munksgaard, 1941–1972.
DgF	Svend Grundtvig, ed. *Danmarks gamle Folkeviser*. 12 vols. Copenhagen: Selskabet til den danske Literaturs Fremme, 1853–1976.
EYL	EYL numbers refer to *kvæði* melodies of texts not included in CCF. See Marianne Clausen. *Løgini / Melodies*. Vol. 8 of *Føroya kvæði: Corpus Carminum Færoensium*. Universitetsjubilæets danske Samfund 559. Hoyvík: Stiðin, 2003.
Fugloyarbók	Copenhagen, Den Arnamagnænske Samling, AM Acc. 4 a.
GKS 2894 I	Copenhagen, Det Kongelige Bibliotek, GKS 2894 I.
NF	M. B. Landstad, ed. *Norske folkeviser*. Christiania [Oslo]: Tönsbergs, 1853.
NKS 345 8vo	Copenhagen, Det Kongelige Bibliotek, NKS 345 8vo.
Sandoyarbók	Copenhagen, Dansk Folkemindesamling, DFS 68.
SMB	Bengt R. Jonsson, Margareta Jersild, and Sven-Bertil Jansson, eds. *Sveriges medeltida ballader*. Stockholm: Svenskt visarkiv, 1983–2001.
TSB	Bengt R. Jonsson, Svale Solheim, and Eva Danielson, eds. *The Types of the Scandinavian Medieval Ballad: A Descriptive Catalogue*. Skrifter utgivna av svenskt visarkiv 5. Stockholm: Svenskt visarkiv, 1978.
Utsyn	L. Heggstad and H. Grüner Nielsen, eds. *Utsyn yver gamall norsk folkevisedikting*. Kristiania [Oslo]: Norli, 1912.
*	Asterisks within the text of the Faroese ballads denote that a reading is conjectural or is an emendation.

PREFACE AND ACKNOWLEDGEMENTS

THE IDEA BEHIND offering a volume of English translations is to encourage more people who do not have Faroese as a native language to learn about the literature, language, and culture of the Faroe Islands. It is hoped that the English translation and notes will be helpful aids in engaging with the original sources. It should also be said that the selection of ballads here (those about the hero Sjúrður, known in Old Norse as Sigurðr Fáfnisbani) should not be perceived as being the best, most sung, or more valued on the Faroes by those participating in the still-living ballad tradition. Indeed, they have been selected because they are amongst those best known abroad and are comparable to material found in the Old Norse world. We therefore hope that the selection will be of particular interest to those working in Nordic, medieval, and Old Norse studies and those interested in Faroese ballads in general.

We would like to thank Universitets-Jubilæets danske Samfund for permission to reproduce the Faroese text of the ballads from volume one of *Føroya kvæði: Corpus Carminum Færoensium*, published by Einar Munksgaard in Copenhagen in 1951.

We acknowledge the support of the Centre for Advanced Study (CAS) in Oslo, Norway, which funded and hosted the Young CAS research project *Ballads Across Borders: The Faroe Islands in the Norse Story-Telling World* during the 2021–2023 academic years, led by Helen F. Leslie-Jacobsen. The generous funding from CAS has made the open access publication of this volume possible. The participants of this project also workshopped the translations of the first three ballads in this book, and we are very grateful for their corrections and comments. We are also grateful to Saskia Cowan for her participation in the second phase of the project in 2024.

We would also like to thank the members of the Research Group for Medieval Philology at the University of Bergen who gave feedback on the introduction, and to fagutvalget i norrøn filologi (the official student group for Old Norse philology at the University of Bergen) for their enthusiasm for the project. Annika Christensen deserves thanks for her feedback on the introduction, copyediting, and for tackling the layout of the ballads into two columns. Fredrik Charpentier Ljungqvist also deserves thanks for help with formatting. Ambra Ventura deserves thanks for correcting the digital edition of the Faroese text against the printed edition. We would like to thank Julia Skinner, Jens Eike Schnall, David Carrillo-Rangel, Signe Nilssen, and Anna Bohlin for their long-term support for the project. We would also like to thank the team at Arc Humanities Press, especially Anna Henderson, Tania Colwell, and Emily Morgan Harless. All remaining errors are unfortunately our own.

BALLADS ON THE FAROE ISLANDS

HELEN F. LESLIE-JACOBSEN

THE FAROE ISLANDS are a small archipelago country in the North Atlantic Ocean with a truly unique story-telling heritage; this introduction and volume of translations explores how this community preserved and transmitted some of the most exciting and enduring stories from Germanic legend. To say "preserved and transmitted" in the past tense is perhaps not completely correct, because the Faroese ballad tradition is still living. The ballads are a key element of the vibrant Faroese folk tradition and the ballads presented in this volume, although they have their roots in the Middle Ages, are still sung and danced in the Faroe Islands to this day.[1] The goal of this volume is simple: to introduce the Faroese ballads preserving material from the Völsung legend to a wider audience and to make them accessible to students, scholars, and those generally interested. Ballads on the Faroe Islands have been collected, written in manuscripts, recorded, and published in print. This introductory essay gives an overview of how this happened, how ballads are present in contemporary Faroese culture, and the characteristics of the Faroese ballad tradition.

The Norse settled on the Faroe Islands permanently in the ninth century, bringing with them their language, culture, and storytelling traditions, which from the Middle Ages were transmitted in the Faroe Islands in ballad form.[2] Faroese ballads are dance narratives, often very lengthy and accompanied by a distinctive ring dance.[3] The Faroese language is descended from Old West Norse, but unlike the Old Norse culture in Iceland, the Faroe Islands did not have a written literary culture in the Middle Ages and early modern period.[4] Danish was the official language of the islands and written Faro-

---

1 For oral poetry to the present on the Faroe Islands, see Marnersdóttir, "From Oral Poetry to Rap."

2 For an excellent overview of Faroese social and cultural history, especially in connection with its literature, see Marnersdóttir and Sigurðardóttir, *Føroysk bókmentasøga*. Otherwise, for an accessible overview in English of Faroese history, see Wylie, *The Faroe Islands*.

3 See Árnadóttir, "Chain Dancing"; Isaksen, "Kvadene," 42–44; Opielka, "Færøerne og den færøske dans"; Jacobsen, *Tekster til den færøske folkevise-dans*, 7–10.

4 From the time of settlement to the late twelfth century, the Faroe Islands were a separate legal entity. They were subject to the Norwegian crown by the 1180s and entered the Kalmar Union in the late fourteenth century as a Norwegian territory. At

ese was not countenanced; nevertheless, the native population developed a rich oral tradition consisting of ballads and folk tales, which helped to preserve the Faroese language in the face of Danish domination. Faroese finally became an official language of the Faroe Islands in 1948 in the Home Rule Act of the Faroe Islands.[5] Prior to this, during the eighteenth and nineteenth centuries, a great period of ballad collecting began on the Faroe Islands, and at this time the ballads were recorded in manuscripts.[6]

Before discussing what is characteristic of the Faroese ballads, we might ask what exactly is a ballad? A ballad is "a learned term for anonymous, Western European epic folk-poetry in oral tradition with couplets or quatrains followed by a refrain." The ballads presented in this volume are more specifically heroic ballads: "folk-ballads in ballad stanza form which tell of champions in the past, often in faraway places, and of their excellent (or villainous) deeds."[7]

Situated in the middle of the west Norse area, the Faroe Islands were far from being culturally isolated and were an integral part of the Germanic storytelling tradition in the Middle Ages and beyond, sharing legendary narrative motifs and content with the general heroic Germanic story-telling tradition in an area that extends from the Nordic countries (Iceland, Faroe Islands, Norway, Sweden, and Denmark) to the British Isles in the west and south to Germany. This can be referred to collectively as medieval Germanic legend—legend that goes across the borders of a single national literature.[8] This material speaks to the close connections between communities across this large area during the entirety of the pre-modern era. In the Faroe Islands, the heroic material took the form of ballads (long dance narratives), preserved in oral tradition and accompanied by a distinctive ring dance.

This volume focuses on the Faroese ballads that tell the story of the figure known in Old Norse-Icelandic as Sigurðr Fáfnisbani. That this medieval legend was found on the Faroe Islands is no surprise: the legend of Sigurd

the end of the Kalmar Union in the sixteenth century, Norway (and thus the Faroe Islands) entered a union with Denmark. The Dano-Norwegian union lasted until 1814, when Norway was ceded to Sweden. However, this did not include the Faroe Islands, Iceland, and Greenland, which remained part of Denmark. The Faroe Islands are still part of the Kingdom of Denmark.

5 Home Rule Act of the Faroe Islands, section 11.

6 See below for information on early Faroese ballad collecting, pp. XX–XX.

7 Nolsøe, "Faroese Balladry," 11, 21.

8 See Ţăranu, "The Elusive Nature of Germanic Heroic Poetry"; Frank, "Germanic Legend."

the Dragon-Slayer was popular all over the medieval north, in an area that included the Faroe Islands, Iceland, Norway, Sweden, Denmark, the British Isles and which stretched down to central Europe in what is now Germany. The story includes several other pre-eminent heroic figures of the Middle Ages, such as Helgi Hundingsbani, Gunnar (Old Norse Gunnarr, a historical king of Burgundy), focuses on the youth, marriage, and death of Sjúrður Fávnisbani (Old Norse Sigurðr Fáfnisbani), his lover Brynhild Buðladóttir (Old Norse Brynhildr Buðladóttir), Sjúrður's slaying of the dragon Fávnir/Frænar (Old Norse Fáfnir), and associated legendary events concerning the Nibelung royal house and their treasure.

Characteristics of the Faroese Ballads

In contrast to most other medieval ballad traditions that we know of, Faroese ballads (*kvæði*) are specially marked out by their great length.[9] It is not uncommon for a ballad to have over one hundred stanzas; indeed, the variants of *Brynhildar táttur* often have around 250 stanzas.[10] This means that each ballad can take several hours to a whole evening to perform. Performance is also a key element when considering the Faroese ballad tradition; these ballads were not simply chanted but rather danced; indeed, one verb denoting performance of ballads is *at dansa* (to dance), where it is understood that you would also be singing, while *at kvøða* (to chant, sing) explicitly means to chant or sing the ballads.[11]

Since heroic Faroese ballads can be so long, they often have several sections known as *tættir* (sg. *táttur*), and each section can function as a standalone ballad and be chanted independently. This is the case with the *Sjúrðar kvæði*, which is divided into three *tættir* (*Regin smiður, Brynhildar táttur*, and *Høgna táttur*). The origin of this construction would seem to be medi-

---

9 There are two types of ballads, *kvæði* and *tættir* (also the word used to refer to ballad sections). *Kvæði* are the long heroic ballads, of which the *Sjúrðar kvæði* is an example. *Tættir* are performed in the same way but are shorter and deal with local affairs rather than the epic concerns of the *kvæði*. For more on the difference between *kvæði* and *tættir*, see Christensen, "'Kvæði í føroyskari samtíð,'" 14–16. For more on *tættir*, see Galvin, "The Many Faces of Satiric Ballads."

10 Stanzas are usually two or four lines, but sometimes more (five, six, seven, nine, or ten). See Dahl, *Bókmentasøga I*, 23, also for rhyme schemes.

11 Cf. Christensen, who writes "The term *kvøða/kvøðing* is used to denote the way the ballad is performed vocally, which is a combination of singing and chanting, as opposed to the Faroese word *syngja*, which refers to singing." Christensen, "'Kvæði í føroyskari samtíð,'" 6.

eval and is comparable with medieval English ballads being divided into *fyttes*, although Mortan Nolsøe suggests that the origin of the structure in the Faroese ballads likely stems from Norwegian heroic ballads of the late Middle Ages.[12]

Historically on the Faroe Islands singing such ballads, folk songs, and spiritual songs would have been a major source of entertainment:

> Winter days were short and the evening long—and if you needed entertainment, there was nowhere to go! The family and other members of the household gathered in the smoke-room (*roykstova*), i.e. the room where there was a fireplace, but with only a hole in the roof to let in light and let out the smoke. There was lots of work in a Faroese household: fishing tackle and other tools needed repairing; wool had to be carded and spun; there was knitting to be done, etc. etc. There were ample opportunity to tell stories and not least to sing, whether *kvæði*, folk songs or spiritual songs. These *kvøldsetur* ("evening gatherings") were of great importance to the oral transmission of legends and songs.[13]

The Faroese folklorist Mortan Nolsøe points out that chanting ballads at home (without the dance) was vital for the oral transmission and learning of folk ballads,[14] and this was known as *sitandi kvøðing* (seated song). As this quotation also illustrates, ballads were not the only source of songs for Faroe Islanders, nor were they only in Faroese, since songs were also introduced from elsewhere, ballads sung in Danish being particularly popular. Faroese ballads are known in Faroese as *kvæði*, while those ballads referred to as a *vísa* are typically those sung in Danish.

The Dance and Melodies

Faroese folk songs and their melodies have been passed down in oral tradition; these encompass *kvæði*, Danish folk songs (*vísur*), spiritual songs, and Kingo singing.[15] Unlike many European ballad traditions, the ballads are unaccompanied song. There were no instruments on the Faroe Islands until around 1900 and no knowledge of notes.[16] Each village would have had a slightly different melody tradition from the next, although not so different

12 Nolsøe, "Faroese Balladry," 23.

13 Clausen, *Andlig vísuløg í Føroyum*, 55.

14 Nolsøe, "Faroese Balladry," 27.

15 Clausen, *Andlig vísuløg í Føroyum*, 55.

16 Clausen, "Melodies to Faroese Kvæði," 43.

that people from different villages could not sing ballads together.[17] Each singer, too, can shape the melody according to the circumstances.[18] There are various melodies recorded for the ballads, these have been transcribed and published by Marianne Clausen.[19] The database of melodies is available online.[20] Unlike the texts of the ballads which have entered print, the melodies of the ballads are still almost always passed on in oral tradition.[21] Although when villages were more isolated they had individual melodies for the ballads, it should be mentioned that with the advent of dancing societies in the Faroe Islands (the first society was established in the 1950s), and easily available recordings of ballads, a lot of the melodies have become more standardized.[22]

One thing that distinguishes the Faroese ballads is that they are chanted to a dance.[23] The dance that accompanies the ballad singing is a chain/ring dance and is inseparable from the lyrics of the ballad in Faroese tradition.[24] This style of dancing is known to date back to the Middle Ages, and the Faroese variant is agreed on by scholars to be medieval in origin, although it is important to point out that both the dance and its cultural significance have changed through time.[25] When the ballads are danced, the leader of the sing-

17 Clausen, *Andlig vísuløg í Føroyum*, 55. Please note that I use singing and chanting interchangeably for the performance of ballad texts.

18 Clausen, "Melodies to Faroese Kvæði," 43.

19 Clausen, *Løgini / Melodies*.

20 Føroyamálsdeild, Bandasavn.

21 Clausen, "Melodies to Faroese Kvæði," 35.

22 Christensen, "'Kvæði í føroyskari samtíð,'" 88. For more on Faroese dancing societies and their cultural importance, see Christensen, "'Kvæði í føroyskari samtíð,'" 88–101. For standardization of melodies, see Christensen, "'Kvæði í føroyskari samtíð,'" 66.

23 Mortan Nolsøe comments that they are not always danced, but when they are not, they are still chanted as if they were being danced. Nolsøe, "Faroese Balladry," 17. The metre of the ballad and the dance go hand in hand. See Christensen, "'Kvæði í føroyskari samtíð,'"19–20; Galbraith, "Meter, Prosody and Performance"; Clausen, "Melodies to Faroese Kvæði." For dancing and other medieval ballad traditions in Scandinavia, see Colbert, *The Birth of the Ballad*, 127–31.

24 This is the normal dance on the Faroes. There were also dancing games (*dansispøl*), which more or less died out around 1900 but have been revived by dancing societies. Clausen, "Melodies to Faroese Kvæði," 59. See especially Andrea Opielka for studies of dancing games: Opielka, "Tanzspiele"; Opielka, *Danse- og sanglege på Færøerne*.

25 Nolsøe, "Faroese Balladry," 17; Opielka, "Færøerne og den færøske dans."

ing or chanting is known as the *skipari* (pl. *skiparar*, which literally means "the person in charge").[26] The *skipari* (or *kvøðari*, meaning the ballad chanter or singer) starts each stanza then the rest of the dancers join in, while the refrain, sung after each stanza, is sung in unison. Historically mostly men led ballads, especially longer ballads, although women could lead shorter ballads. Today women lead almost equally to men.[27] The dance steps are simple: the dancers typically join hands in a chain, taking two steps left and one step right, and repeating this throughout the ballad.[28] Since there are so many ballads in the repertoire, the same ballad will rarely be performed more than once in a season in the dancing societies.[29] When ballads were danced at home, this was still the custom, since it was thought the ballad may become hackneyed if everyone knew it, and it was also possible for a particular *skipari* to be strongly associated with a particular ballad, and only he knew it and sang it.[30]

The traditional dancing season is from Christmas to Shrovetide. However, in modern dancing associations, the normal dancing season is from October to Shrovetide.[31] It is not only ballads in Faroese that were chanted to the dance. Danish folk songs and ballads, as well as newer Danish and Faroese ballads, were also used for dances, plus at Shrovetide and weddings spiritual songs were also danced.[32] Faroese and Danish counting rhymes

26 For more on the *skipari*, see Clausen, "Melodies to Faroese Kvæði," 75; Opielka, "'At få dansen under foden.'"

27 Marnersdóttir, "Women and Ballads," 29.

28 The dancing is started on the left foot. See Christensen, "'Kvæði í føroyskari samtíð,'" 20. There is another dance style, known as *trokingarstev* (Clausen gives the example of it being danced in Sumba), where dancers remained stationary, perhaps dancing on the spot, for the verses and only moving as described during the refrain. Clausen, "Melodies to Faroese Kvæði," 61; Hammershaimb, *Færøsk anthologi*, vol. 1, pp. xlii–xliii. Hammershaimb also mentions *bandadansur*, where the men and women face each other in two lines, with a band between them, dancing stationary during the verses but during the refrain lifting the band into an arch that the other dancers then dance through. Hammershaimb, *Færøsk anthologi*, vol. 1, p. xliii.

29 Kamban, *Kenn mær einki um*, 13; Nolsøe, "Faroese Balladry," 27; Hammershaimb, *Færøsk anthologi*, vol. 1, p. l.

30 Clausen, "Melodies to Faroese Kvæði," 75.

31 Clausen, *Andlig vísuløg í Føroyum*, 51; Nolsøe, "Faroese Balladry," 27; Clausen, "Melodies to Faroese Kvæði," 73; Kamban, *Kenn mær einki um*, 13. Shrovetide is the last period for having fun and games before the restrictions of Lent begin.

32 See Clausen, *Hundredesyv-visebogen*; Clausen, *Andlig vísuløg í Føroyum*, 51.

were also performed, such as the Faroese *Mær gav sankta Mortan* (St. Martin gave to me), which lists twenty Christmas presents.[33]

Style

Faroese ballads have similarities with other medieval ballad traditions when it comes to their style. The "leaping and lingering" in the narrative is commonplace; that is, some aspects of the story are brushed over while other elements retain narrative focus for multiple verses. In the Faroese material, this is also marked by the repetition of certain lines in the section, or by employing very similar constructions that might switch out one word or so, for example, these five stanzas from *Regin smiður* about Sjúrður growing up:

(36)	So var tað við Sjúrða, mikil gav hann vekst, meiri vaks hann í ein mánað, enn onnur børn í seks.	So was it with Sjúrður, that he grew such a lot, he grew more in one month, than other children in six.
(37)	Hann vaks upp hjá síni móður, tað er einki hól, meiri vaks hann í ein mánað, enn onnur børn í tólv.	He grew up with his mother, it's no exaggeration, he grew more in one month, than other children in twelve.
(38)	Hann vaks upp hjá síni móður, hon gav honum gangin hægst, hann royndi meira í ein mánað enn onnur børn í seks.	He grew up with his mother, she gave him the best upbringing, he achieved more in one month than other children in six.
(39)	Hann vaks upp hjá síni móður, miklan fekk hann alva, styrknaði meiri í ein mánað enn onnur børn í tólv.	He grew up with his mother, he got such great strength, he got stronger in one month than other children in twelve.
(40)	Hann vaks upp hjá síni móður, lukkan honum góð, hann vann meira í ein mánað enn onnur børn í tólv.	He grew up with his mother, his luck was good, he achieved more in one month than other children in twelve.

The ballads also employ refrains, and ballads on similar topics may employ the same refrain; for example, the *Sjúrðar kvæði* all have the same, well-known refrain:

33 Clausen, *Andlig vísuløg í Føroyum*, 51. Clausen writes that such counting rhymes were widespread in Europe and are therefore in Faroese oral tradition.

Grani bar gullið av heiði,	Grani carried the gold from the heath,
brá hann sínum brandi av reiði,	he brandished his blade in a fury,
Sjúrður vann av orminum,	Sjúrður defeated the dragon,
Grani bar gullið av heiði.	Grani carried the gold from the heath.

Since the ballads were transmitted in oral tradition, there are many variants of each ballad, which means there are different versions of what is recognisably the same ballad. This variation also occurs in the melodies and refrains, so while the refrain to the *Sjúrðar kvæði* will look the same, it is clear from Clausen's edition of melodies that there is minor variation within the refrain. Indeed, there are many variants of old refrains and some are impossible to make sense of, and some, unlike the obvious connection of the refrain of the *Sjúrðar kvæði* to the stories they tell, bear no relation to the content of the ballad.[34] The refrain is usually repeated between stanzas, however, there is a form called *tvíflættað* in which the lines of the refrain come in between the lines of the stanza.[35] The refrain is not important to the plot of the story, rather it continues the dance and gives the *skipari* breathing room—not only to catch his breath, but also to ready himself mentally for the next verse.[36]

The Medieval Origins of Faroese Ballads

It is scholarly consensus that the Faroese ballads have medieval, oral origins; 191 Faroese ballads have been identified in previous research as being of medieval origin.[37] J. H. Schrøter (1771–1851), a Faroese priest, sent P. E. Müller a list of ballads that were thought to be over one hundred years old, and it was published in Müller's introduction to Lyngbye's *Færøiske Qvæder*.[38] It has been assumed in scholarship that the productive period of Faroese ballads was in the thirteenth or fourteenth to fifteenth centuries, before entering a period of decline. This can be compared to, and is likely influenced by, the traditional view of Icelandic saga production, which supposedly went into decline around 1300 due to the loss of Icelandic independence, thus connecting the value of literary production to political devel-

34 See Dalsgaard, "Remarks on the Refrains"; Dahl, *Bókmentasøga I*, 24.

35 Dahl, *Bókmentasøga I*, 24; Matras, *Føroysk bókmentasøga*, 18.

36 Clausen, *Løgini / Melodies*, 47.

37 Jonsson, Solheim, and Danielson, *Types of the Scandinavian Medieval Ballad*, 318–19.

38 Lyngbye, *Færøiske Qvæder*, 15–20. For more on Schrøter, see Matras, *Føroysk bókmentasøga*, 43–46; Dahl, *Bókmentasøga I*, 68–73.

opments. The view of ballads entering a period of decline should thus be met with scepticism, since this view seems to be connected to the Faroe Islands losing independence to Norway and then Norway (and thus the Faroe Islands) uniting with Denmark at the dissolution of the Kalmar Union at the end of the fourteenth century, rather than any evidence from the ballad corpus itself. Indeed, since we have no records of Faroese ballads from the period in question, there is no evidence at all for a period of decline.[39] As discussed below, the tradition continues to the present day. The Faroese ballads of presumed medieval origin should be treated as the product of an oral culture that would not have come into being without oral transmission and, as such, they should be read as oral poems.

The ballad as an oral poem is in line with how a "medieval" ballad is defined in the introduction to *The Types of the Scandinavian Medieval Ballad* (TSB). This points to a lack of transcriptions from the actual Middle Ages and our reliance on typology and post-medieval sources that have been orally transmitted to compile what we consider to be medieval ballads, although there is a clear indication of change through time.[40] Medieval ballads have also been defined from a stylistic point of view by David Colbert, who lists, firstly, "a strophic, monodic melody and its verbal complement, a strophic text," secondly, "a traditional song… transmitted orally and characterized by variation," thirdly, "a folksong…without known author or authorized original version," fourth, "with narrative content related from an objective point of view," and fifth, "characterized by a limited range of stanzaic forms, and by a formulaic diction and narrative technique (the narrative formulas)."[41] These stylistic aspects also cause us to consider the medieval origins of the Faroese ballad texts, even though they were recorded in post-medieval times.[42]

The medieval origins of the *Sjúrðar kvæði* have recently been restated by Eyðun Andreassen, and those conclusions represent the scholarly consensus against an argument put forward by Peter Hvilshøj Andersen-Vinlandicus,

39 See, for example, Conroy, "Sniolvs Kvæði," 33. For a discussion of the "peak and decline" theory of Icelandic literature, see Glauser, "What Is Dated, and Why?"; Clunies Ross, *The Cambridge Introduction*, 54–57.

40 Jonsson, Solheim, and Danielson, *Types of the Scandinavian Medieval Ballad*, 14; Opielka, "Færøerne og den færøske dans," 2–4.

41 Colbert, *The Birth of the Ballad*, 13–14.

42 Many Scandinavian ballads that are counted as medieval have been recorded in the post-medieval period. For the major national collections, see Grundtvig, *Danmarks gamle folkeviser*; Espeland et al., *Norske mellomalderballadar*, Jonsson et al., *Sveriges medeltida ballader*.

who states that the *Sjúrðar kvæði* are not medieval.[43] Due to their heroic content, longevity and interconnectedness with other material from the Germanic area, the medieval origins of the material they present seem clear, but it is true that the relative age of the medieval ballads is difficult to pin down.

Faroese Ballads in the Early Modern Period Onwards

Faroese ballads have suffered from the same discourse of decline from a late medieval peak that was once popular with reference to Old Icelandic sagas: after the period in which the Faroese ballads were produced in the fourteenth and fifteenth centuries, the ballad tradition went into decline in the early modern period before the ballads were collected in the eighteenth century.[44] However, it is likely that in the early modern period creativity in ballad composition (or recomposition) may simply have taken a different shape. The Faroese ballad tradition is complex and long and was a continuing, creative tradition rather than the victim of post-medieval decline.

Although the Faroese ballads were in oral rather than written tradition in the medieval and early modern periods, Danish print books of ballads were certainly in circulation in the early modern period and influenced the native ballad tradition.[45] There are, for example, signs in the corpus that print culture in the form of imported ballads may have impacted the form of the Faroese ballads. The heroic ballads composed in couplet form likely reflect the influence of the ballads contained in Anders Sørensen Vedel's *Hundredvisebogen* (1591) and Peder Syv's republishing of this work in 1695 (to which he had added one hundred more), which were widely performed on the Faroe Islands.[46] Conroy briefly touches on the difficulties in detecting younger ballads in what is generally termed the medieval corpus and notes that attempts to list features that help determine a relative chronology have been unsuccessful.[47] The role of these Danish ballad books in forming the later life of Faroese ballad tradition in the early modern period is, however, little understood, although it is clear that since some Danish ballads acquired

43 Andreassen, "Sjúrðar kvæði"; Andersen-Vindlandicus, "Origin and Age of Sjúrðar kvæði."

44 Conroy, "Sniolvs Kvæði," 33–34.

45 For the interplay between oral tradition and written ballads, see Jonsson, "Oral Literature, Written Literature."

46 Vedel, "It Hundrede vduaalde Danske Viser;" Vedel and Syv, *Et Hundrede udvalde Danske Viser*; Conroy, "Faroese Literature," 548.

47 Conroy, "Sniolvs Kvæði," 34.

Faroese melodies that they were important in the multimodal tradition, as demonstrated by Marianne Clausen; Clausen has also demonstrated that the Danish ballads formed an integral part of ballad life on the Faroes.[48]

The earliest collections of the ballads in the Faroe Islands were undertaken in the time of Peder Syv, since a small number of sample texts were sent to the Danish scholar Ole Worm in 1639 by the priest Hans Rasmusen.[49] Although these were lost in a fire in 1728, a copy taken by Peder Syv shows that they included "Koralds kvæði," "Torsteins kvæði," "Hermundur Illi," "Samsons kvæði," and "Berrings vísa."[50] In the eighteenth century, the popularity of the imported printed ballads may have encouraged original ballad compositions in the Faroes; there are several ballads from the eighteenth century with known poets (the later ballads deemed to be of post-medieval composition are numbered CCF 192–236).[51] These later ballads include, for example, poems that have been performed to the ring dance, those that have been composed based on historical sources, and satirical ballads about various Faroe Islanders, known as *tættir*, while in the early nineteenth century, satirical ballads tended to have political themes.[52]

We usually count many of the heroic Faroese ballads as being medieval, although they did not start to be written down until the eighteenth century by the Faroe Islander Jens Christian Svabo (1746–1824) in 1781 to 1782.[53] Svabo initiated a great period of ballad collecting on the Faroes. Two important figures in the nineteenth century were J. H. Schrøter (1771–1851), who collected on Suðuroy, and V. U. Hammershaimb, who collected primarily in

48 Clausen, *Vísuløg í Føroyum*; Clausen, *Hundredesyv-visebogen*.

49 Dahl, *Bókmentasøga I*, 62; Solberg, "Balladen und Volksliedern im Norden," 113; Hammershaimb, *Færøsk anthologi*, vol. 1, p. li.

50 Dahl, *Bókmentasøga I*, 62. For a transcription, see the appendix titled "The Oldest Preserved Record of Faroese Ballads" in Andersen-Vindlandicus, "Origin and Age of Sjúrðar kvæði," 128–33.

51 These known poets are listed in Chesnutt and Larsen, *History, Manuscripts, Indexes*, 169–70. The abbreviation CCF refers to edition *Føroya kvæði: Corpus Carminum Færoensium*, edited in a number of volumes published from 1941 onwards. If a number follows CCF, it refers to the number of the ballad in the edition. Note that in some publications, FK is used instead of CCF.

52 See Galvin, "The Many Faces of Satiric Ballads in the Faroe Islands"; Conroy, "Faroese Literature," 549.

53 For more on Svabo, see Dahl, *Bókmentasøga I*, 42–49; Matras, *Føroysk bókmentasøga*, 28–34; Marnersdóttir and Sigurðardóttir, *Føroysk bókmentasøga*, vol. 1, pp. 150–64; Jacobsen, *Úr bókmentasögu okkara*, 10–20; Svabo, *Svabos færøske visehaandskrifter*, vol. 1, pp. v–lxxvii.

1847–1848.[54] Many ballad collections take the name of the island on which the texts were collected.[55] The largest of these collections is *Sandoyarbók* from 1821–1831, by Johannes Clementsen of Sandur, published in two volumes edited by Rikard Long.[56] Later collectors of importance include Jakob Jakobsen (1864–1918), who was collecting around 1900, Jóannes Patursson (1866–1946), who collected in between the wars and who published ballad books in 1922–1945 for the use of dancers, and Mortan Nolsøe (1924–1987), who was central in collecting Faroese ballad audio recordings in the twentieth century (active ca. 1960–1985), collecting approximately 336 ballads—more than any other individual.[57] The earliest ballad collectors wrote the ballads down phonetically since there was no standardized written Faroese language. The ballads were written down by collectors from singers known as informants, which in CCF are two-thirds men and one-third women.[58]

Faroese ballads existed for centuries in oral tradition before being written down. The late recording of Faroese oral literature should likely be seen in connection with the predominance of Danish in the official life of the Faroes. Danish was the language of the church, school, and authorities and until the nineteenth century, and no printed books in Faroese existed. Indeed, the oral ballad tradition was crucial in ensuring Faroese remained as a language in use.[59] It was usual that people were not able to write in Faroese, although, in the twentieth century, the use of Faroese gradually gained acceptance by the Danish authorities. In 1912, a law passed allowing

54 Clausen, *Løgini / Melodies*, 19. For a full analysis of Hammershaimb's work, see Marnersdóttir and Sigurðardóttir, *Føroysk bókmentasøga*, vol. 1, pp. 284–97.

55 For example, Sandoyarbók, Fugloyarbók, and Koltursbók. See Dahl, *Bókmentasøga I*, 64–66.

56 Nolsøe, "Faroese Balladry," 19; í Króki, *Sandoyarbók*, 1968; í Króki, *Sandoyarbók*, 1982. See also Conroy, "'Sandoyarbók'." The name of Johannes Clementsen is rendered in several different ways. The first name is variously spelled as Jóannes, Jóhannes and Johannes, and the surname is Clementsen or Clemensen, or he is known as í Króki.

57 Nolsøe, "Faroese Balladry," 19; Clausen, "Melodies to Faroese Kvæði," 41. For a full analysis of Jakob Jakobsen's work, see Marnersdóttir and Sigurðardóttir, *Føroysk bókmentasøga*, vol. 1, pp. 391–412. In 1925, Patursson published what is known as *Gyltabók* ("The Golden Book") due to the colour of its covers. See Patursson, *Föroysk Kvæði*. He also published the five-volume book of ballads, *Kvæðabók I–V*. For a full analysis of Jóannes Patursson's work, see Marnersdóttir and Sigurðardóttir, *Føroysk bókmentasøga*, vol. 1, pp. 352–91, esp. 383–84.

58 Marnersdóttir, "Women and Ballads," 35. For a list of informants in CCF, see Larsen, "Index of Informants."

59 Hammershaimb, "Færøisk sproglære," 235.

Faroese as a written language to be taught in schools, and while the Bible in Faroese was first published in 1949, there was a hymnbook authorized in 1956 (published 1960), followed by an authorized version of the Bible in 1961.[60] Written Faroese is young.[61]

The ballads were not published until 1822, when H. C. Lyngbye published *Færøiske Qvæder om Sigurd Fofnersbane og hans Æt*, which was also the first book in Faroese.[62] Although Lyngbye also collected ballads, this book is partly published on the basis of Schrøter's collecting, and the manuscript it is based on was published in a critical edition by Matras in 1951.[63] Next came Hammershaimb's two volume *Færöiske Kvæðer* (1851–1855). The first of these volumes is devoted to a Faroese edition of the ballads about Sjúrður, the same ballads translated in this book.[64] Hammershaimb was in contact with the Dane Svend Grundtvig, who was at the time preparing *Danmarks gamle Folkeviser*—the published Danish ballad corpus—and Grundtvig encouraged Hammershaimb to collect more Faroese ballads.[65] Grundtvig then later cooperated with Jørgen Bloch (his brother-in-law) and compiled all the Faroese folk ballads into the large manuscript *Føroya kvæði* (Corpus Carminum Færoensium), which by 1905 ended up as sixteen volumes and two supplements.[66] This collection was printed as six volumes of ballads text from 1941–1972, while volume seven, *History, Manuscripts, Indexes*, was published in 1996 by Chesnutt and Larsen, and volume eight in 2003 by Marianne Clausen, containing the melodies for the whole collection.[67] There are 236 ballads in the six volumes of *Føroya kvæði* and an additional

60 Clausen, *Andlig vísuløg í Føroyum*, 29.

61 For a full analysis of the development of Faroese as a literary language, Faroese literature, and its social and political context, see Marnersdóttir and Sigurðardóttir, *Føroysk bókmentasøga*.

62 Lyngbye, *Færøiske Qvæder*. See Marnersdóttir and Sigurðardóttir, *Føroysk bókmentasøga*, vol. 1, pp. 238–39.

63 Matras, *J. H. Schrøters optegnelser*.

64 Hammershaimb, *Sjúrðar Kvæði*; Hammershaimb, *Færöiske kvæder*.

65 Nolsøe, "Faroese Balladry," 19.

66 Note that Bloch finished this by himself as Grundtvig died in 1883. They produced fifteen volumes together between 1872–1876, and then Bloch prepared volume sixteen and the supplements between 1885–1905. Clausen, *Løgini / Melodies*, 19. See also Jacobsen, *Úr bókmentasögu okkara*, 50–56. For the importance of Bloch's work, see Kjær, "Jørgen Bloch."

67 Grundtvig and Bloch, *Føroya kvæði*; Chesnutt and Larsen, *History, Manuscripts, Indexes*; Clausen, *Løgini / Melodies*.

twenty-six in Clausen's 2003 volume of melodies.[68] However, there are far more ballads present in the Faroese tradition than that, since the tradition also includes ballads in foreign languages, especially Danish.[69] It is also important to note that printed editions of the ballads (especially the early ones) were not widely owned, and therefore, even though printed ballads existed, they were still learnt and transmitted through oral tradition.[70]

Faroese Ballads Today

There is regular discussion about the ballads as cultural heritage on the Faroe Islands today, but all generations have looked back to the good old days. In the afterword to Sandoyarbók (Copenhagen, Dansk Folkemindesamling, DFS 68), written in 1831, one reason Jóannes í Króki gives for collecting is that "the ballads have nearly gone out of use nowadays and the young people prefer new songs. I wanted coming generations of young people to know what their predecessors had in the way of entertainment at their Christmas dancing."[71] However, in 1854, V. U. Hammershaimb wrote that the ballads were still being composed by Faroese farmers, in "clean" language.[72] Although Jóannes did us a great service in collecting the ballads that form the manuscript Sandoyarbók, he need not have worried, since today, the ballad tradition is still living. Brynhild Kamban writes that "kvæði eru sungnar søgur og gott undirhald, og kvøðing og dansur eru framvegis ein livandi partur av føroyskari mentan" (The ballads are sung stories and good entertainment, and chanting ballads and dancing is still a living part of Faroese culture).[73] The importance of the ballad tradition to contemporary Faroese society has been analysed in detail most recently by Annika Christensen. Her thesis argues that "if the ballads are to continue to be a dynamic part of Faroese lived experience, it is crucial that a continuous engagement with

---

68 Further ballads were collected in the twentieth century (not in CCF but listed as EYL in Clausen, *Løgini / Melodies*, 502–97). Versions of ballads have been recorded right into the twenty-first century. A version of *Vermunds kvæði* was recorded in 2001. See Clausen, *Løgini / Melodies*, 584.

69 For the Danish ballad tradition on the Faroes, see Clausen, *Hundredesyvvisebogen*; Clausen, *Vísuløg í Føroyum*.

70 Clausen, "Melodies to Faroese Kvæði," 45.

71 Chesnutt and Larsen, "Descriptive and Analytical Catalogue," 89.

72 Hammershaimb, "Færøisk sproglære," 235. We should probably understand "clean" as meaning grammatically correct or good.

73 Kamban, *Kenn mær einki um*, 13. Translation the author's.

the ballads has to be supported by different means. This includes funding, research, and allowing the ballads to be repurposed and reimagined in Faroese culture." She also points out that ballads are seen as "an important contributing factor to the ways Faroese people socialise, celebrate and understand themselves."[74]

In the twentieth and twenty-first centuries, ballad performances take place in dancing halls organized by dancing associations; they are read and performed in schools and also more generally at other celebrations such as Christmas, New Year, Ólavsøka (the Wake of St. Olav, the Faroese national day), weddings, and other occasions.[75] Ballads, including the tradition, the singing, and the dancing, are a compulsory subject in both primary and secondary schools. The dancing associations also organize separate events for children to learn ballads and dance.[76] The first dancing society was formed in the 1950s, and all associations are a member of the central organization Slái Ring (established 1978), which distributes government funding and is a central organizing point.[77] Christensen pinpoints the importance of the dancing societies as "communal structures that facilitate the ballads as intangible heritage to survive, and potentially, to flourish."[78]

In addition to transmission and preservation of the lived ballad tradition in dancing societies and schools, Christensen has also looked at the importance of other cultural safeguards, such as media transmission and political decisions, for both disseminating and transmitting ballad culture. The Faroese government funds dancing societies, and Christensen points out the importance of the Faroese support for the UNESCO Convention for the Safeguarding of Intangible Cultural Heritage since 2018.[79] Previously, Faroese radio (Útvarp Føroya, started broadcasting in 1957) was an essential platform for disseminating ballads, providing an alternative to dancing societies for people to hear and learn ballads.[80] Ballads continue to be part of the programming for Kringvarp Føroya (the current Faroese radio and TV network). There is the weekly programme Dansival, which combines "bal-

74 Christensen, "'Kvæði í føroyskari samtíð,'" 1, 7.

75 Kamban, *Kenn mær einki um*, 13; Nolsøe, "Faroese Balladry," 27; Clausen, "Melodies to Faroese Kvæði," 73–74.

76 Christensen, "'Kvæði í føroyskari samtíð,'" 62–69, 95–96.

77 Christensen, "'Kvæði í føroyskari samtíð,'" 69, 88–89.

78 Christensen, "'Kvæði í føroyskari samtíð,'" 89.

79 Christensen, "'Kvæði í føroyskari samtíð,'" 5, 59–62, 69.

80 Christensen, "'Kvæði í føroyskari samtíð,'" 37–38.

lad performances and discussions with weekly guests who relate specific ballads or performances that carry a special meaning for them."[81] Christensen's conclusions in her study of the importance of ballads to contemporary Faroese culture are that ballads are a dynamic part of heritage and, as such, allowing traditions to include young people and continue to evolve is crucial.[82] In summary, it is important to appreciate that there has been no break in the Faroese ballad tradition and the ballads are not simply a static phenomenon or set of texts for scholars to analyse. Rather, they are, most importantly, a living tradition on the Faroe Islands.

The Legend of Sigurd the Dragon-Slayer

The legend about Sjúrður finds its best-known form in the Icelandic *Vǫlsunga saga*.[83] It concerns the story of Sigmundr (the father of Sigurðr) being killed, Sigurðr growing up, slaying the dragon Fáfnir, his meeting and engagement to Brynhildr, his marriage to Guðrún, Brynhildr's subsequent revenge for this, and his death at the hands of Guðrún's brothers. When she learns of Sigurðr's death, Brynhildr kills herself. Guðrún is married to King Atli, who invites her brothers to his court and kills them. Guðrún kills her two sons with Atli and feeds them to him, and she and one of her brother's sons kill Atli while he is asleep, and she sets his hall on fire. Guðrún marries King Jonakr and has three more sons, and Guðrún and Sigurðr´s daughter, Svanhildr, is raised with them. King Jormunrek wants to marry Svanhildr but ultimately has her trampled to death. Two of Guðrún's sons kill their brother and then Jormunrek in revenge for Svanhildr's death, but they are stoned to death by his retainers.

The Völsung legend was recorded in different media in different areas, such as on picture stones in Sweden, carved stave-church doors in Norway, in poems and sagas in Iceland, epic poems in Germany, and ballads on the Faroe Islands.[84] The different reflexes of the legend are known collectively

---

81 Christensen, "'Kvæði í føroyskari samtíð,'" 38. For the Dansival website, see Kringvarp Føroya, "Dansival."

82 Christensen, "'Kvæði í føroyskari samtíð,'" 70–100.

83 Finch, *Vǫlsunga Saga*.

84 A full comparison with the regional versions of the Völsung/Nibelung legend is outside the scope of this study. For these variants of the Völsung legend, except the ballads, see, for example: Margeson, "Vǫlsung Legend in Medieval Art"; Blindheim, *Sigurds Saga i middelalderens billedkunst*; Ney, *Bland ormar och drakar*; McKinnell, "The Sigmundr/Sigurðr Story."

in the Norse world as the Völsung legend (from an Icelandic perspective) or the Nibelung legend (from a German perspective).[85] The focus of this volume is on the Faroese ballads connected to the Völsung legend. The most famous Völsung Faroese ballads, the *Sjúrðar kvæði* (composed of the three ballads *Regin smiður*, *Brynhildar táttur*, and *Høgna táttur*) provide us with unparalleled and undervalued material about Sjúrður, Brynhild, and the events and people associated with them. The content of these ballads is connected to, and the material probably to some degree drawn from, Old Icelandic saga material (oral or written) as well as material from further south in Germany (represented in text form in, e.g., the *Nibelungenlied*) and from ballads from the Scandinavian countries. There are also additional Faroese ballads concerning the Völsungs that will be translated here, and they also have analogues in Nordic balladry from the Scandinavian mainland.[86]

The *Sjúrðar kvæði* is composed of three ballads: *Regin the Smith* (*Regin smiður*), *The Ballad of Brynhild* (*Brynhildar táttur*), and *The Ballad of Høgni* (*Høgna táttur*). These three ballads follow one another in manuscripts as a set and are sometimes joined by a fourth, *The Second Ballad of Høgni* (*Annar Høgna táttur*), also known as *The Ballad of Aldrias* (*Aldrias táttur*). The corpus of Faroese ballads about Sjúrður is completed by *The Ballad of Gestur* (*Gests ríma*)—also known as *The Ballad of Ásla* (*Áslu ríma*); *The Ballad of Nornagestur* (*Nornagests ríma*); *Ísmal the Brave Hero* (*Ísmal fræga kempa*); *Sjúrður and the Dwarf Maiden* (*Sjúrður og Dvørgamoy*)—also known as *Dwarf Maiden I* (*Dvørgamoy I*); *The Beautiful Dwarf Maiden* (*Dvørgamoyggin fagra*)—also known as *Dwarf Maiden II* (*Dvørgamoy II*); *Ása the Dwarf Maiden* (*Ása Dvørgamoy*)—also known as *Dwarf Maiden III* (*Dvørgamoy III*); *The Ballad of Kvørfinn* (*Kvørfins táttur*)—also known as *Dwarf Maiden V* (*Dvørgamoy V*); *The Giant of Hólmgarðar* (*Risin úr Hólmgørðum*)—also known as *The Mound Ghost* (*Dysjadólgur*); and finally *The Giant of Leittraberg* (*Risin av Leittrabergi*).[87]

---

85 The former is chosen here, since the Faroes were part of the Norse world.

86 The Nordic ballads *Sivard Snarensvend* (Dan., DgF 2), *Sivard og Brynhild* (Dan., DgF 3), *Frændhævn* (Dan., DgF 4), *Grimhilds Hævn* (Dan., DgF 5), *Kong Diderik og hans kæmper* (DgF 7), *King Diderik og Løven* (Dan., DgF 9), *Sigurð svein* (Norw., NF 9), *Sivert Snarensvend* (Swed., SMB 204), *Regnfred og Kragelil* (Dan., DgF 22), *Karl og Kragelil* (Dan., DgF 23), *Ormekampen* (Dan., DgF 24), and *Lindarormen* (Norw., Utsyn 27) intersect with the same material.

87 The ballad titled *Dwarf Maiden IV* (*Dvørgamoy IV*) in Grundtvig and Bloch, *Føroya kvæði*, vol. 1, pp. 295–96, is not included in this volume of translations because it is a variant (labelled as variant D) of the preceding ballad, *Ása the Dwarf Maiden* (*Ása Dvørgamoy*), also known as *Dwarf Maiden III* (*Dvørgamoy III*). It is noted in

Manuscripts of the Ballads

The ballads printed in CCF are edited from manuscripts in which the ballads were recorded from oral tradition from various informants. Each ballad has a number of variants. Ballad variants can be thought of as different versions of the same ballad. Each ballad variant may have different numbers of stanzas, certain details added or missing in comparison to other variants, and different language used in the narration. When the same stanzas appear in certain sections of the variants, they are often in a slightly different order. All these features are typical of texts originating in oral tradition.

Each variant of a ballad is given a letter in CCF. The ballads making up the *Sjúrðar kvæði* (*Regin smiður, Brynhildar táttur, Høgna táttur,* and often *Aldrias táttur / Annar Høgna táttur*) appear together in manuscripts and so are edited together in groups and assigned the same letters. The variants of the *Sjúrðar kvæði* are labelled A–H. Variant A, for example, comes from the manuscript NKS 345 8vo (Copenhagen, Det Kongelige Bibliotek), while B comes from Sandoyarbók (Copenhagen, Dansk Folkemindesamling, DFS 68), and D from Fugloyarbók (Copenhagen, Den Arnamagnænske Samling, AM Acc. 4 a). Sometimes the variants have subsidiary letters. Aa is the text from NKS 345 8vo, while Ab (not actually printed in CCF for the *Sjúrðar kvæði*) is Lyngbye's published edition of the ballads from 1822.[88] The information about the variants for each ballad and where they are sourced from is given in the content pages to CCF. In this book, we have translated the A variant of each ballad, because that variant is the oldest. This is not to say we perceive the oldest variant as most valuable or somehow as most authentic or best; we simply had to make a selection, and this seemed a sensible way to do it.

There are four sources of the A variants of the ballads translated in this book:

1. NKS 345 8vo: *Regin smiður, Brynhildar táttur, Høgna táttur, Annar Høgna táttur, Gests ríma, Nornagests ríma, Kvørfinns táttur, Risin av Leittrabergi*
2. GKS 2894 I (Copenhagen, Det Kongelige Bibliotek): *Risin í Hólmgørðum*
3. Lyngbye's *Færøiske Qvæder*: *Ísmal fræga kempa*
4. Sandoyarbók: *Sjúrður og Dvørgamoy, Dvørgamoyggin fagra, Ása Dvørgamoy*

---

the edition that it is a side piece or parallel (*sidestykke*) to Ása the Dwarf Maiden recorded on Suðuroy; Grundtvig and Bloch, *Føroya kvæði*, vol. 1, p. 295n1.

88 Lyngbye, *Færøiske Qvæder*.

Ballad	No. of stanzas in A variant	Manuscript	Pp. in CCF vol. 1 (A variant)[89]
Regin smiður	142	NKS 345 8vo	1–8
Brynhildar táttur	271	NKS 345 8vo	8–22
Høgna táttur	177	NKS 345 8vo	22–31
Annar Høgna táttur	123	NKS 345 8vo	31–40
Gests ríma	37	NKS 345 8vo	244–45
Nornagests ríma	34	NKS 345 8vo	248–49
Ísmal fræga kempa	61	Lyngbye's *Færøiske Qvæder*	254–57
Sjúrður og Dvørgamoy	65	Sandoyarbók	263–66
Dvørgamoyggin fagra	60	Sandoyarbók	273–76
Ása Dvørgamoy	67	Sandoyarbók	283–86
Kvørfinns táttur	93	NKS 345 8vo	297–301
Risin í Hólmgørðum	40	GKS 2894 I	311–13
Risin av Leittrabergi	107	NKS 345 8vo	326–31

In each case, for the Faroese text we have used the version printed in CCF, rather than an individual edition of the manuscript or printed book.

NKS 345 8vo and Lyngbye's *Færøiske Qvæder*

NKS 345 8vo is a manuscript written by Johan Henrik Schrøter in 1818 and contains the oldest known versions of many of the ballads to do with Sjúrður.[90] It was sent to H. C. Lyngbye in 1819 and used in the preparation of his *Færøiske Qvæder* (1822). Lyngbye himself has written this information on the title page and provided a list of contents. Schrøter collected the ballads for Lyngbye, who himself had been to the Faroe Islands in 1817 and recorded some ballads from the informant Joen Jacobsen. The ballads Lyngbye had were an incomplete version of the *Sjúrðar kvæði*, which had been identified as such by P. E. Müller. Müller had written to Schrøter about the incomplete ballads. In 1818, Lyngbye sent his incomplete recording to Schrøter and asked him to fill in what was lacking. Schrøter sent variants and

89 All the ballads translated in this book are to be found in CCF, vol. 1: Grundtvig and Bloch, *Føroya kvæði*.

90 The collection is the second oldest Faroese ballad manuscript, the oldest being from Svabo in the eighteenth century, published as Svabo, *Svabos færøske visehaandskrifter*; Matras, *J. H. Schrøters optegnelser*, ix.

an abstract of what was missing to Lyngbye already in 1818, with a promise to send what was missing. His recording of what was missing is now known as the manuscript NKS 345 8vo. Lyngbye's own recording and Schrøter's abstract and variants are lost.[91] The original orthography of the manuscript was published and the language analysed by Christian Matras in 1951.[92]

GKS 2894 I

This manuscript is a fair copy from around 1783 of Jens Chr. Svabo's ballad collection performed in 1781–1782. There are three volumes; the one ballad translated in this book, *Risin í Hólmgørðum*, is from volume one. There are 52 items in the collection, and it was purchased by the crown prince of Denmark, who later went on to become King Frederik VI (r. 1808–1839).[93] The manuscript was published by Christian Matras, who also published the accompanying word list.[94]

Sandoyarbók (DFS 68)

The manuscript is written by Jóannes í Króki (Johannes Clementsen) in 1821–1831, and the ninety ballads are either recorded or, less frequently, copied by him from other texts. Í Króki provides an index that details the date recorded or copied and the name and place of the informants or collector. He also wrote an afterword describing the reasons for his collecting.[95] The manuscript has been published by Rikard Long.[96]

---

91 For details of this story and a manuscript description, see Chesnutt and Larsen, "Descriptive and Analytical Catalogue," 104–8.

92 Matras, *J. H. Schrøters optegnelser*.

93 For details of this story and a manuscript description, see Chesnutt and Larsen, "Descriptive and Analytical Catalogue," 95–98.

94 Svabo, *Svabos færøske visehaandskrifter*; Svabo, *Svabos glossar*. See also Benati, "Jens Christian Svabo's Glossary."

95 For details of this story, a translation of the afterword, and Jóannes' autobiographical description of the collecting, see Chesnutt and Larsen, "Descriptive and Analytical Catalogue," 88–92. Regarding í Króki's (Clementsen's) name, there are several variations in spellings across different sources, where he is referred to as "Klemenson" or "Clemensen" in various scholarly literature; cf. n. 56 for more versions of his name.

96 í Króki, *Sandoyarbók*.

Scholarly Work on the Ballads

The Faroese ballads began to be collected in the eighteenth century by Jens Chr. Svabo, although they were not published at this time. Due to continued work in the nineteenth century by Hammershaimb—a Lutheran minister who established the modern orthography of Faroese—the philologist Jørgen Bloch, and the Danish literary historian and ethnographer Svend Gruntvig (amongst others), the *Føroya kvæði* (CCF), the eight-volume standard edition of the ballads (including registers and melodies), was finally published in print between 1941 and 2003. The eighth volume from 2003 also contains the melodies for the CCF ballads and further ballads that were collected in the twentieth century and labelled EYL rather than CCF.[97] The Faroese ballads are also catalogued in TSB, where they are assigned a tale-type.[98] The CCF and TSB are an important starting point for anybody beginning in Faroese ballad research. CCF vol. 7 provides a catalogue of some of the manuscripts the ballads are recorded in (however not all ballad manuscripts are listed) and registers of first lines, refrains, and medieval ballad types in the Faroese corpus and their analogues, informants, ballad collectors, scribes and owners of manuscripts, known poets, and proper names while TSB offers descriptions of the tale types found in the ballads and a list of the medieval Faroese ballads.[99]

In TSB, six types of ballad emerge: A. ballads of the supernatural; B. legendary ballads; C. historical ballads; D. ballads of chivalry; E. heroic ballads; and F. jocular ballads.[100] Medieval Faroese ballads have been studied almost exclusively by reference to category E, the heroic ballads, which make up half the medieval corpus and number approximately 100.[101] Nevertheless, there are around 90 more ballads from the other categories of ballads that are rarely referenced in the scholarly discourse.

---

97 Clausen, *Løgini / Melodies*, 502–97.

98 Jonsson, Solheim, and Danielson, *Types of the Scandinavian Medieval Ballad.*

99 Chesnutt and Larsen, *History, Manuscripts, Indexes*; Jonsson, Solheim, and Danielson, *Types of the Scandinavian Medieval Ballad.*

100 For a discussion of these ballad categories, see Christensen, "'Kvæði í føroyskari samtíð,'" 16–19. For other divisions of ballads into types, see Dahl, *Bókmentasøga I*, 26–27; Matras, *Føroysk bókmentasøga*, 19–22.

101 Isaksen, "Kvadene," 22; Marnersdóttir and Sigurðardóttir, *Føroysk bókmentasøga*, vol. 1, p. 70.

Translations and editions of individual ballads are thin on the ground.[102] Svabo's recordings were published, and the manuscript collection of ballads DFS 68 (Copenhagen, Dansk Folkemindesamling), known as *Sandoyarbók*, compiled by Jóannes í Króki (i.e., Johannes Clementsen), has been edited and published, and a further compilation by Jóannes í Króki known as *Hentzasavn* has also been edited.[103] The ballads about Sigurðr were collected and translated into Danish by Lyngbye in the early nineteenth century and into English by Smith-Dampier in the early twentieth century, into German in the 1980s, and into Spanish in 2008.[104] There is a lack of modern and comprehensive translations of the ballads, particularly into English (baring the one collected translation of the *Sjúrðar kvæði* into old-fashioned English by Smith-Dampier from 1934), and a lack of introductory and analytical material in ballad scholarship that touches on Faroese material.[105]

From the point of view of Old Norse philology and medieval studies more widely, the Völsung ballads of the Faroe Islands—in particular the *Sjúrðar kvæði*—are an important and undervalued source.[106] That medieval Northern Europe had a thriving and well-developed literary culture is well-known, but research on the different geographical areas has been uneven. Even though these ballads transmit the familiar story of Sigurd the Dragon Slayer, they are seldom mentioned in connection with analyses of the Völsung and Nibelung legends, even when the Icelandic and German textual material and the Norwegian and Swedish visual material are well-trodden patches in medieval studies. The Faroe Islands have a large literary corpus, but the literary tradition of the medieval Faroe Islands is still obscure, and

102 For coverage of translations up to the middle of the 1980s, see Syndergaard, *English Translations of the Scandinavian Medieval Ballads*.

103 Svabo, *Svabos færøske visehaandskrifter*; í Króki, *Sandoyarbók*; Weyhe, *Hentzasavn*.

104 Lyngbye, *Færøiske Qvæder*; Smith-Dampier, *Sigurd the Dragon-Slayer*; González Campo, *Baladas épicas feroesas*. The *Sjúrðar kvæði* in Sandoyarbók were edited with a German glossary by Lockwood, *Die Färöischen Sigurdlieder*. There is also a three-volume edition and translation into German of all three *Sjúrðar kvæði* by Fuss, *Die Faröischen Lieder Der Nibelungensage*.

105 See e.g., Solberg, "Balladen und Volksliedern im Norden," 113–16.

106 It should be mentioned that this retrospective view of the Faroese ballads does not account for the full importance of the ballad tradition in contemporary Faroese society. The ballads were an important aspect of Faroese nation building, as reflected in the work of Simonsen, "Literature, Imagining and Memory," and continue to play an important role in Faroese culture today, as explored in the work of Árnadóttir, "Chain Dancing."

the Faroe Islands are largely absent from the literary history of the Nordic countries. This is despite the Faroe Islands having strong ties culturally, politically, and geographically to all of northern Europe; it thus was likely an important arena for cultural exchange and dissemination.

Previous scholarship has engaged with the Faroese ballads (especially heroic ballads) as derivative of Old Icelandic or mainland Scandinavian literature.[107] The similarity in content has been noted briefly in comparison with other Norse tales.[108] Studies also discuss the oral-formulaic nature of the ballads (the most thorough study is still de Boor from 1918), and more recently Hansen treats repeated motifs in selected Faroese ballads.[109] In his reconstruction of the earliest stages of the Brynhildr legend, Andersson mentions *Brynhildar táttr* only in passing and the ballad is not mentioned in the stemma that anticipates his conclusions.[110] In terms of gender studies, Agneta Ney has written the most important recent monograph on Sigurðr Fáfnisbani from the perspective of the manly ideal in Old Norse literature, and she provides a thorough treatment of the visual material but does not treat the Faroese ballads.[111] Malan Marnersdóttir has written about women and the ballad tradition, while Brynhild Kamban has published her MA thesis on gender and the narratology of the *Sjúrðar kvæði* as a short book.[112] Scholars also situate the ballads in terms of their modern cultural context and their role in nineteenth-century nation-building, although a major recent anthology on the subject includes Norway, Sweden, Iceland, the UK, Germany, and Denmark but not the Faroe Islands.[113] Several ballads and cycles have been treated on an individual basis, for example in the work of Patricia

107 Nolsøe, "Development of the Faroese Heroic Ballad"; Nolsøe, "Forholdet mellom ballade och sagaforelegg"; Nolsøe, "The Faroese Balladry"; Nolsøe, "The Faroese Heroic Ballad"; Nolsøe, "The Heroic Ballad in Faroese Tradition"; Skårup, "De færøske viser om Karl den Store"; Conroy, "Faroese Literature," 548–49; De Vries, *Færøsche balladen.*

108 See recently: Novotná, "Role of the Body"; Korecká, "Óðin Stoyttist í Jørðina Niður"; Árnadóttir, "Den flyvende bejler"; Isaksen, "Kvadene," 24–26; Marnersdóttir and Sigurðardóttir, *Føroysk bókmentasøga*, vol. 1, p. 66.

109 de Boor, *Die Färöischen Lieder*. See also O'Neil, "Oral-Formulaic Structure"; Hansen, *Endurreisn kvæðanna*, 37–54.

110 Andersson, *The Legend of Brynhild*, 23.

111 Ney, *Bland ormar och drakar*.

112 Marnersdóttir, "Women and Ballads"; Kamban, *Kenn mær einki um*.

113 Simonsen, "Literature, Imagining and Memory," 194–222; Lassen, *Det norrøne og det nationale*.

Conroy.[114] In summary, there is still a large scope for further research on the Faroese ballad corpus, and it is the hope that this book will contribute to raising interest in Faroese ballads amongst students and scholars of Nordic literature, including medievalists.

About the Translations in this Book

W. P. Ker writes that "to bring out, in English, anything like the value of the Danish ballads would require the finest poetical skill," and this sentiment can also be applied to Faroese ballads.[115] We have not tried to produce translations with immense literary value in their own right; the intention behind the translation presented here is not to mirror the beauty of the Faroese but rather to aid in understanding it. Therefore, we hope that the reader will approach this book of ballad translations with the idea that reading and making sense of the Faroese should be the primary aim, with the English version as a helpful aid.

The translations offered in this book are prose and are a line-by-line rather than a stanza-by-stanza translation, except on the rare occasions when it simply made no sense in English to retain a literal translation of a line. The aim of this approach is to facilitate easy comparison with the Faroese version of the text and to provide a basis for further study. For this reason, the translations are more literal than poetic. Larry Syndergaard, who has studied English translations of the Scandinavian medieval ballads closely, defines a literal translation as following "the original very closely, with such changes as needed to make the translation idiomatic," and a close translation as following "the original quite closely, with minor substantive changes, very limited structural changes, and limited 'enhancement' or intensification."[116] Our translation strategy likely lands between these; we have added the occasional pronoun or left out the occasional particle in the Faroese that seemed to be purely for metrical purposes rather than meaning. Grammatical tenses can change mid-stanza in the ballads, and here we have chosen to follow the Faroese and change the tense in the English translation. No changes to the stanza order have been made, nor have any changes to the substance of the narrative.

---

114 For example, Conroy, "Sniolvs Kvæði"; Conroy, "'Hernilds Kvæði.'" See also Kleiner and Piotrovsky, "From Epic to Ballad: The Faroese 'Sjúrður Cycle'."

115 Cited in Syndergaard, *English Translations of the Scandinavian Medieval Ballads*, 39.

116 Syndergaard, *English Translations of the Scandinavian Medieval Ballads*, 31.

Very occasionally the order of two lines has been switched in the translation to preserve the sense in English, and this has been indicated in the footnotes. Explication of the narrative has not been added to the stanzas but is instead contained in the footnotes. Sometimes the Faroese makes little sense or is at best difficult to interpret, and these difficulties have also been indicated in the footnotes. The footnotes are intended to orientate the reader in the action of the narrative, to aid with difficult words and readings, and, occasionally, to justify translation choices. The vocabulary used in the ballads contains a number of poetic words (*heiti*) not used in ordinary discourse. These have been marked in the footnotes and translated with the ordinary word in the translation. Kennings found in the ballads have also been explained in the footnotes. We have used the Faroese names exactly as they appear in the ballads in CCF, although in the nominative case in the English. The names are often inconsistent in form, also often within the same ballad (or between the title and the ballad text, for example "Høgni" in the title and "Høgnar" in the text).

Sometimes refrains are not recorded in CCF with the ballad, and if that is the case in the edition, no refrain has been given in the translation. In the cases of those missing refrains, it is possible to consult Clausen's volume of melodies, which gives refrains for the ballad versions she records.[117] It should be noted that different refrains can be used with the same ballad.

117 Clausen, *Løgini / Melodies.*

THE BALLADS

REGIN THE SMITH (REGIN SMIÐUR)

1. Vilja tær nú lýða á, meðan eg man kvøða, um teir ríku kongarnar, sum eg vil nú um røða.	Would you listen now, while I will sing, about those mighty kings, that I will now speak about.
Refrain *Grani bar gullið av heiði,* *brá hann sínum brandi av reiði,* *Sjúrður vann av orminum,* *Grani bar gullið av heiði.*	*Grani carried the gold from the heath,* *he brandished his blade in a fury,* *Sjúrður defeated the dragon,* *Grani carried the gold from the heath.*
2. Sigmundur var ein jallsins son, men hann fekk eina so høgborna konu.	Sigmundur was a son of an earl, but he married such a high-born wife.
3. So glaðiliga drekka tey í ríkinum jól, so fagurliga byggja tey tann ríka kongins stól.	They celebrated so joyfully in the kingdom at Christmas,[1] so beautifully they sat in the throne of the mighty king.
4. Tá var har so mikil ríka manna gongd, ófriður gekk á kongins land.	At that time there was such a great number of mighty men around, war descended on the king's land.
5. Ríða teir í bardagar, suður upp á strand, so reystiliga vardu teir tann ríka kongins land	They rode into battle, in the south on the beach, so bravely they defended the mighty king's land.
6. Løgdu sínum bátunum suður við strand, so listiliga vardu teir tann ríka kongins land	They drew their boats up south at the beach, so merrily[2] they defended the mighty king's land.

---

1 *At drekka jól* literally means "to drink Christmas," but really means "to celebrate Christmas," although it is clear where the emphasis lies in the celebrations.

2 Here we have translated *lystiligur* as "merrily." However, the word could potentially be *listuliga*, meaning "cunningly" or "slyly," since the words *lystiliga* and *listuliga* sound the same. Matras, *J. H. Schrøters optegnelser*, 1, has *listelia*.

7. Ríða teir í bardagin, lótu har sítt lív, eftir livir Hjørdis Sigmundar vív	They ride into the battle, they lost their lives there, Hjørdis is widowed Sigmundur's wife.
8. Stendist tað av bardøgum, eingin kemur heim, eftir livir Hjørdis við sorg og døpul mein.	The battles were fought, no one is coming home, Hjørdis is widowed with grief and great sorrow.[3]
9 Stoytir hon yvir seg kápu bláa, so gongur hon á vánaðin, sum Sigmundur lá.	She casts over herself a blue cloak, she goes onto the field,[4] upon which Sigmundur lay.
10. "Ligg nú heilur, Sigmundur, søti mín, eg man vera í sorgartíð komin at vitja tín.	"Lie unhurt,[5] Sigmundur, my sweet, in this time of grief I have come to attend to you.
11. Hoyr tú, reysti Sigmundur, søti mín, eru tey nakað grøðandi sárini tín?"	Listen, brave Sigmundur, my sweet, can they be healed, your wounds?"

3 *Døpul mein* literally means "double harm."

4 The meaning of *vánaðin*, here translated "the field," is uncertain since the word is unknown elsewhere. In Matras, *J. H. Schrøters optegnelser*, the word is originally spelt as *Vaanajin* (1). We have picked "the field" in the sense of "battlefield" due to the readings in the other variants. In the B variants of the ballad (Ba and Bb), the equivalent word is *garðin*: Grundtvig and Bloch, *Føroya kvæði*, vol. 1, p. 34, st. 10; vol. 1, p. 58, st. 9, meaning "vicinity" or "fenced off area." In variant C, the word is *herin*: Grundtvig and Bloch, *Føroya kvæði*, vol. 1, p. 86, st. 8, meaning "army." In variant D, the word is *valin*: Grundtvig and Bloch, *Føroya kvæði*, vol. 1, p. 106, st. 9, meaning "battlefield." In E the word is *vágnið*: Grundtvig and Bloch, *Føroya kvæði*, vol. 1, p. 140, st. 6., which the editors follow with a (!) since this is also meaningless. In F we find *vølli*: Grundtvig and Bloch, *Føroya kvæði*, vol. 1, p. 165, st. 6. meaning "field"; and in G *heyggin*: Grundtvig and Bloch, *Føroya kvæði*, vol. 1, p. 169, st. 7, meaning "hill." Hammershaimb, which is printed as variant H in CCF, has *völlin*: see *Sjúrðar kvæði*, p. 4, st. 9; Grundtvig and Bloch, *Føroya kvæði*, vol. 1, p. 191, st. 9, meaning "field." Lyngbye has *Veâlin*: *Færøiske Qvæder*, p. 48, st. 9, meaning "battlefield."

5 *Heilur* means "hale" in English, "healthy and sound."

12. "Seint manst tú, Hjørdis,
fáa til tess ráð,
gera tey smyrslini,
sum grøða míni sár.

"It will be too late, Hjørdis
before you're able to
to make those balms
that would heal my wounds.

13. Hundsins synir í randarný
skaðan gjørdu tær,
eitur var í svørðinum,
teir bóru móti mær.

Sons of Hundingur[6] in battle
inflicted the injury on you,
poison was on the swords,
that they carried against me.

14. Áðrenn teir góvu mær
tað fyrsta sár,
sundur gekk mítt svørðið
í lutirnar tvá.

Before they gave me
the first wound,
my sword broke
into two pieces.

15. Sundur gekk mítt svørðið,
og sundur gekk mítt spjót,
Hundsins synir
riðu mær allir ímót.

My sword broke,
and my spear broke,
Sons of Hundingur
all rode against me.

16. Sundur gekk mítt svørðið
í lutir tvá,
tí mundi eg ongan
sigur av teim fáa

My sword broke
into two pieces,
for that reason I won no
victory over them.

17. Tað annað sárið, teir
góvu mær tá,
illa neit í hjartanum,
tað hyggi av tí gár.

The second wound, they
gave me then,
a terrible pain to the heart,
my eyesight is fading because of it.[7]

18. Tað, ið tú hevur í vónum hjá tær,
tað er sveinsbarn,
føð tað væl við ærum upp,
og gev tí Sjúrðar navn.

The child that you are expecting
is a boy-child,
bring it up well with honour,
and give it the name Sjúrður.

19. Tak tú hesar
svørðslutir tvá,
lat tú teir til smiðju bera
ungum soni, tú ár.

Take these
two pieces of sword,
have them taken to a smithy
to the young son you have.

---

6 Here it says "the Hundingur," although Hundingur is a person (in the Völsung legend killed by the hero Helgi Hundingsbani, in some versions of the tale the half-brother of Sigurðr Fáfnisbani).

7 *At gá av* is a verb form used in ballads for *at ganga av*, meaning in this sense "to ease off" or "stop."

20. Av sonnum eg tað sigi nú til tín: hesin sami sonur skal hevna deyða mín	I tell the truth to you now: this same son shall avenge my death.
21. Regin smiður býr fyri handan á, honum skalt tú fáa hesar svørðslutir tvá.	Regin the smith lives on the other side of the river, you shall give him these two pieces of sword.
22. Og so má hann gera tað so reinliga hart, bæði má hann vega við tí steinin og jarn.	And he must make it so very hard, he must be able to split with it both stone and iron.
23. Frænar eitur ormurin, á Glitrarheiði liggur, Regin er ein góður smiður, fáum er hann dyggur.	The dragon is called Frænar, who lies on Glitrarheiði,[8] Regin is a good smith, he is loyal to few.[9]
24. Eg fái ikki, Hjørdis, longur snakkað við teg, hetta man vera deyðastundin, ið komin er á meg."	I'm not able, Hjørdis, to speak with you anymore, this will be my moment of death which has come over me."
25. Grátandi snúðist Hjørdis Sigmundi frá, allar hennara hirðkonur feldu fyri hann tár.	Hjørdis turned crying from Sigmundur, all of her ladies-in-waiting shed tears for him.
26. Grátandi fór nú Hjørdis í sínum sali at sitja, Hjalprek kongur fyrstur og fremstur frúnna kom at vitja.	Crying, Hjørdis now went to sit in her hall, King Hjalprek first and foremost came to visit the queen.
27. Frúgvin gekk sær við barninum níggju mánar sínar, til at teirri stundum leið, hon føðir ein svein so fríðan.	The queen was pregnant for her nine months, until the time came that she gave birth to a beautiful boy.

8 For Glitrarheiði, see Andreassen, "Jesus á Glitrarheiði."

9 Sigmundur is telling Hjørdis not to trust Regin, even though they need his help.

28. Nú er enn sum ofta fyrr,
duld eru døpul mein,
frúgvin er gingin í høgaloft,
hon føðir ein ungan svein

Now it is as so often before,
great sorrow is kept to oneself,
the queen went into the hall,[10]
she gave birth to a young boy.

29. Sveipar hon hann í klæði væl,
tá ið hann kom í heim,
Sjúrða bað hon nevna sær
tann geviliga svein.

She wrapped him well in cloth,
when he came into the world,
she ordered him to be called Sjúrður,
the valiant boy.

30. Barnið varð sveipt í klæði væl,
og gott er til góðan at evna,
síðan bað hon presti bera,
Sjúrða bað hon nevna.

The child was wrapped well in cloth,
it is good to get something good fulfilled,[11]
later she ordered him to be carried to the priest,
she ordered him to be called Sjúrður.

31. Hann varð borin frá kirkjuni
aftur til móður sín,
meira læt hon røkta hann
enn alt sítt gull í skrín.

He was carried from the church
back to his mother,
she took better care of him
than all her gold in the coffers.

32. Barnið varð borið frá kirkjuni
og sett á móðurs fang,
meira legði hon røkt á hann
enn alt sítt gull og sprang.

The child was carried from the church
and placed in his mother's lap,
she tended to him more
than all her gold and land.

33. Barnið varð borið frá kirkjuni
og sett á móðurs knæ,
meiri legði hon røkt á hann
enn alt sítt gull og fæ.

The child was carried from the church
and placed on his mother's knee,
she tended to him more
than all her gold and riches.

34. Sigmundur kongurin
frá henni gekk,
Hjalprek kongurin
hana aftur fekk.

King Sigmundur
went from her,
King Hjalprek
married her after that.

35. Hjalprek kongurin,
tann jallsins son,
hann fekk nú sær
so høgborna konu.

King Hjalprek,
the earl's son,
he now got himself
such a high-born wife.

10 *Høgaloft* is the loft room, although sometimes means simply "hall" in ballads. It is a chamber on the second floor and would have been the most private area.

11 The meaning of this is not very clear. Lyngbye glosses this line as "Og godt er til Lykken at evne" (*Færøiske Qvæder*, 57n29), and it could refer to the fulfilling of Sigmundur's prophecy about the birth of a boy that he made as he was dying.

36. So var tað við Sjúrða, mikil gav hann vekst, meiri vaks hann í ein mánað, enn onnur børn í seks.	So it was with Sjúrður, that he grew such a lot, he grew more in one month, than other children in six.
37. Hann vaks upp hjá síni móður, tað er einki hól, meiri vaks hann í ein mánað, enn onnur børn í tólv.	He grew up with his mother, it's no exaggeration, he grew more in one month, than other children in twelve.
38. Hann vaks upp hjá síni móður, hon gav honum gangin hægst, hann royndi meira í ein mánað enn onnur børn í seks.	He grew up with his mother, she gave him the best upbringing, he achieved more in one month than other children in six.
39. Hann vaks upp hjá síni móður, miklan fekk hann alva, styrknaði meiri í ein mánað enn onnur børn í tólv.	He grew up with his mother, he got such great strength, he got stronger in one month than other children in twelve.
40. Hann vaks upp hjá síni móður, lukkan honum góð, hann vann meira í ein mánað enn onnur børn í tólv.	He grew up with his mother, his luck[12] was good, he achieved more in one month than other children in twelve.
41. Hann vaks upp í ríkinum til geviligan mann, Hjalprek kongurin fostraði hann.	He grew up in the kingdom to a valiant man,[13] King Hjalprek fostered him.
42. Hann vaks upp í ríkinum skjótt og ikki leingi, til hann gjørdist í høggum tungur, hann bardi kongins dreingir.[14]	He grew up in the kingdom quickly and not slowly, until he could deal out heavy blows, he fought the king's men.
43. Hann var sær á leikvøllum, ímillum manna herjar, rívur upp stórar eikikelvar, lemjar summar til heljar.	He was on the playing field, creating havoc amongst men, tears up big oak logs, beats some to death.

12 This is "good luck" in the sense of good fortunes.

13 This means that he grows up into/becomes a valiant man. On the other hand, if you were to read a more Danish sense into this line, it may mean that he grew up in the kingdom of a valiant man.

14 *Drongur* (pl. *dreingir*) is a word for "hero" in the ballads, although ordinarily meaning "boy."

44. Niður settust sveinarnir, vreiðir ið teir vóru: "Líkari var tær faðir at hevnt enn berja os so stórum."	The boys[15] sat down, they were angry: "It would be better to avenge your father than to beat us so badly."
45. Sveinur kastar skildri niður, lystir ei longur at leika, gongur fyri sína sælu móður við reyðar kinnar og bleikar.	The boy throws down the shield, doesn't want to play anymore, goes before his dear[16] mother pale and with red cheeks.
46. Sveinur gekk til móður sína, talar rætt og slætt: "Sig mær sannan faðir at mær, ein hvør vil vita sín ætt.	The boy went to his mother, saying simply: "Tell me who my true father is, everyone wants to know their lineage.
47. Hoyr nú tað, mín sæla móðir, sig mær satt ífrá: varð mín faðir av lívi tikin, ella doyði hann á strá?	Now listen to this, my dear mother, tell me truthfully: was my father killed or did he die in bed?[17]
48. Hoyr tú nú, mín sæla móðir, spyrja má eg nú teg: varð mín faðir við váknum vigin? Dult er tað fyri meg.	Now listen, my dear mother, now I have to ask you: was my father killed with weapons? It is kept[18] from me.
49. Hoyr tú, mín hin sæla móðir, sig mær satt ífrá: er hann enn á vørildini, ið mín faðir vá?"	Listen, my dear mother, tell me truthfully: is he still in the world,[19] the one who slew my father?"
50. "Um hann er í vørildini, ið tín faðir vá, tað verður ikki, meðan tú livir, tú sømdir av honum fár.	"If he's in the world, the one who slew your father, it won't be while you're alive, that you will get redress from him.

---

15 *Sveinar* (sg. *svein*) usually means "boys" but can also refer to the king's men, sometimes footmen. Here we have chosen boy, since Sjúrður is also referred to as a boy in the following stanza.

16 *Sælur* literally means "blessed" but is used in ballads to mean "beloved" or "dear."

17 This literally means "or did he die in the straw," since bed mattresses were stuffed with straw (cf. the English expression "to hit the hay" for going to bed).

18 It is kept a secret from him.

19 *Vørild* is used in ballads for *verøld* (world). Here Sjúrður is asking if this person is still alive.

51. Hundsins synir í randarný teir tín faðir vá, tú manst ikki, meðan tú livir, sømdir av teimum fá."	The sons of Hundingur in battle they slew your father, you won't, while you live, get redress from them."
52. Sveinur svaraði síni móður, alt væl sum hann kundi: "Ofta hevur vaksið ungum rakka hvassar tenn í munni."	The boy answered his mother, as well as he could: "Often a young dog has grown sharp teeth in its mouth."
53. Frúgvin gekk at tí kistuni, sum øll var í gulli tvigin: "Her skalt tú síggja tey herklæði, sum tín varð faðir í vigin."	The lady went to that chest, which was all dipped in gold: "Here you shall see the battle clothes, in which your father was slain."
54. Hon læsir upp ta kistuna, sum nógv var í gull og fæ, hon tekur upp teir svørðslutir og kastar Sjúrða á knæ.	She unlocks that chest, in which was much gold and wealth, she picks up those sword pieces and throws them on Sjúrður's knee.
55. Hon tekur upp ta skjúrtuna, sum øll var í blóði drigin: "Her sært tú nú, mín sæli sonur, hvussu tín varð faðirin vigin."	She picks up that shirt, that was all drenched in blood: "Now you see here, my dear son, how your father was slain."
56. Hon tekur hesar svørðslutir, Sjúrða hon teir fær: "Hetta gav tín hin sæli faðir, ið mikið gott unti mær.	She takes these sword pieces, she gives them to Sjúrður: "Your dear father gave these to me, who loved me very much.
57. Tak tú hesar svørðslutir tvá, lat tú tær eitt annað svørðið av teim slá.	Take these two sword pieces, have yourself another sword made from them.
58. Regin smiður býr fyri handan á, honum skalt tú fáa hesar svørðslutir tvá.	Regin the smith lives on the other side of the river, you shall give him these two pieces of sword.[20]
59. Honum skalt tú fáa hesar svørðslutir tvá, smíða væl og virðiliga, til tú ríða má.	You shall give him these two sword pieces, to forge them well and carefully, you must ride there.

20 Hjørdis repeats Sigmundur's words exactly from st. 21.

60. Frænar eitur ormurin,
á Glitrarheiði liggur,
Regin er ein góður smiður,
fáum er hann dyggur."

The dragon is called Frænar,
who lies on Glitrarheiði,
Regin is a good smith,
he is loyal to few."[21]

61. Tað var hin ungi Sjúrður,
honum mundi einki fresta:
"Hoyr nú tað, mín sæla móðir,
vís mær á veldigan hest!"

That was the young Sjúrður,
he wouldn't delay anything:
"Now listen, my dear mother,
show me[22] a magnificent horse!"

62. "Gakk tú fram at fossinum,
varpa stein í á,
kjós tær hest til handar tann,
sum ikki víkir frá!"

"Proceed to the waterfall,
hurl a rock into the river,
choose that horse for yourself,
that doesn't run away!"

63. Hann gekk sær at fossinum,
kastaði stein í á,
tók sær tann av hestunum,
sum ikki víkti frá.

He went to the waterfall,
threw a rock into the river,
took that one of the horses for himself,
that didn't run away.

64. Hann var í tí ríkinum
ein tann allarbesti,
síðan varð hann kallaður
Grani Sjúrðar hestur.

It was in the kingdom
the best of all of them,
after which it was called
Grani, Sjúrður's horse.

65. Árla var um morgunin
meg man rætt um minna,
Sjúrður kvittar yvir um á
Regin smið at finna.

Early in the morning
if I remember correctly,
Sjúrður leaves across the river
to find Regin the smith.

66. Sjúrður leyp á Grana bak
sama morgun snimma,
so ríður hann sær yvir um á
Regin smið at finna.

Sjúrður jumps on Grani's back
early the same morning,
then he rides across the river
to find Regin the smith.

67. Tað var hin ungi Sjúrður,
ríður fyri dyrnar fram,
Regin kastar smíðinum,
hann tekur jarn í hond.

That was the young Sjúrður,
riding before the doors,
Regin throws his tools down,[23]
he holds iron in his hand.

---

21 Hjørdis repeats Sigmundur's words exactly from st. 23.

22 This is in the sense of "show me to" or "indicate" a horse, to help him find one.

23 It literally says that Regin throws the tools.

68. "Hoyr tú meg nú, Regin,
hetta er fyrsta mín ferð,
ger mær tað, tú Regin smiður,
smíða mær nú eitt svørð!

"Now listen, Regin,
this is my first journey,
do it for me, Regin the smith,
forge me a sword now!

69. Tak nú frá mær hesar
svørðslutir tvá,
tú mást mær eitt javngott
svørð av teimum slá."

Now take from me these
two sword pieces,
you have to forge an equally good
sword from them."

70. "Ver vælkomin, Sjúrður,
tú ert mær so kær,
dvølst í ríkinum nakra tíð
og hesa nátt hjá mær!"

"Welcome, Sjúrður,
you are so dear to me,
stay in this kingdom for some time
and this night with me!"

71. "Eg fái ikki, Regin smiður,
dvølst í nátt hjá tær,
Hjalprek kongur saknast meg
úr hásætinum frá sær.

"I'm not able, Regin the smith,
to stay the night with you,
King Hjalprek misses me
from his high-seat.

72. Smíða mær nú svørðið
skjørt og so reint,
bæði má eg vega við tí
jarnið og so stein."

Now forge me the sword
brittle and so pure,
with it I have to split both
iron and also stone."[24]

73. Regin tók við svørðinum,
og legði hann tað í eld,
einans náttina
hevði hann tað í gerð.

Regin took the sword,
and put it in the fire,
one single night
he worked on it.

74. Einans náttina
hevði hann tað í gerð,
hugaður var nú Sjúrður ungi,
har ið hann fer.

One single night
he worked on it,
young Sjúrður was now eager,
he went there.

75. Árla var um morgunin,
sólin skín so snimma,
Sjúrður loypur á Grana bak
Regin smið at finna.

Early in the morning,
the sun shines so early,
Sjúrður jumps on Grani's back
to find Regin the smith.

76. Sjúrður er riðin
fyri dyrnar fram,
Regin kastar smíði
og tekur sær svørð í hond.

Sjúrður has ridden
before the doors,
Regin throws his tools down
and takes the sword in his hand.

24 This echoes Sigmundur's wishes in st. 22. Cf. also st. 85.

77. "Smíðað havi eg svørðið, gjørt havi eg tað til, bilar tær ei hugurin, lívið leggi eg við.	"I have forged the sword, I have made it, if you are not lacking in courage, then I will give my life as security.[25]
78. Smíðað havi eg svørðið skjørt og so reint, bæði mást tú vega við tí jarn og so stein."	I have forged the sword brittle and so pure, you are able to split with it both iron and also stone."[26]
79. Sjúrður gekk at sterkum steðja, roynir alt við hast, fyrsta høggið, ið hann brá, í tógva lutir brast.	Sjúrður went to a strong anvil, trying it in all haste, the first blow that he swung, it broke in to two pieces.[27]
80. "Deyðan ert tú, Regin smiður, av mær verð, at tú mundi svikið meg í váknagerð."	"Death, Regin the smith, you are worthy of from me, since you would betray me in the making of the weapon."
81. Tekur hann hesar svørðslutir, kastar á Regins knæ, Regin smiður skalv sum eitt liljublað.	He takes these sword pieces, throws them on Regin's knee, Regin the smith trembled like a lily leaf.[28]
82. Legði hann hesar svørðslutir aftur í hans hond, tá skalv hondin á Regin smiði sum eitt liljuvand.	He laid these sword pieces back into his hand,[29] then the hand of Regin the smith trembled like a slender maiden.[30]
83. "Smíðar tú annað svørðið so mær, deyðan mást tú, Regin Smiður, vænta tær.	"If you forge the second sword like that for me, then death, Regin the smith, you must expect.

---

25 Regin seems to be saying here that if Sjúrður would dare to kill him, he vouches for the quality of the sword with his life. He is bluffing here, since he has only spent one night making the sword, which proves to be of poor quality.

26 This echoes Sjúrður's words in st. 72.

27 It is the sword that breaks, not the anvil.

28 This is a particularly unflattering depiction of Regin, since women are often associated with lilies in the ballads. See the stanza below, st. 82.

29 Sjúrður lays the sword pieces into Regin's hand.

30 A *liljuvand* (or *liljuvond*) is a slender maiden in ballads, since *lilja* means "woman" and *vond* means "mast." Lilies are also associated with the Virgin Mary.

84. Tú mást gera tað so reinliga hart, bæði má tað vera tolið og so skarpt.	You must make it so very hard, it must be both resilient and very sharp.
85. Smíða mær svørðið skjørt og so reint, bæði má eg vega við tí jarn og so stein."	Forge the sword for me brittle and so pure, with it I have to split both iron and also stone."[31]
86. "Hoyr tað, Sjúrður ungi, smíði eg tær svørð, hjartað úr orminum vil eg hava í verð.	"Listen, young Sjúrður, if I forge you a sword, the heart of the dragon I want as my portion.[32]
87. Smíði eg tær svørðið, geri eg tað so, hjartað úr orminum leggi eg virðin á."	If I forge you the sword, if I make it like that, the heart of the dragon I claim as payment."
88. Regin gongur at smíðinum, legði svørð í eld, tríati næturnar hevði hann tað í gerð.	Regin goes to the smithing, laid the sword in the fire, thirty nights he worked on it.[33]
89. Tríati næturnar hevði hann tað í gerð, hugurin var um Sjúrða unga og um hansara ferð.	Thirty nights he worked on it, young Sjúrður was thinking about it and about his journey.[34]
90. Tað var um ein árla morgun, sólin skein so víða, Sjúrður kvittar yvir á til Regin smið at ríða.	It was early one morning, the sun shone so widely, Sjúrður leaves across the river to ride to Regin the smith.[35]

31 This is nearly identical to st. 72 (spoken also by Sjúrður), which echoes Sigmundur's words in st. 22.

32 In the ballad they have not explicitly discussed the dragon, although Frænar has been mentioned, but we are to understand that they have discussed killing the dragon already.

33 This is in contrast to the one night Regin worked on the previous sword.

34 This could also mean that Regin was thinking about Sjúrður and his journey. It is not quite clear.

35 Cf. Sjúrður departing in st. 66.

91. Tað var hin snari Sjúrður,
reið fyri dyrnar fram,
Regin kastar smíði
og tekur svørðið í hond.

That was the swift Sjúrður,
rode before the doors,
Regin throws down his tools
and takes the sword in his hand.

92. "Ver vælkomin, Sjúrður,
hvussu er at tí vón?
Góðar hevur tú yvirvánir
í allari ásjón.

"Welcome, Sjúrður,
what are you expecting?
Your advantages are good
it would appear.

93. Ver vælkomin, Sjúrður,
smíðað havi eg svørð,
bilar tær ei hugurin,
tú verður so víða á ferð.

Welcome, Sjúrður,
I have forged a sword,
if you are not lacking in courage,[36]
you will journey far and wide.

94. Smíðað havi eg svørðið
skært og so reint,
bæði mást tú vega við tí
jarnið og so stein."

I have forged the sword
bright and true,
you must split with it both
iron and also stone."

95. Sjúrður gongur at steðjanum
høggur á við fart,
hvørki mátti røkka ella støkka,
so var svørðið hart.

Sjúrður goes to the anvil
strikes with haste,
it must neither snap nor break,
so hard was the sword.

96. So høgg hann Sjúrður
fastliga til,
sundur kleyv hann steðjan
og stabban við.

Then Sjúrður struck
so powerfully,
he split the anvil apart
and also the block underneath.

97. Hann vá ein orm av giltum upp,
annan skamt íhjá,
Gramm kallaði hann svørðið,
á gólvinum lá.

He slew a glittering[37] snake,[38]
and another nearby,
he called the sword Gramm,
that lay on the floor.

---

36 He echoes his words in st. 77.

37 We assume *giltum* is the same as *gyltum*, meaning golden, but also glittering, in the sense that the scales of the dragon are catching the sunlight. Hammershaimb notes for his st. 85 the first and second lines as a variant of the stanza as presented here, and questions whether *af giltum* could be *af kelduni*. See *Sjúrðar Kvæði*, 11n1. This could mean from the bog, marsh or source of river. Lyngbye seems to suggest that this is a gilded snake, and that it could refer to the type of snake. See *Færøiske Qvæder*, 81n90.

38 We have chosen to translate this as snake here, but it could be a dragon (with another nearby). The episode seems to be mentioned too casually for it to be a dragon, however.

98. "Hoyr tú, frægi Sjúrður, av kongaborið vív, fyri tílíkar høvdingar vil eg lata lív.	"Listen, valiant Sjúrður, born of a woman of royal descent,[39] for such chieftains I will give my life.
99. Hoyr tú, frægi Sjúrður, siga mást tú mær, nær tú ríður á Glitrarheiði, eg vil fylgja tær."	Listen, valiant Sjúrður, you must tell me, when you ride to Glitrarheiði, I want to join you."
100. "Fyrst fari eg í randarný Hundsins synir at fella, síðan fari eg á Glitrarheiði, tí mær man einki bella.	"First I will go into battle to slay the sons of Hundingur, then I will go to Glitrarheiði, because nothing will hurt me.
101. Fyrst fari eg í randarný Hundsins synir at finna siðdan ríði eg á Glitrarheiði, tí tað verður mær minna."	First I will go into battle to find the sons of Hundingur then[40] I will ride to Glitrarheiði, because that will be the lesser deed[41] for me."
102. Snarliga vá hann Hundsins synir, snart kom hann aftur úr teirri, stokkut stund hann dvøldist við, hann reið á Glitrarheiði.	Quickly he slew the sons of Hundingur, soon he came back from them, for a fleeting moment he lingered, he rode to Glitrarheiði.
103. Allar vá hann Hundsins synir, væl kom hann aftur frá teim, skammri stund av ríkinum hann reið á Glitrarheiði.	He slew all of the sons of Hundingur, he came back from them safely, after a short time away from the kingdom he rode to Glitrarheiði.
104. Tað var svikarin Regin smiður, hugsar so við sær: "Kvittar tú á Glitrarheiði, eg skal fylgja tær."	That was the traitor Regin the smith, He thinks to himself: "If you leave for Glitrarheiði, I will join you."
105. Tað var hin ungi Sjúrður, ríður fram yvir skóg, møtir honum ein gamal maður settist niður á ló.	That was the young Sjúrður, riding over the forest, an old man meets him he[42] sits down on the sandy beach.

39 *Vív* is a poetic word for woman.

40 *Siðdan* in the Faroese is spelled wrongly; it should be *siðan*. It is spelt *sujan* in the critical edition of the manuscript. See Matras, *J. H. Schrøters optegnelser*, p. 6, st. 101.

41 In the Faroese, "deed" is understood.

42 It is not clear whether Sjúrður or the old man sits down on the beach.

106. Tað var hin ungi Sjúrður, ríður á Glitrarheiði, møtti hann einum gomlum manni mitt á sínari leið.	That was the young Sjúrður, riding to Glitrarheiði, he met an old man in the middle of his journey.
107. Tað var hin ungi Sjúrður, hann situr á baldum hesti, so er mær av sonnum sagt, at tað var Nornagestur.	That was the young Sjúrður, he sits on a bold horse, so I've been truthfully told,[43] that it was Nornagestur.
108. "Hoyr tú, reysti Sjúrður, siga skalt tú mær: hvør er hasin vesæli maður, í fylgi er við tær?"	"Listen, brave Sjúrður, you have to tell me: who is that wretched man accompanying you?"
109. "Regin smiður ormins bróðir hann er, tí er hann ein í hesari ferð."	"He is Regin the smith the dragon's brother, therefore he is on this journey."
110. "Hvør bað teg, Sjúrður, grava gravir tvær? Deyðan hevur sá maður aktað tær."	"Who told you, Sjúrður, to dig two trenches? That man has death intended for you."
111. "Regin legði ráðini, at grava gravir tvær, tí er hann við mær í hesari ferð."	"Regin gave me the advice to dig two trenches, therefore he is with me on this journey."
112. "Hevur Regin biðið teg grava gravir tvær, hann er versti Guds svikari, deyða vil hann teg.	"If Regin has told you to dig two trenches, then he is the worst of God's traitors, he wants death for you.
113. Grav tú nú tógvar, ta triðju har íhjá, ein mun av eitrinum man tað líva tá.	Now dig two, the third nearby, a mouthful of the poison will still be left.

43 The narrator of the ballad saying that they have been told something is part of the genre convention of the ballad and lends credibility to their story. It does not make it conditional or diminish the credibility, but rather makes what they have been told a fact.

114. Grav tú tær tríggjar, ta fjórðu skamt íhjá, síðan skalt tú, Sjúrður, at jørðini náa.	Dig yourself three, the fourth close by, then, Sjúrður, you should lie in the soil.[44]
115. Grav tú gryvjur fýra, um tú verður móður, harvið skalt tú verja teg fyri ormins eiturblóði."	Dig four trenches, if you become tired, in that way you shall defend yourself from the poisonous blood of the dragon."
116. Ormurin er skriðin av gullinum, tað man frættast víða, Sjúrður situr á Grana baki, býr seg til at ríða.	The dragon has slithered off the gold, it was told far and wide, Sjúrður is siting on Grani's back, preparing himself to ride.
117. Ormurin er skriðin av gullinum, langt ger hann skrið, Sjúrður trívur um benjarkolv, hann býr sítt svørðið til.	The dragon has slithered off the gold, he slithers a long way, Sjúrður grasps the sword,[45] he readies the sword.
118. Tríati alin var fossurin, ið ormurin undir lá, høvur og sporl á jørðini, bukt á homrum lá.	The waterfall was thirty ells high[46] that the dragon lay under, head and tail[47] on the ground and the bight[48] on the crags.
119. Tríati alin var fossurin, ið ormurin undir lá, uppi vóru bæði bøksl, og búkur á hamri lá.	The waterfall was thirty ells high that the dragon lay under, both forelimbs[49] were up in the air,[50] and the stomach lay on the crag.

44 This means literally "reach the earth," which we assume means he should lie down in the soil.

45 *Benjarkolvur* is a *heiti* for sword used in the ballads.

46 "High" is understood in the Faroese. An "ell" is an older measurement used in northern Europe, understood as the length of a man's arm from the elbow to the fingertips. This is traditionally understood as being around eighteen inches (45.7 cm), although the measurement was later standardized in different countries to a variety of different lengths.

47 *Sporl* is the same word used for fishtail.

48 The bight where the body of the dragon curves into a loop.

49 *Bøksl* means the front flipper of a whale.

50 We have added "in the air" for clarity here. If the head and tail are on the ground but the body is on the crag, it would imply the dragon is hanging in the air off the cliff.

120. Tað var hin snari Sjúrður,
sínum svørði brá,
hann kleyv tann hin frænarorm
sundur í lutir tvá.

That was the swift[51] Sjúrður,
he brandished his sword,
he split that dragon Frænar[52]
apart in two pieces.

121. Vænt var tað høggið,
ið Sjúrður gav ta stund,
tá skalv bæði leyv og lund
og øll vørildins grund.

That blow was graceful,
that Sjúrður dealt in that moment,
then both leaf and grove trembled
and all the foundations of the world.

122. Tá skalv bæði leyv og lund
og øll vørildins grund,
Sjúrður brá sín bitra brand,
hjó hann í fýra sundur.

Then both leaf and grove trembled
and all the foundations of the world,
Sjúrður drew his sharp sword,[53]
and hacked him apart into four.

123. Tá spurdi ormurin,
i fjørbrotunum lá:
"Hvør var so hin hugdjarvi,
ið vega tordi so?"

Then the dragon asked,
who lay in his death throes:
"Who was the courageous one
who dared to strike like that?"

124. "Sjúrða skalt tú nevna meg,
Sigmundar son,
Hjørdis drottning
móðir nevnd var hon."

"You shall call me Sjúrður,
son of Sigmundur,
Queen Hjørdis
my mother was named."

125. "Hoyr tú tað nú, Sjúrður,
eg sigi tað til tín:
hvør fylgdi tær tann ringa veg
higar nú til mín?"

"Now listen, Sjúrður,
I say this to you:
who accompanied you on the bad road
here to me?"

126. "Regin er tín bróðir,
hann vísti mær veg,
hann er tann versti svikarin,
deyða vildi hann teg."

"Your brother Regin,
he showed me the way,
he is the worst traitor,
he wanted death for you."

127. Til tess svaraði ormurin,
meðan hann fleyt í blóði:
"Drepa mást tú Regin smið,
hóast hann er mín bróðir.

The dragon answered to that,
while he was drenched in blood:
"You have to kill Regin the smith,
even though he is my brother.

---

51 *Snarur* can also mean brave. When it occurs with Sjúrður, functioning almost as a by-name, we have used "swift."

52 *Frænarorm* is not presented as a name in the edition here, but it clearly refers to the dragon Frænar.

53 *Brandur* is a *heiti* used for sword in ballads.

128. Veg tú nú Regin smið, sum tú hevur vigið meg, hann er versti svikarin, deyða vil sjálvan teg."	Slay Regin the smith as you have slain me, he is the worst traitor, he wants death even for you."
129. Stokti hann hjartað, vegin var so trongur, tríati alin var teinurin langur.	He roasted the heart,[54] the road was so narrow, the spit was thirty ells long.
130. Sjúrður gjørdist um hendur heitur, drap sær í munn, fuglar og allskyns djór vórðu honum á máli kunnig.	Sjúrður's hands got hot,[55] he stuck them in his mouth, he began to understand the language of birds and all kinds of animals.[56]
131. Tað var tá Regin smiður, talaði so fyri sær: "Fái eg tað nú, Sjúrður, ið tú lovaði mær?"	Then it was Regin the smith, speaking to himself like this: "Sjúrður, do I now get that which you promised me?"
132. Tá svaraðu vípurnar, uppi sótu í eik: "Sjálvur skalt tú, Sjúrður, eta tína steik."	Then the lapwings answered, that sat in the oak: "Sjúrður, you should eat your roast yourself."
133. Át hann hjartað, av teininum dró, Regin legðist at drekka ormins eiturblóð.	He ate the heart that he drew off the spit, Regin lay down to drink the poisonous blood of the dragon.
134. Regin legðist at drekka ormins eiturblóð, Sjúrður gav honum banasár í spori, sum hann stóð.	Regin lay down to drink the poisonous blood of the dragon, Sjúrður gave him a deadly wound where he stood in the track.[57]

54 Sjúrður is the one roasting the heart here.

55 I.e., he is burning himself. In Icelandic sources this is because he touches the meat to see whether it is done.

56 Although it does not explicitly say this in the ballad, in Old Norse tradition it is the blood of the dragon that Sjúrður inadvertently licks off his hands at this point that enables him to understand the birds.

57 Previously Regin was depicted as lying down. Now, suddenly, he appears to be standing. This is due to the needs of the rhyme.

135.	Tað var hin snari Sjúrður, sínum svørði brá, síðan kleyv hann Regin smið sundur í lutir tvá.	That was the swift Sjúrður, he drew his sword, then he split Regin the smith apart into two pieces.[58]
136.	Mikið mundi Sjúrður gullið ognast tá, tí hann vá tann frænarorm, á Glitraheiði lá.	Then Sjúrður acquired a lot of gold, because he slew the dragon Frænar that lay on Glitrarheiði
137.	Árla var um morgunin, áðrenn upp rann sól, bant hann á Grana bak gullkistur tólv.	Early in the morning, before the sun came up, he tied on Grani's back twelve chests of gold.
138.	Tólv gullkistur hvørjumegin klakk, Sjúrður settist omaná, og so er frásagt.	Twelve chests of gold on each side of the horse, Sjúrður sat himself on top, that's how it's told.
139.	Tólv gullkistur hvørjumegin á, Sjúrður leyp á lendar, og vreiður var Grani tá.	Twelve chests of gold on each side, Sjúrður leapt on the back, and Grani was resentful[59] then.
140.	Tólv gullkistur hvørjumegin klakk, sprakk hann yvir Lindará, so er frásagt.	Twelve chests of gold on each side of the horse, he leapt over Lindará, that's how it's told.
141.	Grani sprakk um díkið, sylgjan sundur gekk, tað er mær av sonnum sagt, at Nornagestur hana fekk.	Grani leapt over the dyke, the buckle burst apart, it has been told to me truthfully that Nornagestur got it.
142.	Nú skal lata ljóði av, eg kvøði ikki longur á sinni, nú skal taka upp annan tátt og víðari leggja í minni.	Now I shall end my song, I sing no longer at present, now to begin the second part of the ballad and continue to remember it.
Refrain	*Grani bar gullið av heiði, brá hann sínum brandi av reiði, Sjúrður vann av orminum, Grani bar gullið av heiði.*	*Grani carried the gold from the heath, he brandished his blade in a fury, Sjúrður defeated the dragon, Grani carried the gold from the heath.*

58 The words used here to describe Regin being chopped in two recall the words used to describe the two pieces of the sword and the splitting of the anvil.

59 *Vreiður* can also mean "angry" or "irate."

THE BALLAD OF BRYNHILD (BRYNHILDAR TÁTTUR)

1.	Eg veit eina rímuna, Buðla skulum vær kalla, hon er bæði mild og mæt, um Hákuns synir allar.	I know of a ballad, we shall call him Buðli, it is both pleasant and powerful,[1] about all of Hákun's sons.[2]
Refrain	*Grani bar gullið av heiði,* *brá hann sínum brandi av reiði,* *Sjúrður vann av orminum,* *Grani bar gullið av heiði.*	*Grani carried the gold from the heath,* *he brandished his blade in a fury,* *Sjúrður defeated the dragon,* *Grani carried the gold from the heath.*
2.	Kongur ræður fyri langa lund, bjarti Buðlin kallast, tívin telur málmaring við sínar hirðir allar.	A king rules a tall grove,[3] he is called fair Buðlin, the chieftain counts armoured nobles[4] amongst all his retinue.[5]
3.	Árla var um morgunin, tímin tað til bar, sjálvur er gingin Buðlin kongur í sín dótturs sal.	It was early in the morning, the time was right,[6] King Buðlin himself goes into his daughter's hall.[7]

---

1 "It" here refers to the ballad or story itself.

2 *Hákun* here is a synonym for king. In other variants, such as variants Bb and D (Grundtvig and Bloch, *Føroya kvæði*, vol. 1, p. 64, st. 3; vol. 1, p. 114, st. 1), it says *Júka synir* (sons of Júki). Júki is Gjúki in Old Norse, King of the Burgundians, head of the clan the Gjúkungar, father of Gunnarr, Hǫgni, Guðormr, and Guðrún. In Matras' edition of Schrøter, it noted that the *Haaguns* of the manuscript has been corrected to *Gjuka* by Lyngbye. Matras, *J. H. Schrøters optegnelser*, p. 10, line 4n.

3 This could also be a long grove; it is referring to his kingdom or land.

4 A *málmari* is an armoured soldier in the ballads. *Málmaringar* is also found in variant Bb (Grundtvig and Bloch, *Føroya kvæði*, vol. 1, p. 64, st. 4) and *málmaring* in variant D (Grundtvig and Bloch, *Føroya kvæði*, vol. 1, p. 114, st. 5). In Matras' edition of Schrøter, it says *Mölm Aar Ring*. Matras, *J. H. Schrøters optegnelser*, p. 10, st. 2. Lyngbye however cannot make sense of this and believes it to mean *Malm aa Rhin* (Rhinens malm), meaning "gold, money." Lyngbye, *Færøiske Qvæder*, 127–28n2. In this interpretation, the king would be counting money with his followers. Hammershaimb, on the other hand, has *málm og ring* (metal and ring). Hammershaimb, *Sjúrðar Kvæði*, p. 16, st. 3.

5 The *hirð* is a retinue, which is a body of people (usually understood to be men) retained in the service of a noble, here king. Cf. the *hirðkonur* (lit. female retainers) who attend to Hjørdis in *Regin smiður*, st. 25.

6 This means it was a good opportunity for the king to visit his daughter because it was early.

7 It is unclear how this stanza got into the edition of variant A (translated here) in Grundtvig and Bloch, *Føroya kvæði*, vol. 1. It is not in the edition of the manuscript by Matras, *J. H. Schrøters optegnelser*, nor is it in Lyngbye, *Færøiske Qvæder*.

4. Brynhild situr á Hildarfjalli,
hon er dóttir Buðla,
sigist so til í bragdartátti,
sól skein hana við skugga.

Brynhild sits on Hildarfjall,
she is the daughter of Buðli,
it is told in *bragdartáttur*,[8]
that the sun shone on her as a shadow.[9]

5. Brynhild situr í stólinum,
kembir hon sítt hár,
fínt er tað sum silki,
gull ber litur á.

Brynhild sits in her throne,
she combs her hair,
it is fine as silk,
the colour is that of gold.

6. Brynhild situr í hallini,
sum ríkir ganga inn,
ongan tykti Buðla dóttir
vera javnlíka sín.

Brynhild sits in the hall,
as the powerful walk in,
Buðli's daughter did not find any of them
to be her equal.[10]

7. Tað var reystur kongurin,
sveipar hann seg í skinn,
so gongur hann í høgaloft
fyri sína dóttur inn.

That was the bold king,
wrapping his cloak[11] around him,
then he walks into the hall[12]
before his daughter.

8. Brynhild situr í stólinum
so jammurliga tvist,
kongurin hann krevur
sína dóttur við list.

Brynhild sits in the throne
so miserably quiet,
the king makes demands of
his daughter with cleverness.[13]

It is, however, very close to st. 11 in variant E of *Brynhildar táttur*. Grundtvig and Bloch, *Føroya kvæði*, vol. 1, p. 146: "Tað var um ein halgan dag, / ið tímin hartil bar, / gingin var hann Buðli kongur / í sín dótturs sal." This version was recorded by Hammershaimb from Hans Johanneson (Sandur, Sandoy). Chesnutt and Larsen, *History, Manuscripts, Indexes*, 79. However, it is not in Hammershaimb, *Sjúrðar Kvæði*.

8 *Bragdartáttur* is also cited in *Høgnar táttur* as a source. Lyngbye interprets *bragdartáttur* to be the name of a lost ballad and suggests it could be the same lay as *Guðrúnarbrǫgð hin fornu*, mentioned in the Old Icelandic *Nornagests þáttr*. Lyngbye, *Færøiske Qvæder*, 41–42. It could, however, be a reference to tales of admirable deeds as told in the *kappakvæði* (heroic ballads), especially those in the *Bragdar tættir* in the *Karlamagnusar kvæði*. See Grundtvig and Bloch, "Bragdar Tættir" (although the content of those *tættir* do not have to do with this one). Cf. the words *bradgagerð* and *bradgaligur* (heroic or valerous deeds) and *bragdamenni* (hero).

9 This is expressing that Brynhild is brighter than the sun, and that the sun becomes like a shadow when it is close to or compared to her.

10 She is rejecting suitors.

11 *Skinn*, literally meaning "hide," sometimes means "cloak" in ballads.

12 *Høgaloft* is a private chamber on the second floor. Cf. st. 27 of *Regin smiður* when Hjørdis gives birth in the *høgaloft*.

13 *List*, translated here as cleverness, means clever in a cunning way. It could potentially have magical connotations and can also mean "art" or "artifice."

9. "Hoyr tað, mín hin sæla dóttir, sig mær satt ífrá: ríður so nakar higar í dag, ið tín stár hugur á?	"Listen, my dear daughter, tell me truthfully: Is there anyone riding here[14] today that you would find appealing?
10. Ríður so nakar higar í dag, ið tín stár hugur á, var hann ei tín onkabróðir, hann skuldi tú fáa."	If there is anyone riding here today that you find appealing, if he wasn't your own beloved brother,[15] you would have him."
11. "Hoyr tað nú, mín sæli faðir, eg sigi tær satt ífrá: so ríður eingin higar í dag, ið mín stár hugur á."	"Now listen, my dear father, I tell you truthfully: No one is riding here today that I find appealing."
12. "Hvør leingi vilt tú, mín sæla dóttir, elva mær tann vanda, at tú noktar hvørjum manni, ið tær býðst til handa?	"How long will you, my dear daughter, continue to cause me such worry, that you refuse every man that offers you their hand?
13. Hvør leingi vilt tú, mín sæla dóttir, eyka mær ta sorg, at tú noktar hvønn at eiga, higar kemur í borg?"	How long will you, my dear daughter, increase my sorrow, that you refuse to marry anyone that comes here to this castle?"
14. "Sjúrður eitur sá maður, Sigmundar son, tað tykti mær vera mín sámi at vera hansara kona."	"Sjúrður is the name of that man, Sigmundur's son, that seemed to me to be fitting for me to be his wife."
15. "Undarliga hevur tú tær ástirnar við tær mett, at tú unnar manni tann, ið tú hevur ikki sætt."	"You have strangely chosen your love, that you love a man who you have not seen."
16. "Tað hava mær nornir skapt, viti tað Gud og menn, níggju vetur unti eg Sjúrða, ósæddan enn.	"The Norns[16] shaped this for me, both God and men know, that for nine winters[17] I have loved Sjúrður, though still unseen.

14 *Higar* is an adverb of direction and means "to here, hither." See also, for example, stt. 10 and 11.

15 *Onkabróðir* is a favourite brother that you love more than the others. This is from Old Norse *einka-* in compounds, denoting something special or particular.

16 The norns are female beings in Old Norse mythology who shape human destinies.

17 This is used to signify "a very long time."

<table>
<tr><td>17. Tað hava mær nornir skapt,
liggur í brósti trá,
níggju vetur Sjúrða unga,
eg ei við eygum sá."</td><td>The Norns shaped this for me,
a desire in my breast,
nine winters young Sjúrður,
I didn't see with my eyes."</td></tr>
<tr><td>18. Til tess svaraði kongurin,
hann drekkur tann mjøðin reina:
"Hvat er hann Sjúrður frægari
enn aðrir danisveinar?</td><td>To that the king answered,
he drinks the pure mead:
"How is Sjúrður better
than other honourable men?[18]</td></tr>
<tr><td>19. Hoyr nú, mín hin sæla dóttir,
so sigi eg tær enn:
hvat er hann Sjúrður frægari
enn aðrir kongins menn?"</td><td>Listen, my dear daughter,
I say to you once again:
how is Sjúrður better
than others of the king's men?"</td></tr>
<tr><td>20. "Tað er hann Sjúrður frægari
enn aðrir kongins menn,
tí hann fellir heidningarnar,
hundrað um í senn.</td><td>"This is how Sjúrður is better
than the others of the king's men,
because he is killing the heathens,
a hundred in one go.[19]</td></tr>
<tr><td>21. Tað er hann Sjúrður frægari
enn aðrir danisveinar,
saðil hans og hestbúni
tað glógvar sum gullið reina.</td><td>This is how Sjúrður is better
than other honourable men,
his saddle and tack
shine like pure gold.</td></tr>
<tr><td>22. Tað er hann Sjúrður frægari
fram fyri aðrar garpar,
saðil hans og teymarnir
tað glógvar av gulli bjarta.</td><td>This is how Sjúrður is better
than other warriors,
his saddle and bridle
shine of bright gold.</td></tr>
<tr><td>23. Hoyrt havi eg frásagt,
ikki var eg hjá,
tá ið hann ormin á Glitrarheiði
við sínum svørði vá.</td><td>I have heard it told,
I was not present,
when he slew the dragon on Glitrarheiði
with his sword.</td></tr>
</table>

18 A *danimaður* is a gentleman or man of honour. It is likely referring back to st. 2, which refers to the king's retinue, although the context here is the suitors.

19 This line is formulaic and found in other ballads in the context of killing a lot of people in one go.

24. Hoyrt havi eg frásagt tí sama sjáldna bragdi, hvussu hann tann frænarorm við svørði niður lagdi.	I have heard it told, in the same remarkable deed, how he felled the dragon Frænir[20] with his sword.
25. Mikið mundi Sjúrður gullið ognast tá, tí hann vá tann frænarorm, á Glitrarheiði lá.	Sjúrður acquired a great quantity of gold, when he slew the dragon Frænir, who lay on Glitrarheidi.
26. Tólv gullkistur hvørjumegin klakk bant hann tað á Grana bak, so er mær frásagt."	Twelve chests of gold on each side of the horse he tied to Grani's back, so I've been told."
27. "Hoyr tú, mín hin sæla dóttir, legg nú til tess ráð, hvussu vit skulu tann mikla mann av øðrum londum fáa!"	"Listen, my dear daughter, tell me the plan,[21] how we will get that great man to come here from other lands!"
28. "Tú skalt lata mær salin byggja, í oyðimark so gera, við so lítlari tænastu skal eg har inni vera.	"You must build a hall for me, in a deserted place, with so few attendants I shall be in there.
29. Og so miklan váðaloga lat tú harum gera, sum teir kunnu dvørgar tveir mest við rúnum skera.	And have such a mighty wall of fire[22] surround it, as good as two dwarves could carve with runes.[23]
30. Hesin sami váðalogi hann man meg so varða, har man eingin ríða á uttan Sjúrður snari."	This same perilous wall of fire will protect me, no one may ride through it except the swift Sjúrður."

20 We have chosen to interpret Frænar as a personal name and as obviously the dragon Fávnir. However, Hammershaimb and Jakobsen gloss *frænarormur* as a glistening dragon or snake. Hammershaimb and Jakobsen, *Færøsk anthologi*, vol. 2, p. 76. Matras interprets Frænar as a personal name. Matras, *J. H. Schrøters optegnelser*, 89.

21 Her father is asking her for advice and wants to discuss this with her. He wants her ideas on how she is going to make Sjúrður come to them.

22 This is a perilous fire surrounding her bower.

23 The dwarves create the wall of fire with runes.

31. Hann læt henni salin tann
í oyðimark so gera,
við so lítlari tænastu
hon skuldi harí vera.

He built her that hall
in a deserted place,
with so few attendants
she should stay in there.

32. Og so miklan váðaloga
læt hann harum gera,
sum teir kundu dvørgar tveir
mest við rúnum skera.

And had such a mighty wall of fire
surround it,
as good as two dwarves
could carve with runes.[24]

33. Og so miklan váðaloga
læt hann harum slá,
ei mundu dvørgarnir
við svikunum ná.

And he had such a mighty wall of fire
made around there,[25]
the dwarves were not able to succeed
with any trickery.

34. Og so miklan váðaloga
læt hann harum vera,
ikki máttu dvørgarnir
burtur við rúnum bera.

And such a mighty wall of fire
he had there be around there,
the dwarves could not
take it away with runes.[26]

35. Stríða teir í Húnalandi
við útdragin knív,
hevur so mangur edilingur
fyri kvinnur latið lív.

They fight in Húnaland[27]
with unsheathed knives,
so many noble men
have lost their lives for women.[28]

36. Árla var um morgunin,
sólin skín so víða,
tað vóru teir Húnakongar,
teir búðu seg út at ríða.

It was early in the morning,
the sun shines far and wide,
as the Hunnish kings
readied themselves to ride.

37. Tað vóru teir Húnakongar,
búðu seg út at ríða,
frægari vóru Júkagarpar,
nú ið teir komu at stríða.

It was the Hunnish kings,
readying themselves to ride,
better were Júki's warriors,
now that they come to battle.

---

24 Here the narrator echoes Brynhild's command in st. 29.

25 The dwarves have built the wall of fire with rune magic.

26 The dwarves are not able to take the fire made with rune magic away.

27 Húnaland is the land of the Huns. The Huns were the enemies of the Burgundians, the Gjúkingar (Gunnarr and his brothers). In the Völsung legend, their sister Guðrún marries Atila the Hun (Atli) after having been married to Sigurðr (the Faroese Sjúrður), but Guðrún later kills Atli.

28 Stt. 35, 36, and 37 have nothing to do really with the immediate action of the ballad, but they do relate to the wider Völsung legend.

38. Árla var um morgunin, sólin skín í fjøll, tað ríður so mangur edilingur í Buðla kongins høll.	It was early in the morning, the sun shines on the mountains, so many a noble man rides to King Buðli's hall.
39. Árla var um morgunin sólin bráar í brún, ríða so frægir edilingar í Buðla kongins tún.	It was early in the morning the sun shines on the horizon, such valiant nobles ride to King Buðli's courtyard.
40. Ríða so mangir edilingar í Buðla kongins tún, Brynhild situr í Hildarstóli, hon ber gull á brún.	So many noble men ride to King Buðli's courtyard, Brynhild sits on the Hildarstólur, she wears gold on her brows.[29]
41. Buðlin kongur í salin gongur, beiðir frúgv við svari: "Komin er hann Gunnar kongur niðan úr Júkagarði.	King Buðlin walks into the hall, asks the lady for an answer: "King Gunnar has come from Júki's court.
42. Hoyr tú, Brynhild dóttir mín, gera skalt tú tað, komin er hann Gunnar kongur, honum sigur tú ja."	Listen, Brynhild my daughter, you will do this,[30] King Gunnar has come, you will say yes to him."
43. Buðlin kongur á gólvi stendur styðjar seg við borð, Brynhild unga dóttir hans hon talar ikki eitt orð.	King Buðlin stands on the floor leaning on the table,[31] Brynhild his young daughter she doesn't speak a word.
44. Brynhild seg úr stóli lyfti, glógvar í gulli reyð, skundaði sær av Buðlins borg, hon gongur á Hildarheyg.	Brynhild rises herself from the chair, she shines with red gold, hurrying away from Buðlin's castle, she goes to Hildarheygur.
45. Grímur og Høgnar Júkason teir møttust á grønum vølli, moyar hvukku í Hildarsali, nú skelvur høga Buðlins høll.	Grímur and Høgnar Júkason they clashed in a green field, maidens were startled in Hildarsalur, now Buðlin's high hall trembles.

29 She is wearing a crown.

30 He is telling her she will obey him.

31 The intention here is to show him threatening her.

46. Grímur og Høgnar Júkason teir slógust við bitrum brandi, Brynhild situr í váðaloga mitt í faðirs síns landi	Grímur and Høgnar Júkason they fought with sharp swords, Brynhild sits within the wall of fire in the middle of her father's land.
47. Settist aftur í gyltan stól, hon smílist undir lín: "Hvør ið heldur á váðalogan, hann skal verða mín."	Sat down again on the gilded throne, she smiles under her linen:[32] "He who rides through the wall of fire shall be mine."
48. Brynhild situr í gyltum stóli, tað hitt væna vív, dregur hon Sjúrð av Norðlondum í Hildarheyg til sín.	Brynhild sits on the gilded throne, that beautiful woman, she draws Sjúrður from the northern lands to her in Hildarheygur.[33]
49. Brynhild situr í Hildarheyg, tað hitt væna vív, dregur hon Sjúrð av Norðlondum sær til sorgartíð.	Brynhild sits in Hildarheygur, that beautiful woman, she draws Sjúrður from the northern lands to her to times of sorrow.[34]
50. Ein dag frættir Sjúrður burtur í onnur lond: Brynhild svevur á Hildarheyggi, hon er biðlavond.	One day Sjúrður hears news away in other lands:[35] Brynhild sleeps on Hildarheygur, she rejects suitors.
51. Sjúrður reið út árla morgun, ei hans fostra visti, eingin veit á morgni at siga, hvar ið hann á kvøldi gistir.	Sjúrður rode out early in the morning, his foster-mother didn't know,[36] no one knows in the morning, where they will stay in the evening.[37]

32 Brynhild being under linen could signify she is dressed in a bridal headdress ready to be married. The headwear of a bride on the wedding day was made of linen, hence Old Norse *ganga und líni*, "to be wedded." See Wikman, "Bröllop," 315. In other ballads this is, however, less obviously the case, since sometimes men are said to be "smiling under linen," which may only be added to provide a parallel to surrounding stanzas in which women are "smiling under linen," wearing a female headdress.

33 Brynhild draws Sjúrður to her by magic.

34 Times of sorrow is not what she is planning but rather the effect—times of sorrow will follow. This is a flashforward in the story.

35 He is abroad, away from home, when he hears the news about Brynhild.

36 It was so secret that he left that even his foster-mother did not know. Usually, Sjúrður is depicted as having a foster-father, and this is how Lyngbye interprets the line, glossing the figure as Hjalprek. Lyngbye, *Færøiske Qvæder*, 148n. However, the form is feminine. It could also mean "foster-daughter," but it is not clear who this would be.

37 This is a common saying in the ballads.

52. Sjúrður reið út árla morgun, gyrdi seg við horni, har sótu tveir villini fuglar á einum summarsmorgni.	Sjúrður rode out early in the morning, girded himself with a horn,[38] there sat two wild birds on a summer morning.
53. Ein dag tóku fuglarnir at mæla millum sín: "Brynhild svevur á Hildarheyggi, og hagar væntar hon tín."	One day the birds started talking between themselves: "Brynhild sleeps on Hildarheygur, and there she's expecting you."
54. Ein dag tóku fuglarnir ímillum sín at mæla: "Brynhild situr á Hildarheyggi, hagar man Sjúrður fara."	One day the birds started talking between themselves: "Brynhild sits on Hildarheygur, Sjúrður will go there."
55. Enn tá frætti Sjúrður, um Húnaland hann fór: Brynhild situr í sínum sali, hon er so heitstór.	Even then Sjúrður heard, as he travelled in Húnaland: Brynhild sits in her hall, she is so haughty
56. Sjúrður kvittar at ríða á Buðla kongins land, gullibúnar handskarnar teir dregur hann sær á hond.	Sjúrður leaves to ride to King Buðli's lands, the gold-threaded gloves he pulls them on his hands.
57. Tólv gullringar hevði hann har íhjá, drottningsringin reyða omaná.	Twelve gold rings he had with him, and the red ring of the queen as well.
58. Tólv gullringar dregur hann sær á hond, síðan kvittar nýtur drongur á Buðla kongins land.	Twelve rings of gold he puts on his arms, then the brave young man leaves for King Buðli's land.
59. So gongur hann Grani grótið so sum sand, eingin kemur tílíkur á Buðla kongins land.	Grani walks across rocks as well as sand, an equal to him will never come to King Buðli's land.
60. So gongur hann Grani í gróti sum á vølli, slíkur kemur ikki aftur á Buðla kongins fjøll.	Grani walks across rocks as well as fields, such a horse won't return to King Buðli's mountains.

38 This is possibly a signalling horn.

61. Hann reið sær so niðarlaga við Júkagørðum fram, úti stóð frúgv Grimhild við so miklan mann.	He rode down so closely by Júki's court, Lady Grimhild stood outside with mighty men.
62. Úti stóð hon Grimhild við so mangan mann, tí hon vildi forvit[n]ast, hvar ið Sjúrður ríður fram.	Grimhild stood outside[39] with so many men, because she was curious about where Sjúrður rode to.
63. Gjarna vil hon síggja tað, hvar ið Sjúrður ríður fram, hon sá ikki á hestbaki ein tíguligari mann.	She would like to see, where Sjúrður rode to, she hadn't seen on horseback a more magnificent man.
64. "Sjúrður, støða tínari ferð og tala við meg, eg eigi mær so væna dóttur, við ástir vil leiða teg.	"Stop your journey Sjúrður and speak with me, I have such a beautiful daughter, who wants to love you.[40]
65. Tú ger væl, snarpi Sjúrður, tú snakka vilt við meg, eg eigi mær so eina dóttur, við ástum leiðir hon teg."	You do well, brave Sjúrður, that you want to speak with me, I have such a daughter, she wants to love you."[41]
66. "Eg stilli ikki mínari ferð, meðan mín gangari rennur, eg fari mær á heyggin fram, sum váðalogin brennur.	"I won't stop my journey, while my steed runs, I am going to the mound, where the wall of fire burns.
67. Eg støðgi ikki mínari ferð, mín gangari rennur so strítt, eg fari mær á heyggin fram at finna tað væna vív.	I won't stop my journey, my steed runs so fast, I am going to the mound to find the beautiful woman.[42]
68. Eg støði ikki mínari ferð, mín gangari rennur í lund, eg fari mær á heyggin fram at skoða tað væna sprund."	I won't stop my journey, my steed runs in a grove, I am going to the mound to see the beautiful woman."[43]

39 *Úti stóð* is a formulaic thing to say. She is waiting for him.

40 This is a parallel to Brynhild—they both fall in love with him without seeing him.

41 She wants to marry him.

42 *Vív* is a *heiti* for a woman.

43 *Sprund* is also a *heiti* for a woman, and therefore mirrors the end of the stanza above.

69. Sjúrður klæðist árla morgun,
hann fór í brynju víða:
"Eg havi so lítið ørindi
í Eysturlond at ríða."

Sjúrður is getting dressed early one morning,
he went in a large coat of mail:[44]
"I have a small errand
I have to ride to the eastern lands."[45]

70. Tað er enn sum ofta fyrr,
biðlar fara at fríggja,
eingin tordi longur fram
enn váðalogan at síggja.

It is yet like often times before,
suitors go to woo,
no one dared to go further
at the sight of the wall of fire.[46]

71. Merkismaður orðum talar,
tungan mælir inna:
"Hvør ið heldur á váðalogan,
hann skal ta jomfrú vinna."

An outstanding man[47] speaks these words,
saying:
"He who crosses the wall of fire,
will win the maiden."

72. Grímur ríður á grønum vølli,
kinn ber hann so baldan,
hann vendi sín hest frá váðaloga,
hann skuldi í bálið halda.

Grímur rides on the green field,[48]
his cheeks are so bold,[49]
he turned his horse away from the wall of fire,
as he was going to cross the fire.[50]

73. Sjúrður frægi til orða tekur,
frá man frættast víða:
"Eg beri tað merki í mítt skjold,
eg skal nú harí ríða."

Brave Sjúrður began to speak,
it was told far and wide:[51]
"I bear that emblem on my shield,[52]
I will now ride through."

---

44 He is wearing a large coat of armour.

45 Here the Faroese writes *Eysturlond* like it is a country with a capital letter, but we have chosen to translate it as "eastern lands."

46 The suitors hesitate when they see the wall of fire, and they turn back.

47 A *merkismaður* is an excellent man with power and influence, and it is a word often used in obituaries. It could, in this context, also mean a flag- or standard-bearer.

48 In st. 45, Grímur clashes with Høgnar.

49 *Baldur* can also mean "fair," and in this context implies that he has a brave-looking face.

50 In this stanza there are two different words for fire. *Logi* refers more to individual flames, while *bál* refers to something like a bonfire.

51 This is a formulaic phrase often used in ballads.

52 Although this is opaque in the ballad, we hear about this in the Icelandic *Vǫlsunga saga*: "Hans skjǫldr var margfaldr ok laugaðr í rauðu gulli ok skrifaðr á einn dreki. Hann var dǫkkbrúnaðr it efra, en fagrrauðr it neðra, ok þann veg var markaðr hans hjálmr ok sǫðull ok vápnrokkr. Hann hafði gullbrynjuna, ok ǫll hans vápn váru gulli búin. Ok því var dreki markaðr á hans vápnum ǫllum at, er hann er sénn, má vita hverr þar ferr af ǫllum þeim er frétt hafa at hann drap þann mikla dreka er Væringjar kalla Fáfni. Ok fyrir því eru vápn hans ǫll gulli búin ok brún at lit, at hann er langt

74. Eingin reið á Brynhilduheyg
uttan Sjúrður snari,
gjøgnum royk og váðaloga,
hann og hestur hans Grani.

None rode onto Brynhilduheygur[53]
but the swift Sjúrður,
through smoke and the wall of fire,
he and his horse Grani.

75. So steig tá Grani á
foldunum fast,
innarlaga í heygginum
tað hóvsporið brast.

Grani leaps so firmly
over the ground,
well up on to the mound
that the hoofbeats were thundering.

76. So stígur Grani
drístuliga fram,
heitur var tann eldurin,
Sjúrða um lendar brann.

Grani strode so
boldly forward,
the fire was hot,
it burnt around Sjúrður's loins.

77. Og so stígur Grani
gjøgnum tann roykin svarta,
hann kom at tí portrinum,
tað skín sum gullið bjarta.

Grani strode
through the black smoke,
he came to the gate
that shines like brilliant gold.

78. Sjúrður reið tann váðaloga,
ið eingin vágdi fyrr,
og við sínum svørðinum,
tá kleyv hann niður dyr.

Sjúrður rode through the wall of fire
that no one had dared to before,
and with his sword,
he split down the door.

79. Og við sínum svørðinum
klývur hann lokur frá,
sá hann, hvar ið Buðlins dóttir
eina í songum lá.

And with his sword
he splits off the latch,
there he saw where Buðli's daughter
lay alone in bed.

80. Sjúrður frægi í salin gongur,
víða um seg hyggur,
sær hann, hvar tað væna vív
eina í songum liggur.

Brave Sjúrður went into the quarters,
looking all around,
he sees there the beautiful woman
lying alone in bed.

---

umfram aðra menn at kurteisi ok allri hœfersku ok náliga at ǫllum hlutum." (His shield was of many thicknesses. It was plated with gold, on it was pictured a dragon. Its upper part was dark brown, and its lower light red, and his helm, saddle and surcoat were emblazoned in the same way. His hauberk was of gold, and all his weapons were decked with gold. And the reason for the dragon being emblazoned on all his weapons was so that all those who had heard that he'd killed the great dragon the Værings called Fafnir, would know on seeing him who he was. And the reason for his weapons being all decked with gold and gleaming bright was that he far excelled others in fine manners, in all the social graces and well-nigh in everything). Finch, *Vǫlsunga Saga*, 40–41.

53 Up on to the mound.

81. Hann sá, hvar tað væna vív
í herklæðunum svav,
Sjúrður tók sín bitra brand,
hann sprettir brynju av.

He saw where the beautiful woman
was sleeping in armour,
Sjúrður took his sharp sword,
he splits the mail coat open.

82. Upp vaknaði Brynhild,
hon hyggin um seg leit:
"Hvør átti tann búgvin brand,
ið brynju av mær beit?"

Brynhild woke up,
she looked around curiously:
"Who owned that splendid sword
that cut my mail coat open?"

83. Upp vaknaði Brynhild,
víða um seg sær:
"Hvør er tann hin djarvi drongur,
ið brynju sprettir av mær?"

Brynhild woke up,
looking all around,
"Who is that courageous hero
who is splitting the mail coat open?"

84. "Riðin eri eg av Norðlondum
higar nú til tín,
Sjúrður Sigmundar sonur,
veldiga søta mín.

"I have ridden from the northern lands
all the way to you,
Sjúrður son of Sigmundur
my magnificent[54] sweet one.

85. Sjúrða skalt tú nevna meg,
Sigmundar svein,
Hjørdis drottningin
hon bar meg í heim."

You shall call me Sjúrður,
Sigmundur's son,
the queen Hjørdis
brought me into the world."

86. Brynhild setist upp undir seg,
smílist undir lín:
"Ver vælkomin av øðrum londum,
Sjúrður, søtin mín!

Brynhild sat up,
smiled to herself under linen:
"Welcome from other lands,
Sjúrður, my sweet one!

87. Hoyr tú tað nú, Sjúrður,
hvør vísti tær leið
gjøgnum royk og váðaloga,
at tú higar reið?"

Now listen, Sjúrður,
who showed you the route
through smoke and the wall of fire,
so that you rode here?"

88. "Ørnin á kvisti
bíðaði hon mín,
hon vísti mær vegin
higar heim til tín."

"The eagle on the branch
waited for me,
she showed me the way
here, home to you."[55]

---

54 He's impressed, as she is mighty.

55 This is an anthropomorphized eagle. In *Vǫlsunga saga*, ch. 25, Sigurðr sees Brynhildr for the first time because his hawk lands on her tower and he goes to fetch it and sees her within, embroidering a picture of his heroic deeds. Finch, *Vǫlsunga Saga*, 42. This is not the episode with the wall of fire.

89. "Hoyr tú, Sjúrður søti mín, ver nú ei so bráð, gakk tær heldur til mín faðir, tak av honum ráð!"	"Listen, Sjúrður my sweet, don't be so hasty. go rather to my father, ask for his decision."[56]
90. "Tú hevur so leingi, frúgv Brynhild, stundað heim til vár, eg fari ei til tín sæla faðir, taki ei av honum ráð.	"You have for so long, lady Brynhild, been longing to come home to us, I will not go to your dear father, will not ask for his decision.
91. Tú hevur so leingi, frúgv Brynhild, stundað á mítt fund, tað søgdu mær alsingarnir gjøgnum grønan lund."	You have so long, lady Brynhild, waited to meet me, it was said to me by the birds,[57] through the green grove."
92. Løgdu tey sínar ástir saman innan mentarfund, tá varð hon Ásla Sjúrðardóttir gitin á teirri stund.	They fell in love at that splendid meeting,[58] then Ásla Sjúrðardóttir was conceived at that moment.
93. Løgdu sínar ástir saman ytst við menjargátt, tá varð Ásla Sjúrðardóttir gitin á teirri nátt	They fell in love by the splendid front gate,[59] then Ásla Sjúrðardóttir was conceived that night.

56 He is to ask him if they can be married.

57 Lyngbye explains *alsingarnir* as "the singing birds." Lyngbye, *Færøiske Qvæder*, 164n92.

58 The meaning of *mentarfundur* is unclear. It could be translated as *mentar-* (fine, splendid, or magnificent) and *fundur*, meaning "meeting" or "rendezvous," as we have chosen here. Hammershaimb (*Sjúrðar Kvæði*, p. 24, st. 93) has *við tàð mentar sprund* for this line, where *sprund* is a poetic word for "woman," and suggests in 24n2 that this could be *menjarsprund*, a word found in other ballads and which means a delightful or wonderful woman. Lyngbye has *mentar Fund*, and his interpretation is that this refers to Brynhild's bower, with the magical flames around it, relating *mentar* to something like the Old Norse *mennt* (art, skill), referring to the artificial flames around Brynhild's quarters. Lyngbye, *Færøiske Qvæder*, 164.

59 This literally means "outermost by the splendid door," likely referring to the gate Sjúrður goes through in st. 77. *Menjar-* references gold and ornaments (cf. Old Norse *men*, meaning "jewels, treasures" in the plural). It is used in many ballad words, such as *menjarbaldur* (chieftain or hero) and *menjargrund* (woman). *Gátt* means "doorway," cf. *út á ytstu gátt* (to the front door). See *Føroysk-ensk orðabók*, s.v. "Ytstur."

94. Allir teir í Buðlins høll
lova tey onkaverka,
innan fyri mentarfund
bundu tey ástin sterka.

All those in Buðlin's hall
are praising the exceptional deed,[60]
at the splendid meeting[61]
they fell deeply in love.[62]

95. Blíðar legði hann armarnar
yvir Brynhildu háls,
eg svørji tann eið á mína trú,
har búði ikki undir falsk.

Gently he laid his arms
over Brynhild's neck,
I swear an oath by all that is sacred,[63]
there is no deceit.

96. Tólv gullringar
legði hann frúnni á fang,
síðan legði hann omaná
tann dýra drottningsring.

Twelve gold rings
he laid in the lady's lap,
then he laid as well
the precious ring of the queen.

97. Tólv gullringar
dró hann frúnni á hond:
"Hetta skal vera tað fyrsta
elskógins band."

Twelve gold rings
he drew onto the lady's arm:
"This shall be the first
bond of love."

98. Guðrun gekk á gullstólin,
tað hitt væna vív,
dró hon Sjúrð av Hildarheyg
í Júkagarð til sín.

Guðrun went to the gold throne,
that beautiful woman,
she drew Sjúrður from Hildarheygur
to Júki's court to herself.

99. Sjúrður situr í stólinum,
niður fyri seg sær:
"Hvat mundi Grimhild drottning
vilja nú mær?

Sjúrður sits in the throne,
looks down in front of himself:
"What was it that Queen Grimhild
wanted with me?

100. Brynhild, tak mær saðil og boksl,
ringabrynju síða,
eg havi so lítið ørindi
burt annarsstaðni at ríða."

Brynhild, fetch me a saddle and bridle,
a long coat of mail,
I have a small errand
to ride away to another place."

---

60 They are praising the exceptional deed of Sjúrður riding through the wall of fire.

61 See st. 92, line 2n, for *mentarfund*.

62 This literally means that they forged strong bonds between them; they are bound deeply in love.

63 Cf. *svørja á sína trú*, swear by all that is sacred, see *Føroysk-ensk orðabók*, s.v. "Trú." Literally this means he is swearing an oath on his faith.

101. Til tess svaraði Brynhild, tekur um hjarta at køla: "Júkin kongur dóttur eigur, við ástir man teg mæla."	To this answered Brynhild, her heart beginning to chill, "King Júkin has a daughter, she wants to love you."[64]
102. "Tað tykir mær vera undarligt, at meg skal tað henda: eg skal allar mínar ástir frá tær, Brynhild, venda."	"I think that is unlikely, that it should happen to me: that I should turn all of my love from you, Brynhild."
103. Til tess svaraði Brynhild av so miklum sút: "Ríð tú ikki tann niðara vegin við Júkagørðum út.	To this answered Brynhild, out of great stress: "Do not ride the lower road to the court of Júki.
104. Hoyr tú tað nú, Sjúrður, eg gevi tær fingurgull, ríð tær ikki til Grimhildu, tí hon er av svikum full."	Now listen, Sjúrður, I give you finger-gold,[65] do not ride to Grimhild, because she is full of deceit."
105. Tað var um ein árla morgun, hann frá Brynhildu reið, møtti hann hennara sæla faðir skamt frá sínari leið.	It was early one morning, he rode away from Brynhild, he met her dear father not far from his path
106. Sjúrður situr á Grana baki, hugin ið hann vendi hagar, sum hennara faðir var, har av vegnum rendi.	Sjúrður sits on Grani's back, he turned his mind to where her father was, there off the road.
107. "Ver vælkomin, Sjúrður, tú tørvt ei boðini senda, fullvæl veit eg tín forløg út, hvørt tær skal ganga til enda.	"Welcome, Sjúrður, you need not send the message, I know full well your destiny, how it will go for you in the end.[66]
108. Tú manst vera á aldri ungur, lívið man tó tær tróta, tú manst ognast Guðruna, Brynhildu ikki njóta.	You may be of a young age, but your life will still be short, you will marry Guðrun, and never have Brynhild.

64 This reflects the final lines of stt. 64 and 65, spoken by Grimhild.

65 "Finger-gold" is a ring.

66 Buðli, Brynhild's father, is speaking this stanza and the two following.

109. Hevur tú Brynhildu tryggan lovað, væl manst tú tað halda, Guðrun blandar valmannadrykk, tað man nú sútir valda."	If you have made a promise to Brynhild, you ought to keep it, Guðrun mixes a drink of forgetfulness, that will cause great sorrow."
110. "Tað tykir mær vera undarligt, at meg skal tað henda: eg skal allar mínar ástir frá Brynhildu venda."	"I think that is unlikely, that it should happen to me: that I should turn all of my love from Brynhild."[67]
111. "Hoyr tú tað nú, Sjúrður, ger tú ei tann skamm, ríð tær ikki so niðarlaga hjá Júkagørðum fram.	"Listen now, Sjúrður, do not commit this shameful act, do not ride so closely to the court of Júki.
112. Ríð tú ikki tann niðara vegin við Júkagarðar fram, ríð tær heldur í erva, har hendir tær ongan skamm.	Do not ride the lower road to Júki's court, rather ride the higher road, there no shame will befall you.
113. Bæði heilur og happadur(!), vit skiljast nú á sinni, Sjúrður, goym væl hesi orð, tú legg tey væl í minni."	Both healthy and lucky we part now at this time, Sjúrður, remember well these words, commit them well to memory."
114. Sjúrður reið á skógvar burtur, tyktist komin í váða, hann sá tað hitt illa djór berjast við bógvar báðar.	Sjúrdur rode away in the woods, it seemed like he was in danger, he saw that evil beast attack with both forelimbs.[68]
115. Hann sá tað hitt illa djór berjast við bógvar báðar, eitur spýði, eldur goysti, næstan stóð í váða.	He saw that evil beast attack with both forelimbs, spewing poison, vomiting fire, nearly in peril.
116. So hvarv tað hitt illa djór burtur úr Sjúrðar eygum, sær hann, hvar ið Grimhild situr, leikar við brondum beygum.	Then that evil beast[69] disappeared before Sjúrður's eyes, he sees where Grimhild sits, playing with bended swords.[70]

67 This is Sjúrður speaking, and it mirrors st. 102, which he speaks to Brynhild.

68 The monster has big forearms and attacks with them both. This has associations with the dragon.

69 The evil beast seems to be Grimhild, who has shapeshifted.

70 It is not entirely clear what *brondum beygum* means. The critical edition of the manuscript has *Braandun bejun*. Matras, *J. H. Schrøters optegnelser*, p. 17, st. 114.

117. Hestin vilti hon undir honum, at hann kundi ikki ganga, hann gjørdi, hann bæði beit og sló og helti til ymsar vangar.	She bewitched the horse under him, so that he could not go on, she[71] made it so he both bit and kicked and threw his head in different directions.
118. Tað var hin ungi Sjúrður, hann skuldi venda frá, Grimhild treiv í teymarnar, at hann skuldi ikki náa.	That was the young Sjúrður, he was trying to turn away, Grimhild grasped the reins, so that he couldn't.
119. Tað er satt, ið talað er, mong er konan eym, tað er mær av sonnum sagt, hon tók í Grana teym.	It is true what they say,[72] many the woman is wretched,[73] it is truthfully told to me, she took hold of Grani's reins.
120. Tí svaraði Sjúrður, kinn bar hann so balda: "Eg veit so ongan av Húnamonnum, mínar teymar torir at halda."	Then Sjúrður answered, his cheeks are so bold:[74] "I know none of the men of the Huns, who dare to hold my reins."

Beygum could mean "bended, bent," or "beautiful." Lyngbye though reads this as *baajun* meaning "both"; Lyngbye, *Færøiske Qvæder*, 172–73. *Brondum* is the dat. pl. of *brandur*, and could mean "swords" or "fire, embers." Lyngbye reads it as "swords," rendering the words "both swords"; Lyngbye, *Færøiske Qvæder*, 172–73. Hammershaimb has *væl lögd við bondum beyjum*; Hammershaimb, *Sjúrðar Kvæði*, 27, st. 129, which he interprets as "smykket med pyntelige band" (adorned with decorative bands); Hammershaimb, *Sjúrðar Kvæði*, 158. The line is somewhat formulaic, and appears for example in *Gongurólvs kvæði* as *bundan við bondum beygum*; Grundtvig and Bloch, *Føroya kvæði*, vol. 1, p. 587, st. 76. The translation "bended swords" in this ballad makes sense if this is reflective of something that could make magic, while if it is fire, it matches with the monster that could perhaps spew fire.

71 Here is seems that the edition in CCF has made a mistake, see Grundtvig and Bloch, *Føroya kvæði*, vol. 1, p. 14. The editors have printed *hann*, which we have faithfully reproduced here. However, this does not make sense, and in the manuscript it is indeed *Hoon* "she" as we have translated here, see Matras, *J. H. Schrøters optegnelser*, p. 17, st. 115.

72 This is a formulaic line that appears in other ballads. It literally means something like "it's true as it's told."

73 *Eymur* can mean "wretched," but it can also mean "loving." In other variants of the ballad it refers to Guðrun's heartbreak, so we have chosen "wretched" here.

74 He is also described this way in st. 72. It means he has a brave-looking face.

121. "Tú støðga tín hest eina lítla stund, og snakka við meg, eg eigi mær eina væna dóttur, við ástir leiðir hon teg.	"Stop your horse for a little while, and speak with me, I have a beautiful daughter, she wants to love you.[75]
122. So er Guðrun dóttir mín, hvar ið hon gongur inn, rósur og so liljur tær skyggja av hennara kinn."	Such is Guðrun my daughter, wherever she goes, roses and lilies shine from her cheeks."
123. "Guðrun hon er dóttir tín, tað er tí ei betur, hon er ikki Brynhildar líki, summar ímót vetur."	"Guðrun she is your daughter, it is therefore no better, she is not Brynhild's equal, summer against winter."
124. Út kom frúgvin Guðrun í einum stakki blá, flættað hár á herðar lá, við silkibondum smá.	Out comes the lady Guðrun in a blue gown,[76] braided hair lay on her shoulders, with small silk ribbons.
125. Guðrun so til orða tekur, tungu bar hon snjalla: "Hava tað, ið annar eigur, tað man lukkast valla.	Guðrun began to speak, she was so eloquent: "To have that which another has,[77] that will hardly go well.
126. Nógvir eru í várum londum kongasynir og jallar, girnast tann, ið onnur eigur, tað man lukkast sjáldan."	There are many in our lands kings' sons and earls, to covet that which another has that will rarely go well."
127. Hon hevði upp sína høgru hond, gav henni høgg á tenn, blóðið dreiv í barmin niður, sóu tað mangir menn.	She raised her right hand, hit her in the mouth,[78] blood flowed down her breast, many men saw it.

75 This is a formulaic line, cf. stt. 64, 65, 101.

76 A *stakkur* is especially best clothes of red or blue silk.

77 *Eiga* also has the sense here of "is married to," and the same is true of the following stanza.

78 This is Grimhild, who hits her daughter Guðrun in the mouth.

128. "Tig tú, Guðrun dóttir mín,
mangt man smæin lissa,
betri var sjálv at biðja
enn góðan mann at missa.

"Hold your tongue, Guðrun my daughter,
there is much that the shy will miss,
it would be better to ask on your own behalf[79]
than to lose a good man.

129. Guðrun, gakk í kjallaran,
blanda mjøð og vín,
og so mikið óminni
tað lat tú har útí.

Guðrun, go to the cellar,
and mix mead and wine,
and so much forgetfulness
you should pour into it.

130. Og so mikið óminni
tað lat tú har útí,
ikki má Sjúrður minnast
til hálvar ástir sínar."

And so much forgetfulness,
you should pour into it,
Sjúrður must not remember
even half of his love."

131. Guðrun gekk í kjallaran,
blandaði mjøð í ker,
bæði snart og skundiliga
inn fyri Sjúrða ber.

Guðrun went to the cellar,
mixed mead in a cup,
both quickly and hurriedly
she carried it in before Sjúrður.

132. Og so mikið óminni
læt hon har útí,
gekk so fyri Sjúrð svein,
bað hann drekka til sín.

And so much forgetfulness
she poured into it,
then went before Sjúrður swain,[80]
asked him to drink a toast to her.

133. Drekka fór so dýran dramm,
drakk av horninum bjarta,
mildingur misti minni sítt,
og brúður úr buðlungs hjarta.

They drank such a magnificent drink,
drank from the bright horn,
the generous one lost his memory,
and the bride disappeared[81] from
the king's[82] heart.

134. Drekka fór sum dýri drammur,
drakk av horninum leingi,
mildingur misti minni sítt,
og bøta man honum eingin.

The drink went down like a costly drink would,
he drank lengthily from the horn,
the generous one lost his memory,
and no one will heal him.

---

79 Grimhild is advising Guðrun to propose to Sjúrður.

80 *Sjúrður svein* is a formulaic way of saying Sjúrður's name.

81 We have added "the" and "disappeared" here. This line should be understood in the context of the one above, so it is implied that he has lost his bride (Brynhild) from his heart. We are following the punctation of the edition in our translation, but it is worth noting that the manuscript has no punctation, and so that added by editors is a form of interpretation.

82 *Buðlungur* is a *heiti* for king or prince in the ballads.

135. Tá ið hann hevði drukkið,
greiddi aftur skál,
mintist ei til frú Brynhild
og ei á hennara mál.

When he had drunk,
he handed back the cup,
he no longer remembered lady Brynhild
and nothing of matters related to her.[83]

136. Tá ið hann hevði drukkið,
greiddi aftur kerið,
mintist ei til Brynhildu,
og ei, hvar hann hevði verið.

When he had drunk,
he handed back the cup,[84]
he did not remember Brynhild,
nor where he had been.

137. Drakk hon drykk og drakk hon tvá
til tann dreingins deyða,
honum kom einki annað í hug
enn Guðruna at eiga.

She drank a drink and she drank two
to the death of the hero,[85]
nothing else came to his mind
but to marry Guðrun.

138. Drakk hon drykk og drakk hon tvá
til tann dreingin svinna,
hiðan út í skemmu gongur
Guðruna at finna.

She drank a drink and she drank two
to the wise[86] hero,
he went from there to the bedroom[87]
to find Guðrun.

139. Sjúrður gekk í skemmu upp,
Guðrun vegin finnur,
frætti tað Brynhild á Hildarheyg,
nú rann henni ónt í sinni.

Sjúrður went up into the bedroom,
finding the way to Guðrun,[88]
when Brynhild in Hildarheygur
heard about it,
she became full of spite.

140. Brynhild gekk av Hildarheyg,
tað hitt væna vív,
kappin gisti Guðruna,
men Sjúrður misti lív.

Brynhild went from Hildarheygur,
that beautiful woman,
the hero slept at Guðrun's,
but Sjúrður lost his life.

141. Brynhild fyri munni mælir,
tár á kinn man fljóta:
"Ikki skal Guðrun Júkadóttir
tann avrekskappan njóta."

Brynhild spoke,
tears streaming down her cheeks:
"Guðrun Júkadóttir will not
have that excellent hero."

---

83 *Mál* could be things related to her, what she has said, or voice. So, the line could mean "nor her voice."

84 Note that the Faroese uses two different words for cup in stt. 135 and 136.

85 This likely means because of this he is going to die in the sense of foreshadowing, rather than signalling her intention to kill him.

86 This is from *svinnur*, a poetic word used to describe someone as intelligent, clever, sensible, or wise, rather than from *svinna*, when someone is diminished, reduced, or has lost weight.

87 We have added "he" here to make it less ambiguous.

88 Grammatically this could also be she who finds her way to him.

142. Brynhild fyri munni mælir, sorgartíð skal eg kalla: "Hava tað, ið onnur eigur, tað skal lukkast valla."	Brynhild spoke, a time of grief I shall call it: "To have that which another has, that shall hardly go well."[89]
143. Møttust tær á miðjari leið, Brynhild og Guðrun Júka, onnur teirra gleðina bar, og onnur harmin sjúka.	They met halfway in the middle, Brynhild and Júki's Guðrun, one of them bore happiness, and the other desperate grief.
144. Tað var Guðrun Júkadóttir, gjørdi so mangt av fári, hon vildi ikki njóta tað vatn, sum rann av Brynhildu hári.	That was Guðrun Júkadóttir, did so much out of foolishness, she didn't want to use the water that ran from Brynhild's hair.[90]
145. Guðrun leyp á ánna út, sum fossurin rann so snarur, tí hon eigur Sjúrða svein, sum høvd yvir allar bar.	Guðrun jumped out into the river, as the cascade ran so fast, because she married Sjúrður swain, who was a head above everyone.[91]
146. Guðrun leyp á ánna út, sum fossurin rann so stríður, tí hon eigur Sjúrða unga, sum ein yvir allar ríður.	Guðrun jumped out into the river, as the cascade was so rough, because she married young Sjúrður, who rides better than everyone else.
147. Mælti tað Guðrun Júkadóttir fyrsta orðið tá: "Hvør gav tær tað fingurgull, eg síggi tínum fingri á?"	Guðrun Júkadóttir then spoke the first word: "Who gave you that finger-gold I see on your finger?"
148. Svaraði Brynhild Buðladóttir, tekur um hjarta at møða: "Vit munnu ognast eina reiggj, vit hava so mangt at røða.	Brynhild Buðladóttir answered, overcome by grief in the heart: "We will experience strife,[92] we have so much to discuss.

89 This echoes what Guðrun says in stt. 125 and 126.

90 This scene with the two women arguing at the river is known as the Quarrel of the Queens in Old Norse studies. See Bryan, "Indirect Aggression."

91 The idea here is that Guðrun goes further out into the river than Brynhild due to her pride.

92 They will both experience grief because they both want the same man and cannot have him. This is the not the strife happening to them together but rather between them.

149. Hetta sama fingurgull, tú sært á fingri mínum, gav mær Sjúrður Sigmundarson, tú vilti við ástum tínum."	This same finger-gold you see on my finger, was given to me by Sjúrður Sigmundarson, who you enchanted with your love."
150. Brynhild tagdi, Guðrun sagdi, fast er snótin stríð: "Hví man mín bróðir Gunnar kongur ei ognast so vænt eitt vív?"	Brynhild was silent, Guðrun spoke, the woman's[93] stubbornness[94] was steadfast, "Why will my brother King Gunnar not marry such a beautiful woman?"
151. Til tess svaraði frú Brynhild, í tungu var hon snjøll: "Eg lovi ikki tógva kongar báðar í einari høll."	To this the lady Brynhild answered, she was eloquent: "I won't love two kings both in one hall."[95]
152. "Sjúrður hevur tín moydóm spilt og brotið Buðlins frama, ríkum kongi givið í vold, og nú havi eg tann sama."	"Sjúrður has taken your virginity and lost Buðlin's favour, you entrusted yourself to the powerful king,[96] and now I have the same one."
153. "Tú tørvt ikki, falssnóta, brigða mær tað svá, fyri títt orð skal Sjúrður doyggja, um eg liva má."	"You don't need, liar,[97] to accuse me like that, for your words Sjúrður shall die, while I must live."
154. "Ikki óttist eg hóttur tínar, tó tú ert í orðum stív, so er eingin í Júkagørðum, ið ríður um Sjúrðar lív."	"I am not frightened by your threats, though you are good with your words, there is no such person in Júki's court, who has power over Sjúrður's life."
155. Grátandi snúðist Brynhild í sín sal at sitja, Gunnar kongur fyrstur og fremstur hennara kom at vitja.	Crying, Brynhild turned to sit in her hall, King Gunnar came first and foremost to visit her.

93 *Snót* is a *heiti* for woman or girl.

94 *Stríð* also has the connotation that she is being bloody-minded.

95 The same hall (her hall).

96 This seems to be a Danish construction similar to *give sig Gud i vold*, "commend oneself to God." Guðrun is saying Brynhild has yielded or entrusted herself to the powerful king and now Guðrun has the same king.

97 A *falssnóta* is a falsifier.

156. "Tú fært einki yndi av mær,
ein manst tú tað vænta,
so leingi eg Sjúrða við eygum síggi,
seint man angur lætta."

"You will get no love from me,
you must not expect that,
as long as I see Sjúrður,[98]
regret[99] dissipates slowly."

157. Brynhild gongur til seingina
av teirri somu grund,
og nú tolir hon fyri Sjúrða
so ónda eina stund.

Brynhild went to bed
for those same reasons,
and now she suffers because of Sjúrður
so terrible a time.

158. Frætti tað Sjúrður Sigmundarson
á teirri somu stund,
sjálvur fór hann at vitja
tað unniliga sprund.

Sjúrður Sigmundarson heard about that
right then,[100]
he went to visit her himself
that beautiful woman.

159. "Tað hevur eingin hunskur riddari
gjørt sum tú,
tú saknaði ikki fljóðið,
tú fyrstur lovaði trú."

"No Hunnish knight has
done as you,
you did not miss the woman[101]
that you first promised to be faithful to."

160. "Hoyr tú, mín hin veldiga søta,
kenn mær einki um,
vendur var mín hugurin
frá hesum ástum tínum."

"Listen, my magnificent sweet one,
do not blame me,[102]
my thoughts were turned
from your love."

161. Tað fyrsta sum hon mundi
Sjúrða við eygum sjá,
tá mundi hon Brynhild
eina unga dóttur fá.

Immediately when she
saw Sjúrður,[103]
Brynhild
had a young daughter.

162. Til tess svaraði Brynhild
fyrst á orði tá:
"Berið mítt barn á ánna út,
eg vil tað ikki sjá."

To this Brynhild replied
the first thing she said:
"Carry my child out into the river,
I don't want to see it."

---

98 Literally "as long as I see Sjúrður with my eyes." This is formulaic.

99 This could also mean "guilt" or "dread."

100 Literally "at that same moment."

101 *Fljóð* is a *heiti* for woman.

102 See Kamban, *Kenn mær einki um*.

103 Literally "saw Sjúrður with her eyes." This is formulaic, cf. st. 156.

163. Tóku tey Áslu Sjúrðardóttur, floyttu oman eftir á, stórar áir og stríðir streymar bóru hana londum frá.	They took Ásla Sjúrðardóttir, floated her on the river, strong rivers and rapid currents carried her from the lands.
164. Brynhild gekk á Hildarheyg, nú ber hon kinn so reyðan, nú á teirri sorgartíð voldi hon Sjúrðar deyða.	Brynhild went to Hildarheygur, now she had such red cheeks, now in those times of sorrow she brought about the death of Sjúrður.
165. Mangur hevur hóttur notið fyri fagurt vív, liðið er nú at evstu stund, Sjúrður missir lív.	Many have endured threats for beautiful women, it has now passed[104] to the final moment, Sjúrður loses his life.
166. Mangur hevur hóttur notið fyri tær fríðu moyar, nú er liðið at síðstu stund, Sjúrður hann skal doyggja.	Many have endured threats for the lovely maidens, now it is the final moment, Sjúrður he shall die.
167. Sjúrður var ein avrekskappi, vá sítt svørð í droyra, og honum voldu kvinnur deyð, sum tit skulu fáa at hoyra.	Sjúrður was an excellent hero, struck his sword in blood,[105] and women caused him to die, as you shall hear about.
168. Sjúrður varð av lívi tikin frá tí gullinum reyða, tað vóru moyar í forðum tíð, sum voldu mannadeyða.	Sjúrður's life was taken from him from the red gold, it was maidens in ancient times, that caused the death of a man.
169. Tað vóru moyar í forðum tíð, gjørdu so mangt tað bragdið, Brynhild unga Buðlins dóttir kemur nú fyrst í kvæðið.	It was maidens in ancient times, who did so many deeds, young Brynhild Buðlin's daughter is now mentioned first in the ballad.
170. Brynhild unga Buðlins dóttir, føgur yvir brún, gullband henni um herðar liggur við flættað hárí snúnum.	Young Brynhild Buðlin's daughter, fair across the brow,[106] a band of gold lies around her shoulders with hair braided in a twist.

104 Time has elapsed.

105 *Droyri* is a poetic word for blood. When he swings his sword, he causes blood to be spilt.

106 She is beautiful.

171. Brynhild gekk í hallina inn av so miklum móði, ikki mundi mæla tað hitt unniliga fljóð.	Brynhild walked into the hall in great anger, she didn't speak a word the beautiful woman.
172. Sjúrður rendi sínum fóti undir frúnnar stól, ikki vildi sitja tað hitt unniliga fljóð.	Sjúrður banged his foot on the lady's chair,[107] it didn't sit well with her the beautiful woman.
173. Høgnar kemur av skógnum heim við hvøssum slíðraspjóti: "Hann skal harðan deyðan tola, ið tær hevur gjørt ímóti."	Høgnar comes home from the forest with a sharp sword:[108] "He shall endure a cruel death, he who has offended you."
174. "Tað er hon Guðrun systir tín, hon voldi mær tað stríð, eg man ongan søtan sova, meðan Sjúrður er á lívi."	"It is your sister Guðrun, she caused me this harm, I will not sleep sweetly, while Sjúrður still lives."
175. Høgnar so til orða tekur: "Nú man tað so vera, Sjúrður er mín heitbróðir, eg kann honum einki gera."	Then Høgnar speaks: "So it's like this, Sjúrður is my sworn brother, I can't do anything to him."
176. "Tú fært einki yndi av mær, ei tørvt tú tað vænta, so leingi eg Sjúrða við eygum síggi seint man angur lætta."	"You will get no love from me, you needn't expect it, as long as I can see Sjúrður regret dissipates slowly."[109]
177. "Tað er einki eykarverk at ganga Sjúrða ímóti, hvar ið hann kemur í váknaskjal, har hevur hann høvur á spjóti."	"It is no easy feat[110] to go against Sjúrður, wherever he comes into combat, he has a head on his spear."

107 Sjúrður kicked her chair, and it is a matter of interpretation whether this was accidental or deliberate.

108 *Slíðraspjót* is a poetic word for sword used in the ballads.

109 This echoes her words in st. 156.

110 We interpret this as Old Norse *akrverk*, "field-work, harvest-work." A close English expression would be "it is no walk in the park." Lyngbye glosses this as "et Arbeide, som man maa egges, opmuntres til" (work that one must be egged on or encouraged to do). Lyngbye, *Færøiske Qvæder*, p. 196, st. 169n.

178. "Tú fært einki yndi av mær, ei tann menjartrá, fyrr enn tú hevur Sjúrð svein tykkara londum frá."	"You will get no love from me,[111] nor that mighty passion, before you have Sjúrður swain off your lands."
179. Tað var Høgnar Júkason, hann stilti stál fyri stokk, yppist ráð av illari dáð, so køld eru kvinnu tokk(!).	That was Høgnar Júkason he put sword before the beam,[112] the consequences of evil scheming have been exposed,[113] so cold is the love of a woman.
180. Brynhild setist í gullstólin, frá man frættast víða, nú skulu teir Húnakongar burtur á skógvin ríða.	Brynhild sat herself in the golden throne, it was told far and wide,[114] now the Hunnish kings shall ride away to the forest.
181. Brynhild situr á Hildarstóli, spælir við gyltum knívi: "Ikki aftur í mína høll, fyrr enn Sjúrður er av lívi!"	Brynhild sits on Hildarstólur, playing with a golden[115] knife:[116] "Do not return to my hall, before Sjúrður has been killed."
182. "Hoyr tú, Brynhild Buðlins dóttir, hví eykar tú os tann vanda, hann er eingin í Húnalandi, Sjúrða kann bestanda.	"Listen, Brynhild daughter of Buðlin, why do you put us mortal danger, there is no one in Húnaland, that can withstand Sjúrður.[117]
183. Hoyr tú, Brynhild Buðlins dóttir, tær tað sigast má, hann er eingin í Húnalandi, ið høggur hans høvur frá."	Listen, Brynhild daughter of Buðlin, it has to be said to you, there is no one in Húnaland, that can chop his head off."

---

111 Cf. stt. 156 and 176.

112 *Stokkur* means "beam," but Lyngbye interprets this word as the Icelandic *stakka*, meaning "hide," and interprets this line as "at sætte Sværdet for Brystet" (he put the sword to the breast). Lyngbye, *Færøiske Qvæder*, p. 199, st. 171n.

113 This is the line as translated by *Føroysk-ensk orðabók*, s.v. "Yppa." The line is translated "a plan arises from the dreadful deed" in *Føroysk-ensk orðabók / Faroese-English Dictionary*, s.v. "Yppa."

114 This is a formulaic phrase. Cf. *Regin smiður*, stt. 73 and 116.

115 Or "gilded."

116 This could be a sword, since *knívur* can be used as a poetic word for sword in ballads.

117 This means to survive a fight with Sjúrður.

184. Brynhild situr í sínum stóli, leikar við gyltum knívi: "Tit fáa einki yndi av mær, fyrr enn Sjúrður er frá lívi."	Brynhild sits in her chair, playing with a golden knife: "You will get no love from me,[118] before Sjúrður has lost his life."
185. "Hoyr tú, Brynhild Buðlins dóttir, legg sjálv til tess ráð, hvussu vit skulu tann mikla mann burtur av lívi fáa!"	"Listen, Brynhild daughter of Buðlin, give us advice,[119] how shall we take the life of that mighty man!"
186. Brynhild fyri munni mælir, sorg um hjarta man røkka: "Gevið Sjúrða salta krás og hartil einki drekka!	Brynhild says, sorrow will reach her heart: "Give Sjúrður salty food,[120] and nothing to drink with it!
187. Tað munnu vera ráðini góð, eg gevi foruttan ekka: latið hann eta salta krás og hartil lítið drekka!"	This is a good plan, I give without fear: let him eat salty food and not much to drink with it!"
188. Sjúrður gongur í hallina inn, vænur er hann og vitur, sum hon Brynhild Buðlins dóttir fyri í stóli situr.	Sjúrður walks into the hall, he is handsome and wise, as Brynhild daughter of Buðlin she sits in her throne.
189. Sjúrður stendur á hallargólvi við gullslagið skjold í hendi, Brynhild unga Buðlins dóttir eyguni frá honum vendi.	Sjúrður stands on the floor in the hall with a gilded shield in his hand, young Brynhild daughter of Buðlin turns her gaze from him.
190. "Gud náði meg í verðini, hvat ið meg skuldi henda: eg skuldi allar mínar ástir, Sjúrður, frá tær venda."	"God have mercy on me in this world, that it might happen to me: that I would all my love, Sjúrður, turn from you."
191. Sjúrður so til orða tekur: "Nú er av tað versta, tá ið eg aftur av skógnum komi, tá skal eg teg festa."	Then Sjúrður begins to speak: "Now the situation is extremely bad, when I return from the forest I will be betrothed to you."

118 Cf. stt. 156 and 176.

119 They need her to help plan what to do to kill Sjúrður.

120 *Krás* has the connotation that the food is delicious and also likely meat.

<table>
<tr><td>192. Svaraði Brynhild Buðlins dóttir,
ber um hjarta ve:
“Hoyr tú, Sjúrður Sigmundarson,
tú festir ikki meg.”</td><td>Brynhild daughter of Buðlin answered,
carrying sorrow[121] in her heart:
“Listen, Sjúrður Sigmundarson,
you won’t be betrothed to me.”</td></tr>
<tr><td>193. Tá var rómur í Buðlins høll,
sveinar ríða út,
Brynhild sat eftir í Hildarstóli,
feldi tár á dúk.</td><td>It was noisy in Buðlin’s hall,
the men rode out,
Brynhild was left behind in Hildarstólur,
shed tears on cloth.</td></tr>
<tr><td>194. Tá var rómur í Buðlins høll,
sveinar drukku vín,
Brynhild eftir í Hildarstóli,
hon feldi tár á lín.</td><td>It was noisy in Buðlin’s hall,
the men were drinking wine,
Brynhild left behind in Hildarstólur,
she shed tears on linen.</td></tr>
<tr><td>195. Buðlin kongur til orða tekur,
fast av móðins ekka:
“Fáið Sjúrða hjálmin tann,
ið hann skal undan drekka!”</td><td>King Buðlin begins to speak,
though from sorrow’s fear:
“Give Sjúrður that helmet,
that he shall drink from!”</td></tr>
<tr><td>196. Brynhild fyri munni mælir,
sorg um hjarta man byggja:
“Hoyr tú tað, mín sæli faðir,
hann skal eftir liggja.”</td><td>Brynhild says,
sorrow in her heart:
“Listen, my dear father,
it shall be left behind.”</td></tr>
<tr><td>197. Tí svaraði Buðlin kongur,
hann heldur á ringi reyða:
“Hoyr tú, Brynhild dóttir mín,
hví elvir tú Sjúrða deyða?”</td><td>King Buðlin answered,
holding onto the red ring:
“Listen, Brynhild my daughter,
why are you causing Sjúrður’s death?”</td></tr>
<tr><td>198. “Eingin unnar so øðrum væl,
at sínum av man hyggja,
ikki skal Sjúrður Sigmundarson
longur í heimum byggja.”</td><td>“No one loves someone else so dearly,
when they ignore them,
Sjúrður Sigmundarson shall not
live in this world any longer.”</td></tr>
<tr><td>199. “Minnist tú, Brynhild dóttir mín,
minnist tú ta tíð,
dróst tú Sjúrð av Norðlondum
ígjøgnum grøna líð?</td><td>“Do you remember, Brynhild my daughter,
do you remember that time,
when you drew Sjúrður from the
northern lands
through the green slopes?</td></tr>
</table>

121 Old Norse *vé* and Danish *ve* means “woe, misery.”

200. Minnist tú, Brynhild dóttir mín, tá ið tú blandaði vín, dróst tú Sjúrða av Norðlondum á Hildarheyg til tín?"	Do you remember, Brynhild my daughter, when you mixed wine, you drew Sjúrður from the northern lands to you on Hildarheygur?"[122]
201. Buðlin kongur av sali gongur eina morguntíð snimma, eftir Brynhild dóttir hans við hond upp undir kinn.	King Buðlin walks from the hall early one morning, Brynhild his daughter is left behind with her head in her hands.
202. Árla var um morgunin, sólin roðar í lund, reystar kempur váknin taka, fárlig vóru sprund.	Early in the morning, the sun rises in the grove, bold warriors take their weapons, women were dangerous.
203. Út ríða teir Júkungar, Sjúrður var í ferð, visti ei av hilmarasvikum, teir bundu ráðagerð.	The Júkungar rode out, Sjúrður on the trip, he knew nothing of the princes'[123] treachery they were plotting.
204. Brynhild gekk á Hildarsal, sá hon út so víða, Sjúrður frægi fyrst og fremst fyri Húnakongum ríður.	Brynhild went to Hildarsalur, she looked out far and wide, brave Sjúrður first and foremost rides before the Hunnish kings.
205. Ríða út úr Buðlins borg, sum teir gjørdu ofta, eftir liggur Sjúrðar svørð heimi á Brynhildu lofti.	They ride out from Buðlin's castle, as they often did, Sjúrður's sword is left behind at home in Brynhild's loft
206. Brynhild settist í gyltan stól av so miklari pínu, møðiliga feldi hon tárini á báðar armar sínar.	Brynhild seats herself in the golden throne in such great torment, sorrowfully she shed tears down both her arms.[124]
207. Brynhild grætur møðiliga, tað hitt væna vív: "Vildi eg Sjúrða við eygum sætt í Hildarsali til mín."	Brynhild cries sorrowfully, that beautiful woman: "I wish I could see Sjúrður in Hildarsalur with me."

122 In st. 27, King Buðli asks for Brynhild's plan to get Sjúrður to her. Then, in stt. 48 and 49, it is told that she drew him to her. There is, however, no mention earlier in the ballad of her having mixed wine in connection with this; this is something that Guðrun does.

123 *Hilmir* is a *heiti* for prince.

124 Women shedding tears down their arms is formulaic in the ballads.

208. Brynhild grætur so møðiliga,
tað hitt væna vív:
"Vildi eg Sjúrða við eygum sætt
í Hildarstóli mínum."

Brynhild cries so sorrowfully,
that beautiful woman:
"I wish I could see Sjúrður
in my Hildarstólur."

209. Brynhild grætur møðiliga,
tað hitt væna vív:
"Far væl, Sjúrður Sigmundarson,
eg síggi teg ei í lívi."

Brynhild cries sorrowfully,
that beautiful woman:
"Farewell, Sjúrður Sigmundarson,
I won't see you alive again."

210. Ríða teir á skógvin burtur,
glaðir foruttan ekka,
teir Sjúrða salta krás
og hartil einki drekka.

They ride to the forest,
happy without fear,
they gave Sjúrður salty food
and nothing to drink with it.[125]

211. Ríða teir á skógvin burtur,
lótu sporar ringla,
Brynhild situr á Hildarstóli
ferðig til at springa.

They ride away to the forest,
their spurs jingle,
Brynhild sits on Hildarstólur
ready to burst.

212. Ríða teir á skógvin burtur,
alt foruttan ekka,
svørji tann eið á mína trú,
at nú lysta teir at drekka.

They ride to the forest,
with no fear,
I swear an oath by all that is sacred,
that they now desire to drink.

213. Drekka undan sínum hjálmi
bæði títt og ofta,
eftir liggur Sjúrðar hjálmur
heimi á Brynhildu lofti.

They drink from their helmets
very often,
Sjúrður's helmet is left behind
at home in Brynhild's loft.

214. Drekka undan sínum hjálmi,
alt foruttan ekka,
Sjúrður situr á Grana baki,
nú lystir hann at drekka.

They drink from their helmets,
totally without fear,
Sjúrður sits on Grani's back,
he now desires to drink.

215. Drekka undan sínum hjálmi,
glaðir foruttan sút,
Sjúrður loysti hjálmbondini,
steig úr saðli út.

They drink from their helmets,
happy without distress,
Sjúrður loosened his helmet straps,[126]
stepped out of his saddle.

125 This enacts Brynhild's plan that she came up with in stt. 186 and 187.

126 One can wonder why Sjúrður still has helmet straps when it is emphasized and important for the plot that he does not have his helmet with him.

216. Sjúrður sá ikki svikara vón,
steig úr gullsaðli út,
skundaði sær at kelduni
glaður foruttan sút.

Sjúrður didn't expect betrayal,
dismounted from his golden saddle,
he hurried to the spring,
happy without distress.

217 Sjúrður legðist at drekka,
sum vatn stóð fyri í brunni,
sjáldan hevur góður kvistur
sprottið av illum runni.

Sjúrður laid down to drink,
as if the water was in a well,
seldom has a good branch
sprouted from a bad bush.[127]

218. Sjúrður legðist at drekka,
sum vatn stóð fyri í veit,
Høgnar átti mækan tann,
á Sjúrðar hálsi beit.

Sjúrður laid down to drink,
the water was before him in a channel,
Høgnar owned the sword,[128]
that cut Sjúrðurs throat

219. Sjúrður legðist at drekka,
góður drongur og nýtur,
Høgnar átti mækan tann,
á Sjúrðar hálsi bítur.

Sjúrður laid down to drink,
a good and brave young man,
Høgnar owned the sword,
that cuts Sjúrður's throat.

220. Høgnar høgg, og Gunnar hjó,
við hvøssum slíðraknívi,
teir gjørdu so mikið níðingsverk,
teir tóku Sjúrða av lívi.

Høgnar slashed, and Gunnar hacked,
with sharp swords,
they did such a great foul deed,
they took Sjúrður's life.

221. Høgnar høgg, og Gunnar hjó,
og tað fór millum dreingir,
hesi ganga tí illdømi
í Húnalandi leingi.

Høgnar slashed, and Gunnar hacked,
and it went like that between the heroes,
these evil incidents were told about
in Húnaland for a long time.

222. Høgnar høgg, og Gunnar hjó,
mest av Brynhildu ráðum,
hevði hann vitað av svikunum,
maður var hann fyri báðum.

Høgnar slashed, and Gunnar hacked,
mostly because of Brynhild's advice,
had he known about the treachery,
he would have won over both of them.

223. Upp slapp hann undan øllum teim,
tungu bar hann so snjalla:
"Hevði eg vitað av svikunum,
mentur var eg fyri allar."

He broke free from all of them,
he was so eloquent:
"Had I known about this treachery,
I would have managed all of you."

127 The final two lines mean "like father, like son," or "a chip off the old block."

128 *Mæki* is a *heiti* for sword used in ballads.

224. Sjúrður knýtir neva sín saman av góðum treysti, sipaði so til Gunnar kong, niður fell hann av hesti.	Sjúrður clenched his fist together powerfully, took a swing at King Gunnar, he fell down from the horse.[129]
225. Sjúrður so til orða tekur: "Nú hava tit meg svikið. Hevði eg havt mítt svørð í hond, tað skuldi betri tikið.	Sjúrður began to speak: "Now you have betrayed me. Had I had my sword in my hand, this would have gone better.
226. Hoyr tú, Høgnar Júkason, nú hevur tú vigið meg, tá var eg á Finnmarkini, ið eg royndi teg."	Listen, Høgnar Júkason, now you have killed me, when I was in Finnmark, I tested you."[130]
227. Sjúrður følnaði á grønum vølli, nú var hann følin og nipin, men hevði hann havt sítt svørð í hond, tað hevði betri tikið.	Sjúrður grew pale on the green field, now he was pallid and crestfallen, but had he had his sword in his hand, that would have gone better.
228. Sjúrður legðist at drekka, so ganga søgur frá, har kom Høgnar Júkason, kleyv hann í lutir tvá.	Sjúrður lay himself down to drink, so the story goes, here came Høgnar Júkason, and split him in two pieces.
229. Eitt kom boð í hallina inn, Brynhildu sigur frá: "Deyður er Sjúrður Sigmundarson, Gunnar kongur vá."	A messanger came into the hall, and told Brynhild: "Sjúrður Sigmundarson is dead, King Gunnar killed him."
230. Eitt kom boð í hallina inn: "Sjúrður hann er vigin." Brynhild fór í svímilsi av Hildarstóli niður.	A messanger came into the hall: "Sjúrður has been killed." Brynhild fainted down from Hildarstólur.
231. Eitt kom boð í hallina inn uttan av grønum vøll, Brynhild fagra í svímilsi av Hildarstóli fell.	A messanger came into the hall, out from the green field, beautiful Brynhild fainted, fell from Hildarstólur.

129 This is not a very heroic portrayal of Gunnar, who is hacking at an unarmed Sjúrður lying down drinking from a channel, while Gunnar is presumably leaning off his horse to hack at him.

130 We have not heard about Sjúrður fighting with Høgnar in Finnmark.

232. Gunnar kongur fyrstur og fremstur
hana mundi vitja,
grátandi fór Brynhild unga
í sína song at sitja.

King Gunnar first and foremost
visited her,[131]
young Brynhild went crying
to sit in her bed.

233. Gunnar kongur í salin gongur,
ber á brynju blá,
Brynhild unga Buðlins dóttir
sjúk av sorgum lá.

King Gunnar went into the chamber,
wearing a black[132] mailcoat,
young Brynhild Buðlin's daughter,
lay sick with sorrow.

234. Brynhild hon í seingini liggur,
Gunnar situr á stokki,
so er skrivað í breiðu bók,
at kaldur er kvinnu tokki.

Brynhild she lay in the bed,
Gunnar sits at the bedside,
so it is written in a large book,[133]
that a woman's love is cold.

235. Gunnar kongur til orða tekur,
heldur at tí gleim:
"Nú skal taka buðlungs lík,
føra til hallar heim."

King Gunnar began to speak,
rather cheerfully:
"Now shall the prince's corpse,
be taken home to its hall."

236. Skiftu sínum hestunum
við so mangan lit,
ikki vildi Grani ganga,
tí hann hevði manns vit.

They changed their horses
of so many a colour,[134]
Grani did not want to walk,[135]
because he had the mind of a person.

237. Teir royndu sínar hestarnar,
hvør við sínum lit,
ikki vildi Grani ganga,
tí hann hevði manns vit.

They tried out their horses,
each its own colour,
Grani did not want to walk,
because he had the mind of a person.

238. Teir skiftu sínum búnaði,
øllum sínum lit,
ikki vildi Grani ganga,
tí hann hevði manns vit.

They changed their attire,
each their own colour,
Grani did not want to walk,
because he had the mind of a person.

131 This mirrors how Hjalprek visited Hjørdis after the death of her husband Sigmundur in *Regin smiður*.

132 In the Faroese it says blue, but bluing armour means to blacken it as an aesthetic choice.

133 This is often interpreted as a reference to an Icelandic saga manuscript.

134 They are changing their tired horses for fresh horses and the horses are of many different colours.

135 This means Grani is not budging, because, as we will see in st. 239, Gunnar is trying to ride him and Grani will only accept Sjúrður.

239. Ikki vildi Grani ganga, tí Gunnar honum reið, fyrr enn hin deyði Sjúrður honum á herðar neig.	Grani did not want to walk, because Gunnar rode him, until the dead Sjúrður was sitting on his withers.[136]
240. Deyðan tóku teir Sjúrða unga, teir lívdu ei nakað eftir, høvuðleysan kappan tann í gullsaðilin settu.	They took the young dead Sjúrður, they didn't spare their efforts, they sat the decapitated hero in the gold saddle.
241. Ikki vildi Grani ganga, Gunnar kongur ríður, fyrr enn frægi Sjúrður í gullbygilin stígur.	Grani did not want to walk, King Gunnar was riding, before the valiant Sjúrður steps into the gold stirrups
242. Deyðan tóku teir Sjúrða unga, kappan tann hin snjalla, tá á teirri somu tíð førdu heim til hallar.	They took the young dead Sjúrður, the eloquent hero, then at the same time they took him home to the hall.
243. Deyðan tóku teir Sjúrða svein, bóru inn á skildri, hevur so mangur latið lív, helst av kvinnu veldi.	They took the dead Sjúrður swain, carried him in on a shield, so many have lost their lives, especially because of women.
244. Deyðan tóku teir Sjúrð svein, løgdu Brynhildu hjá: "Berið Guðrunu Sjúrða, hon eigur hann enn sum áður."	They took the dead Sjúrður swain, laid him next to Brynhild: "Carry Sjúrður to Guðrun, she is married to him now as before."
245. Deyðan tóku teir Sjúrða unga, løgdu hjá Guðrunar síðu, Brynhild unga sá hará, nú gongur hon kyk av kvíðu.	They took the dead young Sjúrður, laid him by Guðrun's side, young Brynhild was watching, now she walks shaking with agony.
246. Brynhild hevði manga nátt sovið á Sjúrðar armi, nú hon hevði hans deyða volt, springur hon kyk av harmi.	Brynhild had for many nights slept in Sjúrður's arms, now she had brought about his death, she dies shaking of grief.
247. Brynhild unti Sjúrða væl, meg man minna enn, kvinnur hava av lívi fingið mangar sterkar menn.	Brynhild loved Sjúrður very much, if I still remember, women have taken the lives of many strong men.

136 The withers of a horse are the front part of its back.

248. Brynhild unti Sjúrða væl,
við allskyns spekt og meingi,
kvinnur hava av lívi fingið
mangar reystar dreingir.

Brynhild loved Sjúrður very much,
with all kinds of gentleness and a lot,[137]
women have taken the lives
of many valiant heroes.

249. Hósins dóttir Kjartan unti
við tann mentilin reyða,
tá ið hon ikki kundi hann fáa,
voldi hon hans deyða.

Hósin's[138] daughter loved Kjartan[139]
with the red clothing,[140]
when she could not have him,
she brought about his death.

250. Hava tit hoyrt frá Ingigerð,
meg man minna enn,
hon legði niður á grønan vøll
tógva sterkar menn.

Have you heard about Ingigerð,[141]
if I still remember,
she killed on the green field
two strong men.

251. Hava tit hoyrt frá Dalitu,
loynir ei mín tunga,
brádliga hon av lívi fekk
tann sterka Samson unga.

Have you heard about Delilah,
I don't try to hide it,
suddenly she took the life
of the young Samson the strong.[142]

252. So gjørdi Ásla Sjúrðardóttir
við høvdingin reyða,
svørji tann eið á mína trú,
hon voldi kong Regnars deyða.

So did Ásla Sjúrðardóttir[143]
with the red chieftain,[144]
I swear an oath by all that is sacred,
she caused King Regnar's death.

---

137 As in, she loved him a lot.

138 His name is Ósvífr in Icelandic, which is similar. See Einar Ól. Sveinsson, *Laxdœla Saga*, 311.

139 This is the story of Guðrún and Kjartan in the Icelandic *Laxdœla saga* and the Faroese *Kjartans tættir* (CCF 23). Grundtvig and Bloch, *Føroya kvæði*, vol. 1, pp. 477–97. See also Kamban, *Kenn mær einki um*, 64–65.

140 Kjartan is given scarlet clothing by the king. See Einar Ól. Sveinsson, *Laxdœla saga*, chap. 40, p. 124. *Mentilin* is *mentarlín*, which is decorated linen. See Hammershaimb and Jakobsen, *Færøsk anthologi*, vol. 2, p. 203, s.v. *mentarlín*.

141 The stanza about Ingigerður is from *Torsteinskvæði* (CCF 99). See Kamban, *Kenn mær einki um*, 65.

142 In the Bible story in Judges 13–16, Delilah betrays Samson by cutting off his hair, which causes him to lose his strength. This ultimately leads to his death. See *Samsons kvæði* (CCF 113); Kamban, *Kenn mær einki um*, 65.

143 Her name is Áslaug in Old Norse, and she is the central character in the Icelandic *Ragnars saga loðbrókar*.

144 These two lines mean that Ásla also betrayed King Regnar (Ragnarr loðbrókar in the Icelandic sagas).

253. Regnar kongur í Eysturlondum
menskur var hann av dreingjum,
Ásla voldi deyða hans,
hon duldi sítt navn so leingi.

Regnar king of the eastern lands
he was brave amongst heroes,
Ásla caused his death,
she concealed her name for so long.[145]

254. So gjørdi Guðrun Júkadóttir,
vil eg for ydur tína,
hon læt burtur av lívi taka
fýra brøður sínar.

So did Guðrun Júkadóttir,
I'll tell you about it,
she had the lives taken
of four of her brothers.[146]

255. So gjørdu moyar í forðum tíð
innan rósinslund,
tá ið tær ikki sín vilja fingu,
voldu tær deyðastund.

So did maidens in ancient times
in the grove of roses,
when they did not get their way,
they caused the hour of death.

256. So gjørdu moyar í forðum tíð,
sum frægir siga frá,
tá ið tær ikki sín vilja fingu,
løgdu tær deyðaráð.

So did maidens in ancient times,
as is famously[147] told,
when they did not get their way,
they laid out deadly plans.

257. Deyðan tóku teir Sjúrða unga,
løgdu Guðrunu á skeyt,
ikki visti brúður, hon vaknaði,
fyrr enn blóð um bæði fleyt.

They took the dead young Sjúrður,
laid him in Guðrun's lap,
the woman[148] didn't realize, she woke up,
before blood drenched them both.[149]

258. Deyðan tóku teir Sjúrð svein,
løgdu Guðrunu hjá,
ikki visti brúður, hon vaknaði,
fyrr enn blóð á lendar lá.

They took the dead Sjúrður,
and laid him beside Guðrun,
the woman didn't realize, she woke up,
before blood covered her loins.[150]

259. Ikki visti brúður, hon vaknaði,
fyrr enn hon í benið brá,
tað var ei so undarligt,
við sorg hon í tað sá.

The woman didn't realize, she woke up,
before she noticed the wound,
it wasn't so strange,
that she saw it with distress.

---

145 Stt. 252–253 refer to *Ragnars kvæði* (CCF 2). For an analysis, see Kamban, *Kenn mær einki um*, 65–66.

146 These are Gunnar and Høgnar who appear in this ballad, and the other two are Gíslar and Jarnar who are mentioned in *Høgnar táttur*, st. 17. Their mother Grímhild wants them to stay at home.

147 *Frægir* here is an adjective and means "famous" or "renowned."

148 *Brúður* is a *heiti* for woman used in ballads; it also means bride.

149 The blood is flowing around them both.

150 Loins are specificied here because they have laid the dead Sjúrður in her lap.

260. Vaknaði Guðrun Júkadóttir, læt so orðum fara: "Síðst mundi eg, Gunnar kongur. svikum av tær vara."	Guðrun Júkadóttir woke up, spoke these words: "You were the last one, King Gunnar, of whom I expected treachery."
261. Guðrun setist upp undir seg, strýkur sveita frá, blóðigan kysti hon munnin tann, á Sjúrðar høvdi lá.	Guðrun sat up in bed, wiped the blood off, she kissed that bloody mouth, on Sjúrður's face.
262. Blóðigan kysti hon munnin tann, á Sjúrðar høvdi lá: "Hetta skal eg, Gunnar, hevna, um eg liva má."	She kissed that bloody mouth, on Sjúrður's face: "This, Gunnar, I will avenge, if I'm able to live on."
263. Guðrun steig úr seingini upp, blóð av henni rann, svørji tann eið av míni trú, hon gekk í loftið fram.	Guðrun got out of bed, the blood ran off her, I swear an oath by all that is sacred, she went to the loft.
264. Guðrun steig úr seingini upp, rendi úr henni blóð, so gekk hon í loftið fram, hon var um hjarta móð.	Guðrun got out of bed, the blood ran from her, she went to the loft, her heart was full of distress
265. Guðrun gekk í loftið fram, hon fór úr stakki reyða, alla sína ævina syrgdi hon Sjúrðar deyða.	Guðrun went to the loft, she took off the red gown,[151] all her life she mourned Sjúrður's death.
266. Brynhild sprakk av harmi, Sjúrður læt sítt lív, tað man merkja meiningin, at Brynhild hon var fríð.	Brynhild died of sorrow, Sjúrður lost his life, it must be noted that the opinion was,[152] that Brynhild was beautiful.
267. Brynhild sprakk av harmi eftir Sjúrðar deyða, góvu Guðrunu gull og fæ og mangar ringar reyðar.	Brynhild died of sorrow after Sjúrður's death, they gave Guðrun gold and property and many red[153] rings.

151 It is likely here that the blood has made her gown red. Alternatively, her gown was red to start with.

152 This refers to the general opinion in the story world.

153 This just signifies gold rings.

268.	"Hoyr tað, Guðrun systir mín, syrg ikki Sjúrðar deyða, Artala kongur í Húnalandi kortar ei gullinum reyða."	"Listen, Guðrun my sister, do not grieve Sjurður's death, King Artala in Húnaland is not lacking in red gold."
269.	"Syrg ikki, syrg ikki, dóttir mín, syrg ikki Sjúrðar deyða, Artala kongur í Húnalandi kortar ei gullið reyða."	"Don't grieve, don't grieve, my daughter, don't grieve the death of Sjúrður, King Artala in Húnaland, is not lacking in red gold."[154]
270.	Svaraði Guðrun Júkadóttir av so tungum stríði: "Tó skal eg hevna Sjúrðar deyða, um eg verði á lívi."	Guðrun Júkadóttir answered from such great animosity: "I'll still avenge Sjúrður's death, if I remain alive."
271.	Nú skal lata ljóði av, eg kvøði ikki longur á sinni, nú skal taka upp triðja tátt og víðari leggja í minni.	Now I shall end my song, I sing no longer at present, now to begin the third part of the ballad and continue to remember it.[155]
Refrain	*Grani bar gullið av heiði,* *brá hann sínum brandi av reiði,* *Sjúrður vann av orminum,* *Grani bar gullið av heiði.*	*Grani carried the gold from the heath,* *he brandished his blade in a fury,* *Sjúrður defeated the dragon,* *Grani carried the gold from the heath.*

154 It must be Guðrun's mother speaking here.

155 This implies continuing to transmit the ballad and to keep it in living memory.

THE BALLAD OF HØGNI (HØGNA TÁTTUR)

1. Artala kongur í Húnalandi, bróti úr bragdartátti, festi Guðruna Júkadóttur, ið Sjúrður snari átti.	King Artala in Húnaland, taken from a heroic ballad,[1] married Guðrun Júkadóttir, who was married to the swift Sjúrður.
Refrain *Grani bar gullið av heiði,* *brá hann sínum brandi av reiði,* *Sjúrður vann av orminum,* *Grani bar gullið av heiði.*	*Grani carried the gold from the heath,* *he brandished his blade in a fury,* *Sjúrður defeated the dragon,* *Grani carried the gold from the heath.*
2. Artala kongur í hallina gongur, vekur upp dreingir snarar: "Nú skal eg festa Guðruna, vit ríða í Júkagarðar."	King Artala walks into the hall, wakes up the brave men: "Now I shall marry Guðrun, we ride to the court of Júki."
3. Artala kongur í Húnalandi ríður fram yvir skóg, úti Guðrun Júkadóttir fyri honum stóð.	King Artala in Húnaland rides through the forest, Guðrun Júkadóttir stood outside before him.
4. "Statt væl, Guðrun Júkadóttir, tú unniliga sprund, nú skínur sól á heiðin lond ígjøgnum grønan lund."	"Well met,[2] Guðrun Júkadóttir, you beautiful woman, now the sun is shining on heathen lands through the green grove."
5. Artala kongur í Húnalandi, sigist í bragdartátti, festi frúgv og førdi heim, sum Sjúrður í forðum átti.	King Artala in Húnaland, it is told in a heroic ballad, married the lady and brought her home, the one that Sjúrður was married to before.
6. Guðrun gekk at borði fram, siga má eg þá stand, hana førdi kongurin við sær til Húnaland.	Guðrun went to the table, I must say at once,[3] the king took her with him to Húnaland.
7. Guðrun var leingi á Húnalandi, kinn bar hon so reyða, nú legði hon ráðini á at hevna Sjúrðar deyða.	Guðrun was in Húnaland for a long time, her cheeks were so red, now she's plotting to avenge Sjúrður's death.

1 See *Brynhildar táttur*, st. 4n.

2 This greeting is a chivalric tribute to her and a mark of respect.

3 It is the singer of the ballad making this comment.

8. Artala kongur í Húnalandi blandar mjøð og vín, býður so øllum Júkungum at drekka heim til sín.	King Artala in Húnaland mixes mead and wine, then invites all of Júki's people to drink at his home.
9. Guðrun býður sínum brøðrum, letur ikki gloyma: sterkar hurðar fyri hallina, og fast við jarni soyma.	Guðrun invites her brothers, won't let them forget: strong doors before the hall, and nailed down firmly with iron.[4]
10. Guðrun býður sínum brøðrum, letur ikki seinka, sterkar hurðar fyri hallisdyr, og fast við jarni leinkja.	Guðrun invites her brothers, won't let it be delayed, strong doors before the hall's doorway, and chained firmly with iron.[5]
11. Guðrun gongur út og inn, letur blanda vín, Høgnar, Gunnar og allar brøður letur hon heinta til sín.	Guðrun goes out and in, has wine mixed, Høgnar, Gunnar, and all the brothers she has brought to her.
12. Høgnar gekk í hallina inn, heldur á búnum brandi: "Nú lystir meg á Húnaland at drekka tann mjøðin blandi."	Høgnar walks into the hall, grasping a readied sword: "Now I desire to go to Húnaland to drink that mixed mead."
13. Grimhild so til orða tekur, tykir í tí tortur: "Um tú fert á Húnaland, ikki kemur tú aftur."	Grimhild begins to speak, thinking there might be be humiliation in it:[6] "If you go to Húnaland, you shan't return."
14. Høgnar stendur fyri breiðum borði, tungan mælir snimma: "Tó skal eg á Húnaland sigur av kappum vinna."	Høgnar stands before a wide table, he responds immediately: "Neverthless in Húnaland I shall win a victory against the champions."

4 The doors are very sturdy.

5 This implies it would be hard to escape.

6 This refers to Grimhild's motivation. This could also mean "pain" as well as humiliation. She might be thinking of the tragedy that will occur, and that she is expecting foul play. On the other hand, Grimhild might be trying to embarrass Høgnar by suggesting he won't win and therefore will not come back. So, you can interpret this line both ways: it could be a warning or she could be trying to embarrass him.

15. Grimhild so til orða tekur,
tykir í tí mein:
"Um tit fara á Húnaland,
eingin kemur heim."

Grimhild begins to speak,
thinking there might be harm in it:
"If all of you[7] go to Húnaland,
no one shall come home."

16. Høgnar stendur á hallargólvi,
hann klæddist í brynju blá:
"Tó skal eg á Húnaland,
tað standist av, hvat ið má."

Høgnar stands on the floor of the hall,
he is dressing in blue[8] armour:
"Nevertheless I shall go to Húnaland,
whatever the consequences might be."

17. "Meðan tú fert á Húnaland,
lat nú tað so gera:
Gíslar og hann Jarnar
skulu heima vera.

"While you go to Húnaland,
let us do this:
Gíslar and Jarnar
shall stay at home.

18. Meðan tú fert á Húnaland
at drekka mjøð og vín,
Gíslar og Jarnar verða eftir
báðir hjá móður sín."

While you go to Húnaland
to drink mead and wine,
Gíslar and Jarnar shall stay behind
both with their mother."

19. Gíslar og hann Jarnar,
Júkungarnir báðir,
fara sær á Húnaland
mót síni móðurs ráðum.

Gíslar and Jarnar,
both the sons of Júki,
are going to Húnaland
against their mother's advice.

20. Gíslar og hann Jarnar,
Júkungarnir tveir,
fóru sær á Húnaland,
fátt kann forða feigum.

Gíslar and Jarnar,
the two sons of Júki,
went to Húnaland,
little[9] can save the doomed.[10]

21. Tað var Høgnar Júkason,
ríður út við strand,
møtti honum ein sævarkvinna
á tann hvíta sand.

It was Høgnar Júkason,
he rides to the beach,
a mermaid met him there
on the white sand.

22. "Hoyr tú inda, sævarkvinna,
sig mær dømin mein,
um eg fari á Húnaland,
komi eg heilur heim?"

"Listen lovely[11] mermaid,
tell me the sorrowful fate,
if I go to Húnaland,
will I come home safely?"

---

7 It literally says "if you go," but we have chosen to add "all of you" to make it clear that "you" is in the plural.

8 This implies that the armour is black.

9 There is little one can do.

10 This is an idiom that is still used in Faroese and appears in several ballads. See *Føroysk-føroysk orðabók*, s.v. "Forða."

11 This is a courtly address that can also be used with men.

23. "Hoyr tú, Høgnar Júkason, eg sigi tær dømin mein, um tú fert á Húnaland, ikki kemur tú heim."	"Listen, Høgnar Júkason, I will tell you the sorrowful fate, if you go to Húnaland, you shan't return."
24. Tað var Høgnar Júkason, sínum svørði brá, hann kleyv hesa sævarkvinnu sundur í lutir tvá.	It was Høgnar Júkason, he brandished his sword, he chopped this mermaid into two pieces.
25. Tekur hann hennara blóðiga høvur, kastar út á sund, skjýtur hann kroppin eftir, sukku bæði til grund.	He takes her bloody head, throws it into the sound, throws[12] the body after it, both sank to the bottom.
26. Tað var Høgnar Júkason, gongur fram við strand, møtti hann einum sævarmanni á tann hvíta sand.	It was Høgnar Júkason, walking along the beach, he met a merman on the white sand.
27. "Hoyr tú inda, sævarmaður, sig mær í tí satt, fari eg á Húnaland, komi eg heilur aftur?"	"Listen lovely merman, tell me truthfully, if I go to Húnaland, will I return safely?"
28. "Hoyr tá, Høgnar Júkason, tað man eg siga satt, um tú fert á Húnaland, um tað tú kemur aftur."	"Listen, Høgnar Júkason, I will tell you truthfully, if you go to Húnaland, you will return."[13]
29. Hann læt knør av lunni draga oman úr tøttum neysti, tá stóð fast í kjalborðum, fram leyp knørurin reysti.	He has a ship[14] dragged off the rollers[15] down from the wind-tight boathouse,[16] the keel strakes[17] were stable, the upright[18] ship leapt forward.

---

12 The two verbs for throw are different in the Faroese.

13 The *um* in the Faroese is likely only a filler, but it could indicate that the merman is non-committal in his answer.

14 A *knørrur* is a big sailing ship.

15 These are wooden rollers (*lunnar*) used when a boat is launched or brought up on shore.

16 This is a formulaic stanza. It means a well-built boathouse.

17 These are the boards that are closest to the keel.

18 The ship looks upright when you look at the stem (the most forward part of the bow, and an extension of the keel). In Faroese boatbuilding, it is important that the

30. Høgnar læt av lunni ganga sína glæstriskeið, skipini hildu í havið út, falkurin drívur av leið.	Høgnar let off the rollers his magnificent ship,[19] the ships sailed out into the ocean, the vessel[20] drifts off course.
31. Høgnar vindur segl í rá, letur so orðum svara, grátandi vendi Grimhild drottning aftur í Júkagarðar.	Høgnar sets sail, and then he answers her, Queen Grimhild turned crying back to Júki's court.
32. So grætur Grimhild drottningin, tað hitt væna vív: "Far væl, Høgnar sonur mín, eg síggi teg ei í lívi."	Queen Grimhild cries,[21] the beautiful woman: "Goodbye, Høgnar my son, I won't see you alive again."
33. Grimhild fyri munni mælir, Høgnar reisir á ferð: "Eg kenni væl Guðruna dóttur mína, er roynd í bágagerð."	Grimhild says, as Høgnar goes on the journey:[22] "I know my daughter Guðrun well, she is experienced in harmful acts."
34. Høgnar talar til Gunnar kong, alt foruttan sút: "Vit vinda nú segl í húna hátt, vit seta í havið út."	Høgnar speaks to King Gunnar, without worries: "Now we are hoisting the sail to the masthead, we are setting course for the sea."
35. Ein kom maður í hallina inn til perlamentið fríða: "Nú síggi eg falk í havi út alt undir tann grøna líða."	A man came into the hall to the beautiful parliament: "Now I see a vessel in the sea under the green hillside."
36. "Sært tú skip eftir havi koma, seglini hvít sum lín, vera man Høgnar Júkason at vitja systur sín."	"Do you see a ship coming across the sea, the sails white as linen, it must be Høgnar Júkason on his way to visit his sister."

---

stem is upright rather than leaning forwards or backwards. If it leans forward, the boat does not look proud, whereas if its leans backwards, the construction of the boat looks too pompous. Upright therefore indicates a well-made boat.

19 A *glæstriskeið* is a word used in ballads meaning a magnificent or splendid ship.

20 A *falkur* literally means "falcon," but in ballads is used poetically to mean a horse or a ship (here it clearly refers to a ship).

21 She is weeping, not crying out.

22 We have added "as" here to provide clarity.

37. Guðrun gekk í grasagarð, reyðargullið bar á hendi, ramar ristir hon rúnirnar, tær út í havið sendi.	Guðrun walked in her garden, red gold on her arms,[23] she carved powerful runes, and sent them out to sea.
38. Ørnir tvær av landi komu, setast á salta sjógv, vaksa tekur vindur í ský, aldan brýtur á lógv.	Two eagles came from the land, sat themselves on the salty ocean, the wind picks up in the clouds, the wave breaks on the sandy beach.
39. Tá var veður á sjónum hart, ógvuligt á at líta, stýrir so Høgnar Júkason, at frá dró mjøllin hvíta.	The weather on the sea was severe then, terrible to behold, Høgnar Júkason steers so that white snow came from the ship.[24]
40. So var veður á sjónum hart, tá ið Høgnar stóð til stýri, Gunnar kongur í lyfting gongur, nú bliknaði drongur dýri.	The weather on the sea was so severe, when Høgnar stood at the helm, King Gunnar walks on the poop deck, the magnificent hero now paled.[25]
41. So var veður á sjónum hart, tað brakar í borð og bondum, sundur gingu jarnárar báðar í Høgna hondum.	The weather on the sea was so severe, the strakes[26] and ribs are creaking, both iron oars broke apart in Høgnar's hands.
42. Tá var veður á sjónum hart, tað knakar í hvørjum stongum, tað var Høgnar Júkason, tók havn í Húnalondum.	The weather on the sea was severe then, every mast is groaning, it was Høgnar Júkason, who landed in Húnaland.
43. Løgdu undir Húnaland eina morguntíð, alt var sum í bál at líta, skeiðir dynja í.	They lay by Húnaland one morning, everything was like looking into a bonfire,[27] the ships thunder in their speed.

23 These are golden rings on her arms.

24 This refers to foam from the waves.

25 This implies Gunnar is going pale from fear in the storm.

26 On a wooden vessel, the strakes are the longitudinal planks that make up the sides of the boat, running from front to rear.

27 The bonfire effect is probably a combination of the creaking noise made by the ships and the redness of the sunrise.

44. Løgdu undir Húnaland
eina morgunstund,
alt var sum í bál at líta,
í tann skeiðadund.

They lay by Húnaland
one morning,
everything was like looking into a bonfire,
due to the noise of the ships.

45. Tá ið teirra snekkja
hon kendi fagurt land,
fyrst steig Høgnar Júkason
sínum fótum á land.

When their ship[28]
approached fair land,
Høgnar Júkason was the first to step
foot on land.

46. Fyrst steig Høgnar Júkason
sínum fótum á land,
Gíslar og Jarnar og Gunnar kongur
undir hans høgru hond.

Høgnar Júkason was the first to step
foot on land,
Gíslar, Jarnar, and King Gunnar
were at his right hand side.

47. Ganga teir frá strondum niðan,
so er greitt fyri mær,
síðan allir Júkagarpar
niðan í grasagarð.

They walked up from the beach,
so I've been told,
then all the heroes of Júki
went up to the garden.

48. Úti í miðjum grasgarði
tungu bóru teir so snjalla,
gingu so í høgar borgir
Júkagarpar allir.

In the middle of the garden[29]
they were so eloquent,
then they went to the high castle
all of Júki's heroes.

49. Úti í miðjum grasgarði
klæddust í brynju dýra,
gingu so í høgu borgir
Júkagarpar fýra.

In the middle of the garden
dressed in expensive armour,
then they went to the high castles
the four heroes of Júki.

50. Tað var Høgnar Júkason,
inn um dyrnar steig,
nú sá hann á Guðrunu,
at ilt undir kinnar beið.

It was Høgnar Júkason,
he stepped through the door,
now he saw from Guðrun,
that there was evil hiding on her face.[30]

51. Segði tað Høgnar Júkason,
inn um dyrnar hyggur:
"Eg síggi tað á Guðrunu,
at ilt undir kinnar byggir."

Høgnar Júkason said,
as he looked through the door:
"I see from Guðrun,
that there's evil hiding on her face."

---

28 *Snekkja* is a *heiti* for ship used in ballads.

29 This is formulaic in ballads.

30 This means that she is plotting something and meant them harm; it literally means "it is evil under her cheeks."

52. Guðrun so til orða tekur:
"Vit erum nú her aleina,
fáið mær bæði skjold og svørð
øllum tykkum at goyma!"

Guðrun begins to speak:
"Now we are here alone,
give me both shield and sword
to store for you all!"

53. Svaraði Høgnar Júkason,
hann heldur á brúnum knívi:
"Frá mær leggi eg ikki
skjøld og svørð,
so leingi eg eri á lívi."

Høgnar Júkason answered,
he grasps a shining[31] knife:
"I won't put away my shield and sword,
as long as I'm alive."

54. Guðrun so til orða tekur,
hon bar tungu snjalla:
"Minnist tú nakað á Sjúrða unga,
tú førdi mær til halla[r]?"

Guðrun begins to speak,
she spoke skillfully:
"Do you remember anything
about young Sjúrður,
whom you brought to me in the hall?"

55. Guðrun so til orða tekur,
illskan í henni breyt:
"Minnist tú nakað Sjúrð hin unga
blóðigan mær í skeyt?"

Guðrun begins to speak,
anger wells up inside of her:
"Do you remember anything
about the young Sjúrður
who you laid all bloody in my lap?"[32]

56. Guðrun so til orða tekur,
ilt undir kinnar beið:
"Frægari maður var Sjúrður kappi,
í gullsporum reið."

Guðrun begins to speak,
there was evil hiding on her face:
"Sjúrður the hero was a better man,
who rode in golden spurs."

57. Guðrun so til orða tekur,
bar um hjarta trá:
"Enn var Sjúrður frægari,
í gullsaðli lá."

Guðrun begins to speak,
carried grief in her heart:
"Sjúrður was still better,
laying in the golden saddle."[33]

58. Høgnar hugsar so við sær,
lítur á ringar reyðar:
"Ei er blítt á brúnarskoru,
minnist á buðlungs deyða."

Høgnar thinks to himself,
looking at the red rings:
"You're not in a good mood,[34]
remembering the king's death."

31 The shining reflects how sharp it is.

32 This happens in *Brynhildar táttur*, stt. 257–258.

33 Guðrun is saying Sjúrður was a better man than them even when he was dead.

34 *Brúnaskor* is the mark between the brows, or the furrowed brow. This literally means that they don't look happy (*blíður*) with a furrowed brow.

59. Høgnar mælir fyri sær, lítur á ringin sín: "Ei er blítt á brúnarskoru, minnist á buðlungs lík."	Høgnar mutters to himself, glancing at his ring:[35] "You're not in a good mood, if you're remembering the king's corpse."
60. Inn kemur Guðrun árla morgun, ilt er skap at eggja, borð stóð breitt við silkidúk, og bjór fyri reystar seggjar.	Guðrun comes in early in the morning, one should not provoke a person of evil disposition, the table was set with a silk tablecloth, and beer for brave men.[36]
61. Inn kom Guðrun árla morgun við hógv og hyggið orð: "Kastið nú vákn og herklæði, tær stígið yvir borð!"	Guðrun came in early in the morning with restraint and cautious words: "Discard your weapons and your armour now, you step over the table!"[37]
62. Svaraði Høgnar Júkason, hann var dreingja maki: "Sjálvir skulum vit váknini goyma, osum til at taka."	Høgnar Júkason answered, he was the equal[38] of the heroes: "We shall keep the weapons ourselves, for us to take."
63. Drekka teir í Húnalandi bæði úti og inni, drekka mjøð og kláran vín glaðir á hvørjum sinni.	They drink in Húnaland both inside and outside, they drink mead and clear wine happy on every occasion.
64. Drekka teir í Húnalandi bæði við gleði og gaman, illa líkar Guðrunu, at einki nertur saman.	They drink in Húnaland with both joy and delight, Guðrun doesn't like that there is no conflict.
65. Drekka teir í tríggjar dagar bæði við gleði og gleim, illa líkar Guðrunu, at einki nertur teim.	They drink for three days with both joy and cheerfulness, Guðrun doesn't like, that there is no conflict.
66. Guðrun lokkar sín unga son við so miklum mæti: "Eg skal geva tær gull og fæ, stillar tú Høgnar av kæti."	Guðrun coaxes her young son with such great authority: "I shall give you gold and property, if you silence Høgnar's laughter."

35 He is looking down, ashamed.

36 *Seggur* is a word used in ballads for a man, warrior, or hero.

37 She wants them to sit at the table unarmed.

38 *Maki* means peer or equal.

67. Guðrun lokkar sín unga son,
í duldum hon hann bað,
hann gekk sær at borðinum,
sum Høgnar fyri sat.

Guðrun coaxes her young son,
she tells him in secret to do it,
he went to the table,
where Høgnar sat.

68. Guðrun lokkar sín unga son,
í duldum hon hann dró,
hann hevði upp sína høgru hond,
Høgnar á nasar sló.

Guðrun coaxes her young son,
she lured him in secret,
he lifted his right hand,
he punched Høgnar on the nose.

69. Sveinur var ungur av aldrinum,
hann taldist, tá ið hon bað,
hann gekk aftur at borðinum,
sum Høgnar fyri sat.

The boy was young of age,
he declined when she told him to,[39]
he went back to the table,
where Høgnar sat.

70. Hann gekk aftur at borðinum,
á Høgnar nasar sló,
voldi tað Guðrun Júkadóttir,
drykkjan varð óró.

He went back to the table,
and punched Høgnar on the nose,
Guðrun Júkadóttir caused it,
the drinking was disturbed.

71. Høgna rann tað heita blóð
bæði úr nøsum og munni,
kappin varð so illa við,
hann ikki við slíkt kundi.

Hot blood ran from Høgnar
from both the nose and the mouth,
the hero was so shocked,
he couldn't let that one go.

72. "Eg fái ei í Húnalandi
drukkið tann mjøðin við grandi,
ótakk havi tann móðirin,
ið so sín son upp vandi."

"In Húnaland I'm not able
to drink the mead without harm,
that mother does not have my thanks
for raising her son like that."

73. Høgnar fram um borðið leyp
við berum spjóti í hendi,
mækin sneiddi búk og bein,
ígjøgnum sveinin rendi.

Høgnar leapt over the table
brandishing a spear in his hand,
the sword[40] cut through stomach and bone,
it ran through the boy.

74. Tað var Høgnar Júkason,
sínum svørði brá,
hann tók hennara unga son,
hjó honum bulin frá.

It was Høgnar Júkason,
who brandished his sword,
he took her young son,
he hacked his torso off.

---

39 At first, he is hesitant to take action and doesn't want to, but Guðrun forces him to. This points back to her authority.

40 *Mæki* is a *heiti* used in the ballads for "sword."

75. Høgnar tók sín búgvin brand, sneiðir bulin frá, kastar høvdið á hallargólv, so Artala kongur sá.	Høgnar took his readied sword, and cut the torso off, he throws the head on the hall floor, so that King Artala saw it.
76. Guðrun gekk for Artala kong, sigur honum frá: "Deyður er okra ungi sonur, helst av Høgna ráð.	Guðrun went before King Artala, and tells him: "Our young son is dead, probably Høgnar's doing.
77. Eg man ei í Húnalandi longur við tær stýra, um tú gert ikki nakrar sømdir eftir tann dreingin dýra."	I will not rule Húnaland with you any longer, if you don't take redress for that dear boy."
78. "Hoyr tú tað, mín veldiga søta, lat nú tað so vera, sjálvur er hann tín onkarbróðir, eg kann honum einki gera."	"Listen, my dearly beloved, let it be, he is himself your dear brother,[41] I can't harm him."
79. "Tú skalt ikki, Artala kongur, leingi ríki stýra, vilt tú ongar sømdir taka eftir tann dreingin dýra."	"King Artala, you won't rule this kingdom for long, if you don't take redress for that dear boy."
80. "Hoyr tú, Guðrun søta mín, tað vil eg ei trúgva, at tú vilt nú tínum brøðrum svik til handar snúgva.	"Listen, Guðrun my sweet, I can't believe, that you now want to deceive your brothers.
81. Tá ið teir vógu hann Sjúrð svein, Guðrun søta mín, tá vóru Gíslar og Jarnar børn heima hjá móður sín."	When they killed the young Sjúrður, Guðrun my sweet, Gíslar and Jarnar were children at home with their mother."
82. Guðrun so til orða tekur: "Tað skal eg nú valda, Gíslar og hann Jarnar ungi báðir skulu gjalda."	Guðrun then spoke: "It is my decision now, that Gíslar and young Jarnar shall both pay."
83. Mælti tað Guðrun Júkadóttir: "Tað man einki saka, Gíslar og Jarnar og allar brøður skal eg av lívi taka."	Guðrun Júkadóttir spoke: "It doesn't matter, Gíslar and Jarnar and all my brothers I shall take their lives."

41 *Onka-* is used to denote a favourite of something, the most loved.

84. "Tað er einki eykarverk at ganga Høgna ímóti, hvar ið hann kemur í víggj at standa, har hevur hann høvur á spjóti.	"It is no easy feat to go against Høgnar, whenever he comes into battle, he has a head on a spear.[42]
85. Hoyr tú tað, mín veldiga søta, legg sjálv til tess ráð, hvussu vit skulu teir miklu menn burtur av lívi fá!"	Listen to this, my dearly beloved, make a plot yourself, how shall we take the lives of these mighty men!"[43]
86. "Taka skal tríggjar aldirshúðir, rýða tær í blóði, falla so tungt á Júkagarpar, troyttir av miklum móði."	"You shall take three skins,[44] smear them with blood, attack Júki's heroes so ferociously, tired from great anger."
87. Guðrun stendur fyri breiðum borði, mælir um tann vanda: "Nú skulu tit, Júkagarpar, á aldirshúðir ganga."	Guðrun stands before the wide table, speaking about that danger: "Now you, Júki's heroes, shall walk on the skins."
88. Upp steig Høgnar Júkason, tungu bar hann so snjalla, talar yvir breiða borð fyri teir brøður allar.	Høgnar Júkason stood up, he was so eloquent, speaking over the wide table to all the brothers.
89. Upp steig Høgnar Júkason, blandað hevði vín: "Gíslar og Jarnar fara báðir aftur til móður sín."	Høgnar Júkason stood up, he had mixed wine: "Gíslar and Jarnar both go back to their mother."
90. Upp steig Høgnar Júkason, letur so orðum svara: "Gíslar og Jarnar fara báðir aftur í Júkagarðar."	Høgnar Júkason stood up, answered with these words: "Gíslar and Jarnar both go back to the court of Júki."

42 This echoes *Brynhildar táttur*, stt. 182–183, when Brynhild is telling Høgnar to kill Sjúrður and he replies that it is very difficult to kill him.

43 This echoes *Brynhildar táttur*, st. 185, when Høgnar asks Brynhild for a plan on how to kill Sjúrður.

44 The skins are slippery, and walking over them is a test. If they fall, they will be easier to kill. *Aldirshúð* is an unusual word and is likely related to Old Norse *ǫldungahúð/ǫldungshúð*. An *ǫldungr* is an old bull, so it is probably the skin of an old bull.

91. Guðrun stendur fyri breiðum borði,
mælir um tann vanda:
"Gíslar og hann Jarnar ungi,
allir skulu ganga."

Guðrun stands before the wide table,
speaks of that danger:
"Gíslar and young Jarnar,
all shall walk."[45]

92. "Gíslar og hann Jarnar ungi
vóru ikki hjá,
Gunnar og eg Høgnar
vóru teir, Sjúrðin vá.

"Gíslar and young Jarnar
weren't there,
Gunnar and I, Høgnar,
were the ones that slew Sjúrður.

93. Gunnar og eg Høgnar
tóku Sjúrða av lívi,
tá vóru Gíslar og Jarnar børn
heima hjá móður síni.

Gunnar and I, Høgnar,
took Sjúrður's life,
Gíslar and Jarnar were children then
at home with their mother.

94. Gunnar og eg Høgnar
vógu tann kappan reysta,
Gíslar og hann Jarnar ungi
ikki harav vistu.

Gunnar and I, Høgnar,
slew that mighty hero,
Gíslar and young Jarnar
didn't know anything about it.

95. Gunnar og eg Høgnar
vit vógu Sjúrða við listi,
tá vóru Gíslar og Jarnar børn,
lógu hjá móðurs brósti."

Gunnar and I, Høgnar,
we slew Sjúrður with cunning,
Gíslar and Jarnar were children then,
laying at their mother's breast."

96. Gíslar og hann Jarnar
mundu á húðir ganga,
allir sóu teir falla niður,
eingin sá teir upp standa.

Gíslar and Jarnar
walked on the skins,
all saw them fall down,
no one saw them rise.[46]

97. Guðrun stendur fyri breiðum borði,
mælir um tann vanda:
"Nú skal Gunnar bróðir mín
aftur á húðir ganga."

Guðrun stands before the wide table,
speaks about that danger:
"Now Gunnar my brother shall
walk on the skins again."

98. Tað var Gunnar Júkason,
hann mundi á húðir ganga,
allir sóu hann niður falla,
eingin sá hann upp standa.

It was Gunnar Júkason,
he walked on the skins,
all saw him fall down,
no one saw him rise.

---

45 Guðrun demands that all her brothers shall walk across the skins. Høgnar has realized that his younger brothers are in danger and is trying to save them.

46 The children have been killed.

99. Guðrun stendur fyri breiða borði,
nú ber hon kinn so reyðan:
"Hoyr tú, Høgnar bróðir mín,
nú hevni eg Sjúrðar deyða."

Guðrun stands before the wide table,
her cheeks are now so red:
"Listen, Høgnar my brother,
now I'm avenging the death of Sjúrður."

100. Upp steig Høgnar Júkason,
brandin yvir seg bar,
so er mær av sonnum sagt,
slíkt gongur hans hugi nær.

Høgnar Júkason stood up,
carried the sword above himself,[47]
so I've been truthfully told,
such things touch a nerve.[48]

101. Guðrun stendur fyri breiða borði,
kinn ber hon so balda:
"Nú skal Høgnar bróðir mín
aftur á húðir ganga."

Guðrun stands before the wide table,
her cheeks are so bold:[49]
"Now Høgnar my brother will
walk on the skins again."

102. "Betri var í Júkagørðum
at drekka tann mjøð í blandi,
enn sum at ganga á aldir[s]húðir
og standa í stórum vanda."

"It would have been better to be
at the court of Júki
to drink that mixed mead,
than to walk on the skins
and be in great danger."

103. Høgnar tekur nú brandin tann,
vil eg fyri tygur tína,
gongur so í loftið fram,
hann mintist á móður sína.

Høgnar now takes that sword,
I'll tell you about it,[50]
he then walks forward with it in the air,[51]
he was remembering his mother.[52]

104. Upp steig Høgnar Júkason,
heldur á dragið svørð:
"Eg skal ganga á aldirshúðir,
og vita, hvussu fer."

Høgnar Júkason stood up,
grasping a brandished sword:
"I shall walk on the skins,
and see how it goes."

105. Høgnar gekk á aldirshúðir,
nú mundi tað so vera,
ikki bar nú fóturin við,
tað tykti honum einki at gera.

Høgnar walked on the skins,
now it seemed to be that
the foot didn't touch it,[53]
it didn't seem to effect him.

---

47 Høgnar is carrying the sword above himself because he is angry and defensive.

48 Høgnar is upset because Guðrun has killed his brothers.

49 This means she is displaying a lot of courage.

50 This is the narrator speaking.

51 Høgnar is still holding the sword above him. This is presumably so that if he falls, he will still have his sword above himself to defend himself.

52 Either he is remembering his mother's warning or thinking about how sad his mother would be to lose all her children.

53 Høgnar did not fall. It would appear he jumped over the skins if his foot wasn't touching them.

106. Tað var Høgnar Júkason, hann ræð yvir húðir støkka: "Ei mundi eg í Húnalandi fyrstur undan røkka."	It was Høgnar Júkason, he leapt over the skins: "In Húnaland I would not be the first one to yield."
107. Tað var Høgnar Júkason, hann tekur við húðir at støðga: "Ei man eg í Húnalandi tann fyrsta undan røkka."	It was Høgnar Júkason, he stops by the skins:[54] "In Húnaland I would not be the first one to yield."
108. Guðrun kemur út árla morgun, gramt var henni í huga, heilan sær hon Høgnar standa, ei hava ráðini dugað.	Guðrun comes out early in the morning, she was angry, she sees Høgnar standing unharmed, her schemes hadn't worked.
109. Høgnar stendur í grasgarði, bindur upp hjálmin sín: "Áðrenn dagur at kvøldi kemur, drekka vit blóð sum vín."	Høgnar stands in the garden, fastening his helmet: "Before the day becomes evening, we'll drink blood like wine."
110. Árla var um morgunin, tað roðar fyri sól, tá hevði Guðrun Júkadóttir brynjað út hundrað tólv.	Early in the morning the sun is rising, Guðrun Júkadótttir had then armoured twelve hundred men.
111. Árla var um morgunin, sólin skín á grótið, tað var Høgnar Júkason, hann ríður teim øllum ímóti.	Early in the morning, the sun shone on the rocks, it was Høgnar Júkason, he rides against them all.
112. Tað var Høgnar Júkason, ríður teimum øllum ímóti, búkar fullu á jørðina, sum tey varpa gróti.	It was Høgnar Júkason, he rides against them all, innards fell to the ground, as they throw rocks.
113. Høgnar ríður í bardagin, roynir góðar gripir, niður feldi hann kongins menn, tíggju fyri hvørja sipan.	Høgnar rides into battle, uses good arms,[55] he felled the king's men, ten with every swipe.

54 He hesitates.

55 Høgnar is literally using precious treasures or things; this likely indicates that he is using fancy, adorned weaponry.

114. Hundar tutu, úlvar goyggja, ørnin hyggi læsti, hundrað heilt og hartil hálvt tað fellur í annað kastið.	Dogs howled, wolves bark,[56] the eagle locked its sight, an entire hundred and half again fall in the second attack.
115. Vigið fekk hann Húnamenn við svørð og bitrar eggjar, tað var Høgnar Júkason, hann hopar til hallarveggja.	He slew the Huns with sword and bitter edges, it was Høgnar Júkason, he retreats to the walls of the hall.
116. Guðrun kemur út árla morgun, sól tók fagurt at branda, heilan sær hon bróður sín á leikvøllinum ganga.	Guðrun comes out early in the morning, the sun is shining beautifully, she sees her brother unharmed walking on the battlefield.
117. Guðrun so til orða tekur, sólin brá tá víða: "Hoyr tú, Høgnar bróðir mín, tú skalt á skógin ríða.	Guðrun then speaks, the sun was shining far and wide: "Listen, Høgnar my brother, you shall ride to the forest.
118. Tú skalt ríða á skógin burtur, eystur um Lindará, har skalt tú tey undur síggja, sum tú í forðum vá."	You shall ride away to the forest, east of the Lindará, there you will see those wonders, that you slew in the past."
119. Árla var um morgunin, sólin fagurt rann, tað var Høgnar Júkason, hann ríður á skógin fram.	Early in the morning, the sun shone beautifully, it was Høgnar Júkason, he rides through the forest.
120. Høgnar ríður á skógin fram, eystur um Lindará, har mundi hann tey undur síggja, hann í forðum vá.	Høgnar rides through the forest, east of the Lindará, there he would see those wonders, that he slew in the past.
121. Har sá hann tann stóra hest leypa sær av grundum, voldi tað Guðrun Júkadóttir, ið illgerningar kundi.	There he saw that great horse leap off the ground, Guðrun Júkadóttir caused it, who knew witchcraft.
122. Tungan tók at tala, letur so orðum víkja: "Illa gjørdi tú, Høgnar, tá tú vart við meg at svíkja.	He began to speak,[57] saying these words: "It was an evil deed you did, Høgnar, when you betrayed me.[58]

56 This is backwards—it is dogs that bark and wolves that howl.

57 Literally "the tongue started to speak."

58 The dead Sjúrður is speaking from the saddle of the horse.

123. Mær unti Brynhild Buðlins dóttir,
tað hitt væna vív,
mær unti Guðrun Júkadóttir,
harfyri læt eg lív.

Brynhild Buðlin's daughter loved me,
that beautiful woman,
Guðrun Júkadóttir loved me,
therefore I lost my life.

124. Tað var Brynhild Buðlins dóttir,
sprakk eftir mín deyða,
tá skifti tú Guðrunu gull og fæ
og mangar ringar reyðar."

It was Brynhild Buðlin's daughter,
she died of grief after my death,
at that time you gave[59] gold and property
to Guðrun
and many red[60] rings."[61]

125. Høgnar ríður á grønum vølli,
víða um seg sá,
mikið var tá buðlungs lív,
í gullsaðlinum lá.

Høgnar rides on the green field,
he looked around himself,
the king's body was large,
laying in the golden saddle.

126. "Tak nú hetta rúnarbelti,
bint um tínar lendar,
tað kann øllum lásum læsa,
allar sútir rinda.

"Take this runic belt now,
fasten it around your hips,
it can lock all locks,
and drive away all sorrow.

127. Tak tú hetta rúnarbelti,
sett við gulli reyða,
eg fekk tað á Hildarheyg
eftir ta dvørgamoy deyða.

Take this runic belt,
set with red gold,
I got it on Hildarheygur
from that dead dwarf maiden.

128. Hoyr tú, Høgnar Júkason,
ríð nú til hallar heim,
eg fari mær á heiðin skóg,
so tung eru míni mein."

Listen, Høgnar Júkason,
ride home to the hall now,
I will go to the heathen forest,
so severe are my injuries."

129. Guðrun kemur út árla morgun,
sólin brann so víða,
sær hon Høgnar Júkason
aftur av skógnum ríða.

Guðrun comes out early in the morning,
the sun shone far and wide,
she sees Høgnar Júkason
ride back from the forest.

130. Árla var um morgunin,
roðar fyri sól,
tá hevði Guðrun Júkadóttir
brynjað út hundrað tólv.

Early in the morning,
the sun is rising,
Guðrun Júkadóttir had then
armoured twelve hundred men.[62]

---

59 *Skifta* has the sense of objects being parcelled out or divided amongst people as inheritance.

60 Red indicates golden.

61 This happens in *Brynhildar táttur*, st. 267.

62 This repeats st. 110.

131. Árla var um morgunin, sólin skein á grótið, tað var Høgnar Júkason, hann ríður teim øllum ímóti.	Early in the morning, the sun shone on the rocks, it was Høgnar Júkason, he rides against them all.[63]
132. Tað var Høgnar Júkason, hann ríður teimum øllum ímóti, búkar fullu á jørðina, sum tey varpa gróti.	It was Høgnar Júkason, he rides against them all, innards fell to the ground, as they throw rocks.[64]
133. Høgnar ríður í bardagin, roynir góðar gripir, niður feldi hann kongins menn, tíggju í hvørji sipan.	Høgnar rides into battle, uses good arms, he felled the king's men, ten with each swipe.[65]
134. Hundar tutu, úlvar goyggja, ørnin hyggi læsti, hundrað heilt og hartil hálvt tey fullu í annað kastið.	Dogs howled, wolves bark, the eagle locked its sight, a whole hundred and half again they fell in the second attack.[66]
135. Høgnar ríður í bardagin: "Hetta man lítið bata, tað, ið eg um dagin vegi, villir hon upp um nætur."	Høgnar rides into battle: "This makes little difference, those who I slay during the day she brings back to life at night."
136. Høgnar ríður í bardagin, har yppist ein illur siður: "Nú leiðist mær í Húnalandi at høgga teir trælir niður."	Høgnar rides into battle, evil[67] is arising there: "In Húnaland I'm fed up of chopping down slaves."
137. Tað var Guðrun Júkadóttir, talar til sveinin sín: "Gakk til Tíðrik Tatlarason, og bið hann koma til mín."	It was Guðrun Júkadóttir, speaking to her servant: "Go to Tíðrikur Tatlarason, and ask him to come to me."
138. Sveinur fór á skógin burtur við hógv og hyggið orð: "Guðrun bað tygum koma til sín at drekka yvir borð."	The servant went to the forest with restraint and cautious words: "Guðrun asks you come to her to drink over the table."

63 This repeats st. 111.

64 This repeats st. 112.

65 This repeats st. 113.

66 This repeats st. 114.

67 Literally "an evil custom."

139. Tað var Guðrun Júkadóttir, letur nú blanda vín, býður so Tíðriki Tatlarasoni í hallina inn til sín.	It was Guðrun Júkadóttir, she has wine mixed, then welcomes Tíðrikur Tatlarason to her in the hall.
140. "Ver vælkomin, Tíðrikur Tatlarason, fullvæl eg á teg troysti, hevði tú Høgnar av lívi tikið, tað var eitt manndómsroysni."	"Welcome Tíðrikur Tatlarason, I trust in you wholly, had you taken Høgnar's life, it would be a manly deed."
141. "Hoyr tú, Guðrun Júkadóttir, eyka mær ei tann vanda, hvussu skal eg mót Høgnari stríða, ið einki vákn kann granda?"	"Listen, Guðrun Júkadóttir, don't put me in such danger, how should I fight against Høgnar, whom no weapons can hurt?"
142. "Hoyr tú, Tíðrikur Tatlarason, tú ert ein kempa so sterk, hevði tú Høgnar av lívi fingið, tað var eitt manndómsverk."	"Listen, Tíðrikur Tatlarason, you are a hero so strong, had you taken Høgnar's life, it would be a manly deed."
143. "Tað er einki eykarverk at ganga Høgna ímóti: hvar ið hann kemur á vágarvøll, har hevur hann høvur á spjóti.	"It is no easy feat to go against Høgnar: wherever he comes on the battlefield, he has a head on his spear.[68]
144. Tað er ikki ein ella tveir, standa í tí verki, eingin møtir honum á jørð, deyður er Sjúrður sterki.	It is not one or two, that succeed in that deed, none on earth are his equal, the strong Sjúrður is dead.
145. Mangur hevur lívið latið - sigist í hesum kvæði - eingin møtir honum á jørð, deyður er Sjúrður frægi."	Many have lost their lives - it is said in this ballad - none on earth are his equal, the valiant Sjúrður is dead."
146. Tíðrikur upp frá borði stígur, hann tekur um brandin svarta: "Eg vinni einki á Høgnari." Nú gránaði drottning bjarta.	Tíðrikur stands up from the table, he grasps the black sword: "I won't win against Høgnar." Now the beautiful queen went grey.[69]

68 Cf. what is said about both Sjúrður in *Brynhildar táttur*, st. 177, and about Høgnar in *Høgnar táttur*, st. 84,

69 She went pale.

147. "Hoyr tú, Tíðrikur Tatlarason," brúður mælir av kvíða, "eg gevi tær bæði gull og fæ, vilt tú mót Høgnari ríða."	"Listen, Tíðrikur Tatlarason," the woman speaks in anguish, "I will give you both gold and property, if you ride against Høgnar."
148. Upp stóð Tíðrikur Tatlarason, hann heldur á dragið svørð: "Flúgva skal eg í loftið fram og vita, hvussu fer."	Tíðrikur Tatlarason stands up, he grasps a drawn sword: "I shall fly through the sky and see how it goes."
149. Tíðrikur hvarv úr Hólmgørðum, fáir finnast slíkir, hann kom aftur annað sinni í flogdreka líki.	Tíðrikur vanished from Hólmgarðar, there are few like him, he came back a second time in the likeness of a flying dragon.
150. Tíðrikur fór í stríðið burtur, fáir finnast slíkir, hann kom aftur uttan borg í flogdreka líki.	Tíðrikur went away to battle, there are few like him, he returned to outside the castle in the likeness of a flying dragon.
151. Tíðrikur fleyg í loftið fram við sínar stríðu streingir, Høgnar stendur í tungum stríð, nú ristir hann reystar dreingir.	Tíðrikur flew through the sky, with his strong wings,[70] Høgnar stands in a ferocious battle, now he slices up brave heroes.
152. Høgnar ríður á grønum vølli tað harða stál at klúgva, sær hann Tíðrik Tatlarason í luftini yvir sær flúgva.	Høgnar rides on the green field to split that hard steel,[71] he sees Tíðrikur Tatlarason fly in the sky above him.
153. Høgnar tók sítt góða svørð, hann skjýtur tað leið av hendi, hann vendi sítt svørð so í loftið fram, ígjøgnum Tíðrikin rendi.	Høgnar took his good sword, he throws it from his hand, he then turned his sword through the sky, it ran through Tíðrikur.
154. Tá ið hann eftir jørðini fór, var hann sum sótið svarta, hann hevði mongum manni bágað, men nú stóð brandur í hjarta.	When he went over the ground, he was like black soot, he had injured many men, but now there was a sword in his heart.[72]

70 The Faroese says "strings" not "wings," but this does not seem to make sense. It could be a misremembering of the word, which would be *veingir*. *Streingir* probably crept in due to the alliteration with *stríðu*. Lyngbye also translates it as wings. Lyngbye, *Færøiske Qvæder*, 278n151.

71 This must refer to armour.

72 This stanza is referring to the dragon (Tíðrikur).

155. Eitur spýði tann svarti dreki
niður á Høgna brynju,
hann varð ei við váknum vigin,
fyri tað læt hann synja.

The black dragon spewed poison
down on Høgnar's armour,
he was not slain with weapons,
that he would refuse.

156. Tungt er tað í heiminum
størri sorgir at bíða,
eitur bar hann í brynju síni,
so fast í hjarta at svíða.

It is difficult in the world
to wait for a greater sorrow,[73]
he carried poison in his armour
it burns his heart severely.

157. Høgnar so til orða tekur:
"Eg berjist ikki longur,
eitur gongur at hjartanum."
Tá følnaði nýtur drongur.

Høgnar begins to speak:
"I fight no longer,
poison flows towards my heart."
Then the brave hero went pale.

158. Fallnir eru Húnamenn
við svørð og bitrar eggjar,
nú hopaði frægi av Júkagørpum
so fast til hallarveggja.

Huns have fallen
by sword and bitter edges,
now the valiant hero of Júki is forced back
firmly to the walls of the hall.[74]

159. Guðrun kemur út árla morgun,
gramt var henni í huga,
heilan sær hon Høgnar standa,
ei hava svikini dugað.

Guðrun comes out early in the morning,
she was angry,
she sees Høgnar standing unharmed,[75]
the schemes haven't worked.

160. Høgnar hopaði at hallarveggi
brandin yvir seg bar,
Guðrun stendur í grasgarði,
hon tennur saman skar.

Høgnar was leaning on the walls of the hall,
carrying his sword above himself,
Guðrun stands in the garden,
she grinds her teeth together.

161. "Hoyr tú, Guðrun systir mín,
tað skalt tú mær lova,
læna mær Helvík jallsins dóttur
í nátt á armi at sova!

"Listen, Guðrun my sister,
this you will permit me,
lend me Helvík the jarl's daughter
to sleep in her arms tonight!

162. Ikki havi eg fingið sár,
nú grið vil eg ei tiggja,
læna mær eina jall[s]dóttur
í nátt á armi at liggja!"

I have not received a wound,[76]
now I will not be given mercy,[77]
lend me a jarl's daughter
to lie in her arms tonight!"

---

73 This anticipates Høgnar's death.

74 This echoes st. 115. This may mean that he is standing using the walls as support.

75 Although the audience knows that Høgnar has been harmed, Guðrun does not know that.

76 Høgnar is lying. He knows he is going to die.

77 He will not be allowed to leave alive.

163. Høgnar so aftur til orða tekur: "Tann grið eg av tær tiggja, læna mær Helvík jallsins dóttur í nátt av harmi at liggja!"	Then Høgnar began to speak again: "That favour I will ask of you, lend me Helvík the jarl's daughter to lie with due to distress tonight!"[78]
164. Guðrun so fyri munni mælir, kinn ber hon so reyða: "Fáa skalt tú nú jallsins dóttur, tú gongur nú snart til deyða."	Guðrun then speaks, her cheeks are so red: "Now you shall get the jarl's daughter, you'll be dead soon."
165. Lógu tey í sínari song við allskyns spekt og mæti: "Vit eiga osum ein ungan son, til gulls og landa at gæta."	They lay in their bed with all kinds of good sense and good reputation: "We shall have ourselves a young son, to inherit the gold and lands."
166. Hann gat við frúnni ungan son á teirri somu nátt, Høgnar risti rúnirnar, og tað man lesast brátt.	He conceived a young son with the woman on the same night, Høgnar carved the runes, and it is read immediately.[79]
167. "Tú manst ognast ungan son, Høgnar skalt tú kalla, eg gevi honum tað búna svørð, ið faðir mín søkti úr fjalli.	"You will have a young son, you shall call him Høgnar, I give him the splendid sword, that my father got from inside the mountain.
168. Hoyr tú, Helvík jallsins dóttir, hvat eg nú sigi til tín, síggj so til, um ei langa tíð hann hevnir faðir sín.	Listen, Helvík daughter of the jarl, what I now tell you, see to it that in not too long he avenges his father.
169. Hoyr tú, Helvík jallsins dóttir, eg sigi tey orðini hátt, nú hevur kongurin sveinsbarn gitið á hesi somu nátt.	Listen, Helvík daughter of the jarl, I'm telling you these words proudly, the king has conceived a boychild on this same night.
170. ú manst ognast ungan son, Guðrun vil hann pína, tak tú hennara unga son, og legg í vøggu tína!	You will have a young son, Guðrun will torment him, take her young son, and put him in your cradle!

78 She should be allowed to lie with him due to the stress or distress of the situation.

79 This likely means that the inscription was obvious and could be read without difficulty. It has to be read quickly because he is dying.

171.	Hoyr tú, Helvík jallsins dóttir, brúka nakra list, lat mína systur Guðruna um dyrnar ganga fyrst!	Listen, Helvík daughter of the jarl, use some cunning, let my sister Guðrun walk through the door first!
172.	Hoyr tú, Helvík jallsins dóttir, eg sigi tær satt ífrá: tá ið svein er tólv ár gamal, tú gakk fyri Lindará!	Listen, Helvík daughter of the jarl, I tell you truthfully: when the boy is twelve years old, walk to the Lindará!
173.	Hoyr tú tað, mín veldiga søta, eg tali tey orð til tín, tá ið tín sonur er tólv ár gamal, tá kennir hann móður sína.	Listen, my dearly beloved, I speak these words to you, when your son is twelve years old, he will recognize his mother.
174.	Tak tú hetta rúnarbelti, bint um tínar lendar, tað kann øllum lásum læsa, allar sútir rinda."	Take this runic belt, fasten it around your hips, it can lock all locks, and drive away all sorrows."
175.	Tá segði Høgnar Júkason: "Nú verst ikki longur, nú gongur eitrið at hjartanum." So følnaði nýtur drongur.	Høgnar Júkason then said: "Now it's not bearable any longer, now the poison flows to my heart." Then the brave hero died.
176.	Høgnar leyt tá lata lív, búðu um hann sum dreyg, vældu nú um so virðiliga, løgdu nú lík í heyg.	Then Høgnar had to lose his life, they dressed his corpse, now cared for so carefully, they laid the corpse in a mound.[80]
177.	Helvík leyt tá síggja á, Høgnar mundi doyggja, síðan gróv hon tann dreyg í heyg, sum dreingir dalin hoyggja.	Helvík then had to look on, Høgnar was dying, then she buried that corpse in a mound, that boys in the valley make hay on.
Refrain	*Grani bar gullið av heiði,* *brá hann sínum brandi av reiði,* *Sjúrður vann av orminum,* *Grani bar gullið av heiði.*	*Grani carried the gold from the heath,* *he brandished his blade in a fury,* *Sjúrður defeated the dragon,* *Grani carried the gold from the heath.*

80 This is a barrow, or burial mound.

THE SECOND BALLAD OF HØGNI OR *THE BALLAD OF ALDRIAS* (*ANNAR HØGNA TÁTTUR* OR *ALDRIAS TÁTTUR*)

1. Tær ganga sær við børnunum níu mánar sínar, til at teirri stundum líður, tær føða sveinar fríðar.	They are pregnant for nine months each, until that time arrives, they give birth to beautiful boys.[1]
2. Helvík ungan sonin ár, tung mundi sorgin falla, síðan bað hon presti bera, Høgnar bað hon kalla.	Helvík has a young son, great grief will befall them,[2] then she ordered him to be carried to the priest, she ordered him to be called Høgnar.
3. Guðrun ungan sonin ár, tung man sorgin falla, síðan bað hon presti bera, Svein bað móðir kalla.	Guðrun had a young son, great grief will befall them, then she ordered him to be carried to the priest, the mother ordered him to be called Svein.[3]
4. Lógu tær í síni song, lætta tekur vanda, nú er liðið at teirri tíð, báðar skulu út ganga.	They lie each in their beds, the pain subsides, now that time has come, both shall go outside.
5. Inni sótu tær í dagar, inni sótu tær í tvá, inntil tann hin triðja, tær skuldu út gá.	They sat inside for days, they sat inside for two, until the third, they should go outside.
6. Tað er Guðrun Júkadóttir, brúkar mikla list, biður nú Helvík jallsins dóttur at durum ganga fyrst.	That is Guðrun Júkadóttir, uses great cunning, now asks Helvík, daughter of the jarl, to walk to the door first.
7. Guðrun so til orða tekur, fyrsta orðið tá: "Hoyr tú, Helvík jalsins dóttir, tú skalt út fyri gá."	Then Guðrun begins to speak, the first word: "Listen, Helvík, daughter of the jarl, you shall go out first."

1 This follows on from the action in *Høgnar táttur*, where Helvík and Guðrun seem to be pregnant at the same time.

2 This foreshadows what will come.

3 Svein is written with a lowercase *s* in the edition.

8. Svaraði Helvík jallsins dóttir, læt tá angist og vanda: "Tú bert hægri høvur enn eg, fyri bør tær at ganga."	Helvík, daughter of the jarl, answered, she sounded afraid and troubled: "You have a higher head than me,[4] you ought to go out first."
9. Svaraði Helvík jallsins dóttir í annað orðið tá: "Tú bert hægri krónu enn eg, tú mást út fyri gá."	Helvík, the daughter of the jarl, said secondly: "You are wearing a higher crown than I, you must go out first."
10. Hon átti sær ein ungan son, Guðrun vildi hann pína, hon tók hennara egna son, legði aftur í vøggu sína.	She had a young son, Guðrun wanted to cause him pain, she took her own son, laid him back in his crib.[5]
11. Guðrun mundi út ganga fyrst, øllum tykti undur, hon tók hennara unga son, beit honum barkan sundur.	Guðrun went out first, everyone found it strange, she took her young son,[6] she cut his throat.[7]
12. Árla var um morgunin, sól tók fagurt at skína, Guðrun sneiðir høvur av onkarbarni sínum.	It was early in the morning, the sun began to shine beautifully, Guðrun cuts the head off her dear child.[8]
13. Inn kom Guðrun árla morgun, fell so væl í lag, hon tók út sín lítin knív, hon sneiddi høvdið av.	Guðrun came in early in the morning, it came so easily to her, she took out her small knife, she cut the head off.
14. So er sagt frá Høgnari, Gud gav honum vekst, meiri vaks hann í ein mánað, enn onnur børn í seks.	So it is told about Høgnar, God made him grow, he grew more in one month, than other children in six.[9]

---

4 She is telling her she is higher in status or standing than her and should go out first.

5 Guðrun has gone out first, and Helvík takes the opportunity to switch their babies.

6 Grammatically it is clear that Guðrun is cutting the throat of what she believes to be Helvík's son, not her own.

7 It is implied here by *sundr* that not only does she cut his throat, but she actually cuts it in two, cutting his head off, as confirmed by the following stanza.

8 Grammatically it is now made clear that Guðrun has actually cut the head off her own child, believing it to be Helvík's child. That Helvík has effected Høgnar's plan, laid out at the end of *Høgnar táttur*, to save the life of their child is thus conveyed grammatically in the ballad.

9 This echoes the description of Sjúrður growing in *Regin smiður*.

15. Hann vaks upp í ríkinum, tann geviliga mann, Húnalandskongurin fostraði hann.	He grew up in the kingdom, the valiant man, the king of Húnaland fostered him.
16. Árla var um morgunin, sólin fagurt brá, tað var Helvík jallsins dóttir, hon ríður til Lindará.	It was early in the morning, the sun shines beautifully, it was Helvík, daughter of the jarl, she rides to the Lindará.
17. Tað var Helvík jallsins dóttir, so ganga søgur frá, møtti hon sínum unga soni eystan fyri Lindará.	It was Helvík, daughter of the jarl, so the story goes, she met her young son, east of the Lindará.[10]
18. Helvík so til orða tekur, smílist undir lín: "Tað svørji eg á sannan Gud, at tú ert sonur mín."	Helvík began to speak, smiling under linen: "I swear by the true God, that you are my son."
19. Svaraði Høgnar Høgnason, hann stendur í mannamúgva: "Eg havi ikki sætt eina lágari konu kunna so væl at lúgva."	Høgnar Høgnason answered, he stands in a crowd of people: "I have not seen a woman of a lower class be able to lie so well."
20. "Tak tú út tín lítin knív, hygg, ið væl hann bítur, tína móður í armin sker, vita, um [í] hjarta nítur!"	"Take out your little knife, see how well it cuts, it cuts[11] your mother in the arm, see whether it pains you."
21. Hann dró út sín lítin knív, hyggur, væl hann beit, sína móður í armin skar, so fast í hjarta neit.	He pulled out his little knife, looks, it cuts well, it cut his mother in the arm, it pained him terribly.
22. Svaraði Høgnar Høgnason, smílist undir lín: "Tað síggi eg á sjálvum mær, at tú ert móðir mín."	Høgnar Høgnason answered, smiles under linen: "I feel it in myself, that you are my mother."

10 Following Høgnar's plan in *Høgnar táttur*, we must assume the ballad has jumped forward twelve years here.

11 The words for cut in this stanza are different in the Faroese, the first from *bíta* and the second from *skera*.

23. Helvík so til orða tekur, smílist undir lín: "Síggj so til um ei langa tíð, tú hevnir faðir tín!"	Helvík then begins to speak, smiles under linen: "See to it that in not too long you avenge your father!"
24. Hon tekur upp tað rúnarkelv, sínum soni fær: "Hetta gav tín hin sæli faðir, ið mikið gott unti mær."	She takes the runestick, gives it to her son: "Your dear father gave this to me, who loved me dearly."[12]
25. Sveinur tók við rúnarkelvi, niður fyri seg sá, brast hans belti, litin ið hann brá.	The boy took the runestick, he looked down before him, his belt burst,[13] colour flamed from his face.
26. Brast hans belti, litin ið hann brá, hann sá sín hin faðirs deyða standa har uppá.	His belt burst, colour flamed from his face, he saw his father's death,[14] it tells here.
27. "Tak tú hetta rúnarbelti, bint um tínar lendar, tað kann øllum lásum læsa allar sútir rinda.	"Take this runebelt, tie it round your hips, it can lock all locks, drive away all sorrows.
28. Tá tú kemur til hallar heim, síðla ella snimma, síggj so til í langa tíð, lat ongan á tær finna!"	When you come home to the hall, late or early, see to it that for a long time, let no one find you!"
29. Árla var um morgunin, sólin skein so víða, tað var Høgnar *Høgnason, hann vildi til hallar ríða.	It was early in the morning, the sun shone far and wide, it was Høgnar Høgnason, he wanted to ride to the hall.
30. Sveinur gekk í hallina inn, hann skuldi ljósið skara, brendi gjøgnum fótarblað, hann tók seg ikki vara.	The boy went into the hall, he should trim the light, it burnt through his foot,[15] he wasn't being careful.

12 This echoes the scene where Hjørdis gives Sjúrður the broken pieces of Sigmundur's sword in *Regin smiður*.

13 In Old Norse literature, legendary heroes and gods swell when extremely emotional.

14 The runestick is evidently magical and is able to show him the past event.

15 The *fótarblað* is the surface of the foot.

31. Sveinur var ungur av aldrinum,
hann skuldi skara ljós,
brendi gjøgnum fótarblað,
og niður í hallargólv.

The boy was young of age,
he should trim the light,
it burnt through his foot,
and down to the floor of the hall.

32. Artala kongur til orða tekur,
mjøður í blandi rennur:
"Hugsa nú ikki, svein, so djúpt,
tú gáar ei, tú brennur."

King Artala begins to speak,
the mixed mead runs:
"Don't think so deeply, Svein,[16]
you don't notice that you are burning."

33. Tí svaraði Artala kongur,
*ryður í brósti rennur:
"Hvat hugsar tú, svein, so djúpt,
tú sansar ei, at tú brennur?"

Because of that King Artala answered,
coughing up phlegm:[17]
"What are you thinking about so deeply, Svein,
you don't realize that you're burning?"

34. "Tað hugsi eg, Artala kongur,
at tú eigur miklan eyð,
tað verður helst á tínari ævi,
at tú tiggur vatn og breyð."

"I am thinking, King Artala,
that you possess great riches,
it will probably happen in your lifetime,
that you will have to beg for water and bread."

35. Tí svaraði Artala kongur:
"Eg eigi miklan eyð,
tað verður ikki á mínari ævi,
eg tiggi vatn og breyð."

Because of this King Artala answered:
"I possess great riches,
it won't happen in my lifetime,
that I will beg for water and bread."

36. "Tað hugsi eg, harra mín,
hóast tú eigur miklan eyð:
tað kann verða á tíni ævi,
tú tiggur vatn og breyð."

"I am thinking, my lord,
even though you possess great riches:
that it can happen in your lifetime,
that you beg for water and bread."

37. "Tað hugsi eg, harra svein,
eg eigi so miklan eyð,
tað verður ikki á míni ævi,
eg biði vatn og breyð.

"I am thinking, master Svein,
I possess such great riches,
that it won't happen in my lifetime,
that I ask for water and bread.

38. Mikið eigi eg gull og fæ,
hartil annan eyð,
ikki verður tað á mínari ævi,
at eg tiggi vatn og breyð."

I possess a lot of gold and property,
in addition to other riches,
it won't happen in my lifetime,
that I beg for water and bread."

---

16 The narrator is acknowledging him as Høgnar Høgnason, but the other characters do not know that yet, apart from his mother.

17 The king may be choking on his drink from shock here, seeing the boy he thinks is his son burning.

39. Árla var um morgunin,
sól tók fagurt at skína:
"Vilt tú nakað, Artala kongur,
í dag á skógvin ríða?"

It was early in the morning,
the sun began to shine so beautifully:
"King Artala, do you want to
ride into the forest today?"

40. Árla var um morgunin,
fell so væl í lag,
lysta teir á skógvin burtur,
sveinur og kongurin báðir.

It was early in the morning,
it came to him so easily,
they want to go off to the forest,
both the boy and the king.

41. Tað er enn sum ofta fyrr,
mangur skortar fíggja,
ganga teir til gullbjørgið
tað mikla gull at síggja.

It is yet as often times before,
many look at their riches,
they go to the gold cliff,
to look at the great quantity of gold.

42. Ríða teir á skógvin burtur,
fríðir í huga full,
hann vísti honum á húsið tað,
ið ta[k]t var innan við gull.

They ride off into the forest,
carefree in their courage,[18]
he showed him that house
that was thatched with gold.

43. Tí svaraði Artala kongur
fyrsta orðið tá:
"Hoyr tú tað nú, harra svein,
tú skalt her fyrri inn gá."

Because of this King Artala answered
then said firstly:
"Listen to this, master Svein,
you shall walk in first."[19]

44. Tí svaraði harra svein
í annað orðið tá:
"Tú bert hægri krónuna,
tú skalt inn fyri gá."

Because of that master Svein answered,
then said secondly:
"You are wearing a higher crown,
you shall walk in first."

45. Artala kongur í Húnalandi
inn um dyrnar sá,
tað var inda harra svein,
hann smelti hurð í lás.

King Artala in Húnaland
looked around the door,
it was dear master Svein,
he slammed the door shut.

46. Sveinur var ungur av aldrinum,
lætt var honum til máls,
tað er mær av sonnum sagt,
hann smelti hurð í lás.

Sveinur was young of age,
he spoke so eloquently,
it is truthfully told to me,
he slammed the door shut.[20]

---

18 Here we interpret *í huga full* akin to Old Norse *hugfullr*, meaning full of courage.

19 This exchange about walking in first echoes that of Helvík and Guðrun at the beginning of the ballad.

20 Sveinur has trapped Artala in the house.

47. "Bæði eigur tú, Artala kongur, gull og miklan eyð, tað kann verða á tínari ævi, at tú tiggur vatn og breyð.	"You, King Artala, possess both gold and great riches, it can happen in your lifetime, that you beg for water and bread.
48. Tað hugsi eg nú, harra mín, hóast tú eigur miklan eyð, vilt tú nú nakað, Artala kongur, tiggja vatn og breyð?"	Now I think, my lord, even though you possess a lot of riches, do you want, King Artala, to beg for water and bread?"
49. "Tað hugsi eg, harra svein, at eg eigi miklan eyð, gjarna vil eg nú, harra svein, tiggja av tær vatn og breyð."	"I am thinking that, master Svein, that I possess great riches, now, master Svein, I will gladly beg water and bread from you."
50. Høgnar gekk av gullbjørginum eina morgun snimma, svørji tann eið á mína trú, har læsti hann kongin inni.	Høgnar went from the gold cliff early one morning, I swear an oath on my faith, he locked the king inside.
51. Tað var Høgnar Høgnason, mikið gull hann fekk, hann kom ikki aftur í gullbjørgið, fyrr enn kongurin skarpur hekk.	It was Høgnar Høgnason, he got a lot of gold, he didn't come back to the gold cliff before the king drooped,[21] shrivelled up.[22]
52. Høgni gisti sína móður síðla dags á kvøldi, síðan reið hann haðani burtur til kongin í Danaveldi.	Høgnar[23] stayed the night with his dear mother late one evening, then he rode away from there to the king in Denmark.
53. Tað er satt, ið talað er, mong er konan eym, Guðrun gongur um allan heim, hon heldur í Grana teym.	It is true what they say, many the woman is wretched, Guðrun walks around the world, she holds Grani's reins.

21 *Hanga* means "hang," but it can also mean drooped or wilted. It seems to mean that here, since there is no indication that King Artala was hanged.

22 The king has died, shrunk, and shrivelled from lack of the water and bread Høgnar has been taunting him about.

23 Høgni in the Faroese, rather than Høgnar, is a mistake in CCF, although we have reproduced it faithfully here. It is Høgnar in the manuscript. See Matras, *J. H. Schrøters optegnelser*, p. 43, st. 51.

THE BALLAD OF GESTUR OR THE BALLAD OF ÁSLA (GESTS RÍMA OR ÁSLU RÍMA)

1.	Gestur gekk sær niðan við á, *– at dansa –* fann upp á, hvar ið harpan lá.	Gestur went up by the river, *– to dance –* hit upon where the harp lay.[1]
Refrain	*Og væl er mær ansað,* *her vil eg á gólvið fram at dansa,* *hóast tú vilt mær lív í vanda,* *væl er mær ansað.*	*And I am well looked after,* *I will go on the floor to dance here,*[2] *even if you want to endanger my life,* *I am well looked after.*
2.	Gestur gjørdi sær meiri ómak, harpuna tók hann þá sítt bak.	Gestur made a good effort,[3] he carried the harp on his back.
3.	Gestur gekk seg í ein garð, gisti moy, sum kelling var.	Gestur went to a farm, stayed the night at a maiden's, who was a hag.
4.	"Gestur, dvølst hjá mær í nátt! Haki kemur av skógnum brátt."	"Gestur, stay with me tonight! Haki comes from the forest soon."
5.	Gestur livir við lítið veldi, harpuna setir hann fram at eldi.	Gestur had little power over the situation,[4] he puts the harp by the fire.
6.	Gestur dvaldist hjá henni á nátt. Haki kom av skógnum brátt.	Gestur stayed the night with her. Haki came from the forest shortly afterwards.
7.	Kelling talar orðum brátt: "Vit skulu drepa Gest í nátt."	The hag suddenly speaks these words: "We shall kill Gestur tonight."[5]
8.	"Eg drepi ikki henda mann, eg veit onga sak við hann."	"I will not kill this man, I have no issue with him."[6]

1 He finds a harp.

2 This is referring to the singer of the ballad, going on to the floor to dance a Faroese ballad dance.

3 This means that he took trouble or pains over it.

4 Literally "Gestur lives with little power."

5 These words are spoken to Haki.

6 This is Haki speaking.

9. "Vilt tú ikki drepa hann, Gestur skal vera mín egin mann."	"If you won't kill him, then Gestur shall be my own man."[7]
10. Kelling var í ráðum verst, hon fór upp at drepa Gest.	The hag was the worst in her schemes, she went up to kill Gestur.
11. Kelling eigur ein lítlan knív, snarliga skildi hon Gest við lív.	The hag has a small knife, quickly she parted Gestur from his life.
12. Hon breyt upp harpuna eftir hans deyð, hon fann eina moy í skarlak reyð.	She broke the harp up after his death, she found a maiden dressed in scarlet red.
13. "Tú skalt liva við lítla pínu, eita Kráka, dóttir mín."	"You shall live with little pain,[8] and be named Kráka, my daughter."
14. "Hóast eg livi við lítla pínu, eg eiti ei Kráka, dóttir tín."	"Even if I live with little pain, I'm not named Kráka, your daughter."
15. Ragnar legði skip undir brúgv, so gingu teir í Haka tún.	Ragnar[9] landed the ship by the landing stage,[10] then they went in Haki's courtyard.
16. Ragnar legði skip undir flaka, so ganga teir við breyð at baka.	Ragnar landed the ship by a raft, then they went with bread to have it baked.
17. Tað kom ein jomfrú inn og rann, teir stardu á hana, meðan breyðið brann.	A maiden came in and ran, they stared at her, while the bread burnt.
18. Hon stoytti yvir hana bryggjukar: "Kráka, tú skalt sitja har!"	She poured a brewing vessel over her: "Kráka, you shall sit there!"

7 She plans to kill him herself.

8 You shall have an easy life.

9 Ása eventually becomes Ragnar's wife in the Old Norse material.

10 This could also mean "bridge," but since the next stanza says they landed by a raft, a landing stage (which is a floating flat structure that acts as a bridge to the land for the loading and offloading of boats) seems reasonable.

19. Hon stoytti av sær bryggjukar: "Fái tann skamm, ið situr har!"	She shakes the brewing vessel off herself: "Shame on the one who sits there!"
20. Kelling sló sína dóttur á grúgvu, tá datt av henni nævurhúgva.	The hag struck her daughter down onto the hearth, then a birch bark hat fell off her.
21. "Hoyr tú kelling, sjáldan blíð, hví slært tú so fagurt vív?	"Listen hag, seldom kind, why do you hit such a beautiful woman?
22. Hoyr tað, kelling, sjáldan góð, Hví slært tú so fagurt fljóð?"	Listen, hag, seldom good, why do you hit such a beautiful woman?"[11]
23, "Í forðum var eg vænari fljóð, morð og mans lát av mær stóð."	"In the past I was a more charming woman, murder and manslaughter were caused by me."[12]
24. Sveinar stiltu stál for stokk, slitu eitt hár úr moynnar lokk.	The footmen stopped the steel before the beam, they tore out a hair from the maiden's lock.
25. Sveipa teir tað út í ein klút, teir bóru tað so til skipa út	They wrapped it in a cloth, then they carried it to the ship.[13]
26. Ragnar talar orðum snilt: "Tit hava alla vára føðslu spilt."	Ragnar speaks these sensible words: "You have spoiled all our food."
27. "Tað kom ein jomfrú inn og rann, vit stardu pá hana, meðan breyðið brann.	"A maiden came in and ran, we stared at her, while the bread burnt.
28. Vit hava sætt so vænt eitt vív, tað var fagrari enn Tóra í Líð.	We have seen such a beautiful woman, who is fairer than Tóra í Líð.[14]

11 The words for "woman" in stt. 21 and 22 are different, but they are both *heiti* used for woman.

12 She is saying Kráka got off lightly with her punishment. She has in the past killed Gestur.

13 This would seem to refer to the burnt bread.

14 The name means Tóra on the hillside. Tóra was the first wife of Ragnar, but she is now dead.

29.	Vit hava sætt so vænt eitt sprund, tað var fagrari enn Tóra í Lund."	We have seen such a beautiful woman, who is fairer than Tóra í Lund."[15]
30.	"Sveinar, haldið tit meg fyri háð, tit skulu allir á gálgan gá!	"Footmen, if you are mocking me, you shall all go to the gallows!
31.	Sveinar, halda tit meg fyri spott, tit skulu allir á gálgan brátt!"	Footmen, if you are ridiculing me, you will soon be at the gallows!"
32.	Sveinar stiltu stál for stokk, teir vístu eitt hár úr moynnar lokk.	The footmen stopped the steel before the beam, they showed a hair from the maiden's lock.
33.	"Farið heim og sigið henni frá: Ragnar kongur vil hana sjá!"	"Go home and tell her: King Ragnar wants to see her!"
34.	Teir fóru heim og søgdu henni frá: "Ragnar kongur vil teg sjá."	They went home and told her: "King Ragnar wants to see you."
35.	Ás[l]a gár í grøna líð, kallar við sær lítin hýð.	Ás[l]a walks on the green hillside, calls a little dog to her.[16]
36.	Ás[l]a gár í grønan lund, kallar við sær lítin hund.	Ás[l]a walks in the green grove, calls a little dog to her.
37.	Ás[l]a gár á kirkjubakka, *– at dansa –* kallar við sær lítin rakka.	Ás[l]a walks on the church bank,[17] *– to dance –* calls to her a little young dog.
Refrain	*Og væl er mær ansað,* *her vil eg á gólvið fram at dansa,* *hóast tú vilt mær lív í vanda,* *væl er mær ansað.*	*And I am well looked after,* *I will go on the floor to dance here,*[18] *even if you want to endanger my life,* *I am well looked after.*

15 The name means Tóra in the grove.

16 A *hýð* is a dog. See Fróðskaparsetur Føroya, Orðkort, s.v. "Hyð."

17 This is "bank" as in "hill."

18 This is referring to the singer of the ballad, going on to the floor to dance a Faroese ballad dance.

THE BALLAD OF NORNAGESTUR (NORNAGESTS RÍMA)

1. Eitt er frøðið um Nornagest, *– tú tarvt einki ráð geva í vanda –* tílíkum góðum gekk tað best. *– Hvør tann svein geri so.*	There is a ballad[1] about Nornagestur, *– you don't need to give advice when you're in peril –* such a good man, it went the best way. *– Every man does it like that.*
2. Oksar tólv vóru leiddir á torg, og so fram á fríðu borg.	Twelve oxen were led to the market, and then onwards to a beautiful castle.
3. Kongurin aktar at høgga teim, tílíkum góðum gekk tað við gleim.	The king intends to kill them, such a good kill, it happened with merriment.[2]
4. Kongurin hjó so mikið høgg, eitt bragdarbrá við benjardøgg.	The king landed such a great blow, a heroic draw of the sword with blood.[3]
5. Allir duttu deyðir niður, øksin stóð í stokki við.	All fell down dead, the axe stood in the chopping block.
6. Allir lovaðu hilmar høgg, og blóðið dreiv um benjardøgg.	Everyone praised the prince's blow, and the blood flowed over blood.[4]
7. Kongurin krevur kallin blítt: "Hví lovar tú ikki høggið mítt?"	The king demands of the old man in a friendly way: "Why do you not praise my blow?"
8. "Yvrið, harri, var høggið títt, í forðum sá eg vænari slíkt."	"Your blow was an angry one, sir, in the past I have seen more graceful blows than that."
9. "Kannst tú siga frá Sjúrða svein, hann var seg frægur av fornum ein?"	"Can you tell the story of Sjúrður svein, he was a famous man of the past?"

1 *Frøðið* is the subject matter of a poem or ballad.

2 *Gleimur* is a poetic word used in ballads, meaning gaiety, cheerful, merry.

3 This is a kenning used in ballads. *Ben* is a word used in ballads meaning a fatal wound, while *døgg* means "dew," "dew of the wound," together meaning "blood."

4 The two words for "blood" are different here. The first is literally "blood" while the second is the same kenning used for blood in st. 4.

10. "Tað kann eg siga Sjúrða frá, tílíkan ongan við eygum sá.	"I can tell the story of Sjúrður, no one has seen such a man.
11. Tá skalv bæði leyv og lundur, ormin høgg hann í miðjum sundur.	Both leaf and grove shook, when he chopped the dragon apart through the middle.
12. Høgni var ein heiðursmann, ljótan av lit so kendi eg hann.	Høgni was an honourable man, I knew him to be ugly in complexion.[5]
13. Høgni var ein heiðursmann, døkkan av liti kendi eg hann.	Høgni was an honourable man, I knew him to be dark in complexion.
14. Gunnar var so reystur og ríkur, fróður og blíður og Grimhild líkur.	Gunnar was so strong and powerful, wise and kind and like Grimhild.
15. Gamal og gráur og Grimhild líkur, seint man føðast annar slíkur.	Old and grey and like Grimhild, it will be a long time before another like him is born.
16. Riðu teir um díkið heim, Gunnar og Høgni og Sjúrður svein.	They rode home around the marsh, Gunnar and Høgni and Sjúrður svein.
17. Gunnars hestur sprakk um fyrst, gjørdi so Gunnari góða list.	Gunnar's horse jumped over first, Gunnar did such a well-calculated jump.
18. Høgna hestur sprakk um tá, Grani fastur í feni lá.	Then Høgni's horse jumped, Grani lay stuck in the fen.
19. Ofta havi eg inn um díkið trott bæði dag og døkka nátt.	I have often trodden in the marsh both in the daytime and in the dark night.
20. Allir stóðu úr søðlum teir, Gunnar og Høgni og Sjúrður svein.	All dismounted from their saddles, Gunnar and Høgni and Sjúrður svein.

---

5 Being dark and ugly (see the following stanza, st. 13) is used to visually convey someone being evil.

21. Allir toga á dýran hest, Sjúrður togar á teymar mest.	All are pulling on their precious horses, Sjúrður is pulling on the reins the most.
22. "Gestur, ger mær viljan ein, tú fá mín góða gangara rein!"	"Gestur, do one thing for me, you get my good steed clean!"
23. Riðu so fram at eini á, eingin kundi til manna sjá.	They then rode by a river, no one could see anyone else.
24. Eg tváaði hans bróst og bringugrein, hans lær og legg og longu bein.	I washed his chest and sternum, his thighs and lower legs and long legs.
25. Góðan gangara gjørdi eg rein, síðan hevði Sjúrður svein.	I made the good steed clean, afterwards Sjúrður svein took me as his squire.
26. Riðu so fram á Fávnis ból, har skein gull, sum geisar av sól.	They rode to Fávnir's lair, gold shone there like rays of the sun.
27. Eitt var hár í hala á hest, tað var favn og feti mest.	There was a hair in the tail of the horse, that was a fathom and a foot in size.[6]
28. Tað var favn og feti sítt og glógvaði rætt sum silvur hvítt.	It was a fathom and a foot long and sparkled just as white silver.
29. Kongurin gav honum skaft og skeið, og sjálvur segði hann kalli leið.	The king gave him shaft[7] and ship, and he himself told the man the way.
30. Frakkaland við váknum vítt tað er longd úr lívið mítt.	Scouting land widely with weaponry,[8] that is the extent of my life.

6 This indicates the immense size of the horse.

7 The king gave him weapons.

8 This line is uncertain. In the manuscript, what is *Frakkaland* in CCF is actually *Frökka land* in the manuscript. Matras, *J. H. Schrøters optegnelser*, p. 58, st. 15. Here we follow Lyngbye's suggestion that *Frökka* is the same as *frætta*, meaning to scout.

31. Tað er longd úr lívið mítt, tí havi í forðum farið vítt.	That is the extent of my life, therefore I have travelled far and wide in the past.
32. Leingi kavaði kurtis mann, beint á blýggið niður hann fann.	The courteous[9] man dived for a long time, directly down to the lead that he found.[10]
33. Kørnar prestur skírdi hann, tann læt lív, sum ljósið brann.	Kørnar the priest baptized him, he died as the candle burnt out.[11]
34. Tá ið ljós í lyktu var brent, *– tú tarvt einki í ráð geva í vanda –* tá var lív og levnað ent." *– Hvør tann svein geri so.*	When the candle in the lantern was burnt out, *– you don't need to give advice when you're in peril –* then life and living was ended."[12] *– Every man does it like that.*

Lyngbye, *Færøiske Qvæder*, 365n42. It remains a possibility, however, that this could be a reference to France (*Frakland*).

9 This would appear to be the courtly Old Norse word *kurteiss*. Lyngbye, however, notes that Faroese people have explained it to him as it being "Scotlander," although he is not able to make sense of this (and nor are we). Lyngbye, *Færøiske Qvæder*, 365n44.

10 "Lead" appears to be the lead lantern in which he keeps his candle. The idea is that Nornagestur has lost his candle and finds it at the bottom of the sea. This is made clear in Hammershaimb's version. See Hammershaimb, *Sjúrðar Kvæði*, p. 73, stt. 39–42.

11 In the Old Icelandic *Nornagestsþáttr*, Nornagestur is received by King Ólafr Trygvasson, who suggests that Nornagestur, as a relic of the heathen past from the time of Sigurðr Fáfnisbani, should be allowed to die by extinguishing his candle, which he keeps in the frame of his harp.

12 We have faithfully followed the punctuation of the printed edition here, but it would seem the final quotation mark is in the wrong place. It likely should be at the end of st. 31.

ÍSMAL THE BRAVE HERO (ÍSMAL FRÆGA KEMPA)

1. Mangar bróta á havinum
brattar og bráðar bylgjur,
tað kom Ísmali fyrst í hug
Hermund sín at spyrja.

Many steep and high waves
break on the sea,
the first thing that occurred to Ísmal
was to ask his Hermundur.[1]

Refrain *Grani bar gullið av heiði,*
brá hann sínum brandi av reiði,
Sjúrður vann av orminum,
og Grani bar gullið av heiði.

Grani carried the gold from the heath,
he brandished his blade in a fury,
Sjúrður defeated the dragon,
Grani carried the gold from the heath.

2. Tað kom Ísmali fyrst í hug
Hermund sín at spyrja:
"Vit skulu ríða í kongins garð
Hjálpreks dóttur at biðja."

The first thing that occured to Ísmal
was to ask his Hermundur:
"We shall ride to the king's court
to ask for Hjálprek's daughter."[2]

3. Úti í miðjum grasgarði
akslar hann sítt skinn,
og so búgvin gongur hann
í høgar hallir inn.

In the middle of the garden
he throws his cloak on,
and clothed like that he
walks into the high halls.

4. Og so búgvin gongur hann
í høgar hallir inn,
sum Hjalprek kongur at borði sat
við manna hundrað fimm.

And clothed like that he walks
into the high halls,
where King Hjalprek sat at the table
with five hundred men.

5. Ísmal stendur á hallargólvi
við silkikneptari húgvu,
kinnin er reyð sum hummarklógv
og eygað blátt sum í dúgvu.

Ísmal stands on the floor of the hall
with a silk-buttoned hat,
his cheek is as red as a lobster claw
and his eye as blue as a dove's.

6. Ísmal stendur á hallargólvi,
ber fram kvøðu sína:
"Sit heil, reystur kongurin,
tú gev mær dóttur tína!"

Ísmal stands on the floor of the hall,
he presents his offer of marriage:
"Sit hale,[3] bold king,
give me your daughter!"

7.Leingi sat hann kongurin
og hugsaði um tað ráð,
hvussu hann skuldi Ísmali
eitt hánligt andsvar fá.

The king sat for a long time
thinking about the proposal,
how he should give Ísmal
a mocking reply.

---

1 Hermundur seems to be the name of his squire or one of his trusted men.

2 To ask for her in marriage.

3 This means healthy and unharmed.

8. "Jomfrúgvin eigur ein raskan
bróður,
eitur Sjúrður frægi,
stóð hann tær til høgru hand,
hann tóktist vera tín maki."

"The maiden has a brave brother
called the valiant Sjúrður,
if he stood by your right handside,
he would seem your equal."[4]

9. Tað var Svanhild sólarljóma,
inn í hallina gekk,
tað fyrsta hon Ísmal við eygum sá,
hon yndi til hann fekk.

It was Svanhild sólarljómi,[5]
she walked into the hall,
when she first laid eyes on Ísmal,
she fell in love with him.

10. Leingi sat hann kongurin
og hugsaði har uppá,
hvussu hann skuldi Ísmali
eitt blídligt andsvar fá.

The king sat for a long time
thinking on the issue,
how he should give Ísmal
a friendly answer.

11. Tá svaraði Hjalprek kongur
alt foruttan ekka:
"Tær gevi eg nú mína dóttur
og hartil brúdleypsdrekka."

Then King Hjalprek answered
without worry:
"Now I give my daughter to you
and the wedding feast[6] as well."

12. Ísmal stendur á hallargólvi
gyrdi seg og vendi,
festi Svanhildu sólarljóma,
Hjalprek kongur sendi.

Ísmal stands on the floor of the hall
girded[7] himself and turned,
he was betrothed to Svanhild sólarljómi,[8]
King Hjalprek sent for him.

13. Ísmal stendur á hallargólvi,
á flestøllum veit hann skil:
"Hvør skal bjóða Sjúrða
mína samkoming til?"

Ísmal stands on the floor of the hall,
he is cunning in most things:
"Who shall invite Sjúrður
to my wedding gathering?"[9]

---

4 This likely indicate Sjúrður is just a youth, but already the equal of Ísmal.

5 Her byname means "sunshine."

6 This literally means "wedding drink" and is probably referring to the alcohol to toast the wedding with.

7 This could be, for example, with a sword, or he has dressed himself up.

8 The idea is that he is betrothed to Svanhild then and there, standing in the hall.

9 *Samkoming* is a gathering of people but also is used specifically to refer to a wedding in the sense of a "coming together" of a couple.

14. Tí svaraði Hjalprek kongur, tann hin ríki alvur: "Eg veit einki annað ráð, enn tær bjóðið honum sjálvur."	To that King Hjalprek answered, that mighty man:[10] "I know of no other possibility, than you invite him yourself."
15. Ísmal leyp á góðan gangara, burtur á skógvin reið, møtti honum Sjúrður Sigmundarson mitt á sínari leið.	Ísmal leapt onto a good horse, rode away to the forest, he met Sjúrður Sigmundarson in the middle of his path.
16. Møtti honum Sjúrður Sigmundarson mitt á sínari leið, tað er mær av sonnum sagt, hann var ikki 'brûnabaj.'	He met Sjúrður Sigmundarson in the middle of his path, it is truthfully told to me, that he didn't look happy.[11]
17. Ísmal stendur á grønum vølli, á flestøllum veit hann skil: "Tær bjóði eg nú, Sjúrður, mína samkoming til."	Ísmal stands on a green field, in most things he is cunning: "Now I invite you, Sjúrður, to my wedding gathering."
18. Svaraði Sjúrður Sigmundarson, hann situr á baldum hesti: "Hvaðan av londum er tann frúgv, ið tær havið, Ísmal, fest?"	Sjúrður Sigmundarson answered, he sits on a bold horse: "What kingdom is that lady from, that you, Ísmal, are betrothed to?"
19. "Hjalprek kongur, hennara faðir, frúgv Hjørdis hennara móðir, tað er mær av sonnum sagt, at tær eruð jomfrúgvans bróðir."	"King Hjalprekur is her father, lady Hjørdis is her mother, it is truthfully told to me, that you're the maiden's brother."
20. "Hevur tú mína systur fest og eg ikki til tess frætt, eg skal teg við lurkum lemja, tú bíður ei annan rætt."	"If you've been betrothed to my sister without me having been told about it, I shall beat you with clubs, you can't expect anything else."

10 An *alvur* is a mighty, powerful man.

11 Lyngbye glosses *brûnabaj* as "mild at see til" (gentle to look at). Lyngbye, *Færøiske Qvæder*, 106n16. That Sjúrður doesn't look happy when he encounters Ísmal implies that Sjúrður already knows what has happened and what will happen, i.e., that he knows the future.

21. "Hóað eg havi tína systur fest og tú ikki til tess frætt, áðrenn tú meg við lurkum lemur, eg bjóði tær annan rætt.	"Though I have been betrothed to your sister and you haven't been told, before you beat me with clubs, I will offer you another option.
22. Eg havi tína systur fest, tó eg teg ei kendi, áðrenn tú meg við lurkum lemur, sveittast tær um enni."	I have been betrothed to your sister, though I didn't know you, before you've beaten me with clubs, you will be sweating on your forehead."
23. "Hevur tú mína systur fest, høvisk yvir allar kvinnur, hoyr tú, Ísmal, fræga kempa, tú skalt mær treytir vinna."	"If you have been betrothed to my sister, more courteous than all other women, hear this Ísmal, brave hero, you have to complete some hard tasks[12] for me."
24. Svaraði Ísmal, fræga kempa, vaksin yvir allar seggjar: "Hvat eitur tann fyrsta treyt, ið tær skuluð um meg leggja?"	Ísmal the brave hero answered, better than all other warriors: "What is the first task[13] that you will set for me?"
25. "Fram út í tann grøna skógv har liggja ormar seks, allar skalt tú deyðar hava, tú stígur á brúðarbekk.	"Out in the green forest there are six dragons, you shall kill all of them, before you sit in the wedding seat.[14]
26. Fram út í tann grøna skógv har liggja ormar tólv, allar skalt tú deyðar hava, tú stígur á brúðargólv."	In the green forest there are twelve dragons, you shall kill all of them, before you stand on the wedding floor."[15]
27. "Fram út í tann grøna skógv har liggja ormar tveir, sig mær, Sjúrður Sigmundarson, hvussu langir eru teir?"	"In the green forest, there are two dragons, tell me, Sjúrður Sigmundarson, how long are they?"

12 This is in the sense of difficult trials.

13 In CCF, for this line there is no opening quotation mark and the first letter of *Hvat* is in lowercase.

14 This means before he gets married.

15 Literally "stand on the bridal floor."

28. "Ein er átjan alin langur, annar tríggjar og tjúgu, øll mín hirð er vitnisfør, eg sigi tær sanna søgu."	"One is eighteen ells long, the second is twenty three, all of my retinue can be witnesses to this, I'm telling you a true story."
29. "Er hann átjan alin langur, annar tríggjar ella tvá, eri eg sonur Samsons sterka, ræðist eg ikki tá."	"If it's eighteen ells long, and the second is three or two, if I'm the son of Samson the strong, then I will not fear anything."
30. Allar vá hann ormarnar, tað tókti honum ongan vanda, Finna spýði eitur á hann, hann náddi ikki haðan at ganga.	He slew all the dragons, it didn't seem difficult to him, Finna[16] breathed poison on him, he didn't manage to walk away from there.
31. Tað var Sjúrður Sigmundarson, hann heim í garðin fór, úti er Svanhild sólarljóma, hon fyri honum stóð.	It was Sjúrður Sigmundarson, he went home to the court, Svanhild sólarljómi is outside, she stands before him.
32. Sjúrður gekk í borgina, og gott er í honum alvið, so settist hann í hásætið, so borgin øll hon skalv.	Sjúrður went into the castle, and there is great strength in him, then he sat himself in the high seat, so that the whole castle shook.
33. "Plaga so, faðir, høviskir menn sína dóttur so geva, eg vildi títt hálsbein sundur í sjey varð sligið við mínum neva."	"Is it usual father, for courteous men to give away their daughter like that, I would that your neck bone was broken into seven pieces by my fist."
34. Fram kom Svanhild sólarljóma, høvisk yvir allar kvinnur: "Hevur tú, Sjúrður, lagt tað ráð, Ísmali treytir at vinna?"	Svanhild sólarljómi came forward, more courteous than all other women: "Have you devised such a plot, Sjúrður, that Ísmal should perform deeds for you?"
35. "Gakk tú burtur frá mínum eygum, eg vil teg ikki hoyra, sámir tað ei mín búgvin brand at rjóða í kvinnudroyra!"	"Get out of my sight, I don't want to listen to you, it isn't seemly for my readied sword to be reddened by women's blood!"[17]

16 Finna (presumably the same as Finnur) is the name of one of the dragons.

17 *Droyri* is a word used in ballads for blood.

36. Tað var Svanhild sólarljóma, tekur so høgt at gráta, eftir spurdi Sjúrður, í hví hon mundi so láta.	It was Svanhild sólarljóma, she begins to cry so loudly, Sjúrður asked, why she made such noise.
37. "Gakk tú burtur frá mínum eygum, grát ikki longur á sínni, enn var maður mentur fyri moyggj, *ið ei var maður minni!"	"Get out of my sight, don't cry any longer, still the man was capable for the sake of the maiden, he was not a lesser man than I!"[18]
38. Sjúrður leyp á góða gangara, hann *var dreingja maki, so ríður hann á skógvar burtur fyri systur sínar sakir.	Sjúrður leapt on his good horse, he was the heroes' equal, then he rides off to the forest for his sister's sake.
39. Ísmal liggur á grønum vølli, staddur í ormavanda, fegin er hann, at hann hoyrir Grana hóvar ganga.	Ísmal lies on a green field, he is in danger from the dragons, he is happy when he hears the sound of Grani's hooves.
40. Ísmal liggur á grønum vølli, staddur í ormablóði, fegin er hann, at hann hoyrir Grana bresta hóvum.	Ísmal lies on a green field, lying in dragon's blood, he is happy when he hears Grani beating his hooves.
41. Tekur hann hann í saðilin upp og sára um hann kvíðar, leitar nú í tasku síni smyrsl á hann at ríða.	He takes him up onto the saddle dreading his wounds, he searches in his bag for ointment to rub him with.
42. Tekur hann hann í saðilin upp, førir hann heim til hallar: "Tak við, Svanhild sólarljóma, grøð tann garpin snjalla!"	He takes him up onto the saddle, takes him home to the hall: "Take him, Svanhild sólarljómi, heal the bold hero!"

18 Sjúrður is saying that Ísmal was worthy of the maiden and was almost as strong as he is.

43. Hon grøddi hann í dagar,
hon grøddi hann í tvá,
fyrsta dag í fjórðu viku
fór hann í brynju blá.

She healed him for days,
she healed him for two,
on the first day of the fourth week
he put on his blue armour.

44. Fyrsta dag í fjórðu viku
fór hann í brynju nýggja,
leiddi hon hann í hallina inn,
so vænur var garpi at síggja.

On the first day of the fourth week
he put on his new armour,
she led him into the hall,
the hero was so handsome to look at.

45. Lótu tá til brúdleyps laða,
tá var ei at tvørra,
átjan borgum boðið var,
tólv hundrað menn úr hvørji.

Then they had the wedding prepared,
then nothing could be in short supply,
eighteen castles were invited,
twelve hundred men from each.

46. Lótu tá til brúdleyps laða,
næst var komið til sams,
átjan borgum boðið var,
og har var kongur av Frans.

Then they had the wedding prepared,
everything had almost come together,
eighteen castles were invited,
and there was the king of France.[19]

47. Ikki fattaðist Ísmali
brúðarmannin ein,
við høgru hand gekk Hjalprek
kongur
og vinstru Gunnar svein.

Ísmal wasn't lacking
in bridesmen,
on his right handside walked King Hjalpek
and on his left the young Gunnar.

48. Ikki fattaðist Svanhildu
brúðarkonur prúðar,
við høgru hand gekk Gunnhild
Buðla
og vinstru Grimhild Júka.

Svanhild wasn't lacking in
beautiful bridesmaids,
on her right hand walked Buðli's Gunnhild
and on her left Júki's Grimhild.

49. Ikki fattaðist Svanhildu
brúðarmoyggjar prúðar,
við høgru hand gekk Brynhild
Buðla
og vinstru Guðrun Júka.

Svanhild wasn't lacking in
beautiful bridesmaids,
on her right hand side walked Buðli's
Brynhild
and on her left Júki's Guðrun.

19 *Frans* here for *Frakland*. Lyngbye notes this is for the sake of the rhyme. Lyngbye, *Færøiske Qvæder*, 118n46.

50. Har var maður, ið harpu slerdi, nevndur Ørvaroddur, Hjálmar, kappi frægi, við Sjúrða moyggjar studdi.	There was a man, who played the harp, named Ørvaroddur,[20] Hjálmar,[21] the bold hero, supported Sjúrður's maidens.[22]
51. Tríati vóru silvursteyp og annaðslíkt av skálum, tað leyp av í kongins høll, tá ið alt var sett í máli.	There were thirty silver goblets, and other bowls like them, there was an over abundance in the king's hall, when all the goods had been put in place.
52. Tríati silvurføt, og nýsmídd vóru øll, Sjúrður stendur á hallargólvi, hann sigur frá gørpum snjøllum.	Thirty dishes of silver, and all were newly forged, Sjúrður stands on the hall floor, he tells of bold heroes.
53. So stardi hann Sjúrður á Brynhildar mál, hann breyt yvir borðinum forgylta mjaðarskál.	Sjúrður then stared at Brynhild's conversation, he broke over the table a gilded mead cup.
54. Drukkið varð teirra brúdleypið, hirðin var so fegin, sum tann fuglur, á viði situr, er um tann ljósa dag.	Their wedding was celebrated, the retinue was as happy as the bird that sits in a tree is at the light of day.[23]
55. Tríati vóru kerti tendrað, og fjøruti vóru logar, fylgdu teirri ríku frúgv fyrstu nátt at sova.	Thirty candles were lit, and there were forty flames,[24] they escorted the mighty lady to sleep on the first night.

20 This is the Old Norse character Ǫrvar Oddr, the protagonist of the Icelandic *Ǫrvar Odds saga*, who also appears, for example, in the ballad *Arngríms synir* (CCF 16).

21 This is the Old Norse character Hjálmarr, who appears in both the Icelandic *Ǫrvar Odds saga* and *Hervarar saga*, and who also appears for example in the ballad *Arngríms synir* (CCF 16).

22 It seems Hjálmar and Sjúrður escorted the bride's party.

23 This seems to refer to the dawn chorus.

24 This likely means forty torches.

56.	Tríati vóru kerti tendrað og hartil vaksljós, Hjalprek kongur og hirðin øll tey fylgdu í svøvnhús.	Thirty candles were lit and wax candles as well, King Hjalprek and the whole retinue they escorted them to the sleeping house.
57.	Har varð urgan í garðin troðin, harpur og mikil meingi, Hjalprek kongur og hirðin øll tey fylgdu teim til seingir.	The organ was played in the garden, harps and a large crowd, King Hjalprek and the whole retinue they escorted them to bed.
58.	Drukkið varð teirra brúdleypið, og kátt var teirra lív, bæði gingu í eina song, Ísmal og hans vív.	Their wedding was celebrated and they lived happily together, both went into one bed, Ísmal and his wife.
59.	Drukkið varð teirra brúdleypið bæði væl og leingi, kom so mangur ein hovmann til sum fjøður í fuglaveingjum.	Their wedding was celebrated both well and lengthily, so many a courtier came there as there are feathers in birds' wings.
60.	Drukkið varð teirra brúdleypið, og so er komið til mín, síðan fór hvør, sum biðin var, haðan heim til sín.	Their wedding was celebrated, so it has been told to me,[25] then each that was invited went from there to their own home.
61.	Nú skal lata ljóði av, eg kvøði ikki longur á sinni, nú skal taka upp annan tátt og ítari leggja í minni.	Now I shall end my song, I sing no longer at present, now to begin the second part of the ballad and continue to remember it.
Refrain	*Grani bar gullið av heiði,* *brá hann sínum brandi av reiði,* *Sjúrður vann av orminum,* *og Grani bar gullið av heiði.*	*Grani carried the gold from the heath,* *he brandished his blade in a fury,* *Sjúrður defeated the dragon,* *Grani carried the gold from the heath.*

25 Literally "so has it come to me."

SJÚRÐUR AND THE DWARF MAIDEN OR DWARF MAIDEN I (SJÚRÐUR OG DVØRGAMOY OR DVØRGAMOY I)

1. Eg veit eina rímuna, inni hevur ligið leingi: Hjalprekur fyri ríki ræður, reystar hevur hann dreingir.	I know of a ballad, that has lain inside me for a long time:[1] Hjalprekur rules a kingdom, he has such bold heroes.
2. Raskar hevur hann dreingirnar og hartil mangar sveinar, ein ber yvir allar teir, hann glógvar í gulli reina.	He has such bold heroes, and many footmen as well,[2] one is above them all, he shines in pure gold.[3]
3. Mangar hevur hann sveinar, alir teir upp við gavni, ein ber yvir allar teir, Sjúrður nevndur á navni.	He has many heroes, entertains them with pleasure, one is above them all, Sjúrður is his name.
4. Hoyrt havi [eg] av gamal tíð, at *arin er eitt fok, nú skal ríma um Sjúrð hin unga, hansara fyrsta tok.	I have heard it from olden times, that the arrow is as quick as lightning,[4] now to compose verses about Sjúrður the young, about his first expedition.[5]
5. Snarliga kann *arin flúgva eina langa leið, nú skal kvøða um Sjúrð hin unga, tá hann fyrst út reið.	The arrow can fly quickly for a long way, now to sing[6] about Sjúrður the young, when he rode out the first time.

---

1 It does not say "me" in the original, but we are assuming that this means that the "rhyme" has lain inside the singer for a long time, waiting for an opportunity to be performed.

2 Here we have translated *sveinar* as footmen to distinguish them from the men, *dreingir*, mentioned in the line above, which we have translated as heroes. However, *sveinar* can also mean heroes, so it is not entirely clear here what the two terms are referring to. However, the main point is that the king has lots of men. In st. 3, for example, we have translated *sveinar* as heroes.

3 We understand him shining in gold to mean that his clothes and equipment were gold, i.e., luxurious.

4 We have understood *ar* as *ör*, meaning arrow. Hammershaimb has *örnin* (eagle) and notes that others sing *haran* (the hare). Hammershaimb, *Sjúrðar Kvæði*, 80 st. 1.

5 We have understood *tok* here as the Danish word *togt*, meaning expedition or raid, like that the Vikings went on.

6 *Kvøða* implies dancing and chanting the ballad.

6. Árla var um morgunin,
sólin skín so víða,
Sjúrður klæðist for síni song,
hann býr seg út at ríða.

Early in the morning,
the sun shone so widely,
Sjúrður dresses himself in front of his bed,
he readies himself to ride.

7. Út varð loystur gangarin
undir hallarvegg,
prýddur var hann við skarlak
niður á hóvarskegg.

The horse was untied
under the wall of the hall,
it was adorned with scarlet cloth
down to the fetlocks.

8. Út varð loystur gangarin,
ið Sjúrður skuldi á ríða,
hann var prýddur við skarlak
niður á miðal síðu.

The horse was untied,
that Sjúrður would ride on,
it was adorned with scarlet cloth
down to the middle of its side.

9. Sjúrður klæðist for síni [song],
letst í brynju nýggja:
"Nú lystir meg á skógvin fram
undurverk at síggja."

Sjúrður dresses himself in front of his bed,
puts on his new armour:
"Now I want to go into the forest
to see marvels."[7]

10. Sjúrður klæðist for síni song,
hann fekk so mikið í huga:
"Nú lystir meg á skógvin fram
undurverk at skoða."

Sjúrður dresses himself in front of his bed,
he wanted to so much:[8]
"Now I want to go into the forest
to see marvels."[9]

11. Sjúrður reið á skógvin fram
bæði av illsku [og] bræði,
hvørki kundi fyri hann koma
kristið ella heiðið.

Sjúrður rode into the forest
both in anger and in a temper,
neither Christans nor heathens
could stand in his way.[10]

12. Sjúrður reið á skógvin fram
fult í dagar tríggjar,
einki ting tað kundi hann
hvørki hoyra ei síggja.

Sjúrður rode in the forest
for three full days,
he could neither
see nor hear anything.

13. So reið hann tann fjórða dag,
tóktist vera í trota,
tá ið dagur at kvøldi kom,
sá hann ein stóran flota.

Then he rode on the fourth day,
he was completely worn out,
when the day came to evening,
he saw a great fleet.

7 The closing quotation mark on this line is missing in CCF.

8 This could also be "he had so much on his mind."

9 The verb for "see" is different in stt. 9 and 10 (*síggja* and *skoða*).

10 The final two lines of the stanzas are the other way round in the Faroese but reversed here to preserve meaning in the translation.

14. Tað var Sjúrður Sigmundarson, stillar síni ferð, hann sær har í hasum flota gull við búgvið svørð.	It was Sjúrður Sigmundarson, he stops his journey, there he sees in that fleet gold by readied sword.
15. Sjúrður stillar síni ferð ei í góðan tíma, hann sær har [í] hasum flota teirra skjøldar skína.	Sjúrður stops his journey not at a good time,[11] there in that fleet he sees that their shields shine.
16. Tað er Sjúrður Sigmundarson, tekur til sítt svørð: "Nú skal ríða longur fram at vita, hvøssu fer."	It is Sjúrður Sigmundarson, he grabs his sword: "Now I'll ride further ahead to see how it goes."
17. Sjúrður mundi til teir fara, tað var ei til dans, hann sær sita fyri sær ein heilan dvørgakrans.	Sjúrður would go to them, it was not to dance,[12] he sees sitting in front of him a whole ring of dwarves.
18. Hyggur hann upp á dvørgarnar, teir hyggja upp á hann, hvørgin partur talaði, tóktist teim einki stand.	He looks up at the dwarves, they look up at him, neither party spoke, it seemed to them to be no disturbance.
19. Svaraði ein av dvørgunum, hann bar ikki kinnar bleikar: "Hvat eru tíni ørindi? Ert tú komin at leika?"	One of the dwarves responded, he didn't have pale cheeks: "What brings you here? Have you come to play?"
20. Svaraði annar av dvørgunum, hann bar ikki kinnar bleikar: "Ert tú komin at stríðast her, ella ert tú komin at leika?"	One of the dwarves responded, he didn't have pale cheeks: "Have you come to fight here, or have you come to play?"
21. Sjúrður situr á sínum hesti, ongan veg kann fara, enntá tegir Sjúrður til, tordi ei aftur at svara.	Sjúrður sits on his horse, can't go anywhere, even so Sjúrður is silent, he didn't dare to answer back.

---

11 Presumably this is not a good time to stop his journey because he is completely exhausted.

12 This is a meta reflection on the ballad being sung at this time; the people singing the ballad are in a ring dancing, while Sjúrður sees a circle of dwarves and will not be dancing with them.

22. Hundrað vóru dvørgarnir, væl, tað var ikki fleiri, allir upp á Sjúrðin sóu bæði av illsku og reiði.	There were a hundred dwarves, it was good that there weren't more, all looked up at Sjúrður both in anger and in a temper.
23. Hugsaði Sjúrður Sigmundarson: "Eg skal ikki hjartað selja, gerið, hvat tykkum sýnist best, tit skulu korini velja."	Sjúrður Sigmundarson thought: "I shall not part with the heart,[13] do what seems best for you, you shall choose the terms."[14]
24. Upp steig ein av dvørgunum, hvessir hann sítt spjót, ógvuligur annar tá, hann snúðist honum imót.	One of the dwarves stepped up, he sharpens his spear, then another terrible-looking dwarf[15] turned towards him.
25. Høggini vanka mong og tung, syngur á dvørgabrynju, hann sær hvørki himmal ei jørð, tey yvir honum dynja.	The blows fly, many and heavy, they sing on dwarven armour, he sees neither heaven nor earth, they thunder above him.[16]
26. Høggini vanka mong og tung, summir falla á grúgvu, hann sær hvørki himmal ei jørð, tey yvir honum flúgva.	The blows fly, many and heavy, some fall on his face, he sees neither heaven nor earth, they fly above him.[17]
27. Har kom ein av dvørgunum fast av miklum móði, hann hevði upp sína høgru hond, Sjúrða á nasar sló.	There came one of the dwarves, though in a mighty rage, he had his right hand raised, he hit Sjúrður on the nose.
28. Tá fekk Sjúrður av dvørgum høgg, tann hin menskur mann, blóðið undan brynjuni niður á saðil rann.	Then Sjúrður received a blow from the dwarves, that bold man, the blood ran down the armour down onto the saddle.

13 The meaning of this line is unclear. He seems to be saying he does not want to be killed here.

14 The "you" here is in the plural.

15 It says "he" in the Faroese, but we have added "dwarf" for clarity.

16 The "they" here refers to the blows.

17 Again, the "they" here refers to the blows.

29. Yvrið dregur at Sjúrði, søgur ganga frá, dregur út sítt búgvið svørð og tað í loftið brá.	Sjúrður becomes incensed, tales are told of it, he draws his readied sword and brandishes it in the air.
30. Ógvuliga Sjúrður høgg, tað syngur á gyltum ringi: "Hetta er tað fyrsta sár, eg havi á skógnum fingið."	Sjúrður hews mightily, it sings on golden rings:[18] "This is the first wound, I've received in the forest."
31. Sjúrður brá sín bitra brand, tað mundi ongan vara, sleri so til dvørgin tann, hann feldi hann niður til jarðar.	Sjúrður brandishes his sharp sword, no one would have guessed it,[19] then he dealt a blow to that dwarf, he felled him to the ground.
32. Har kom fram ein annar dvørgur, Sjúrði mundi hann siga: "Slá tú ongan fleiri dvørg, hann var ei av várum liði!	There appeared a second dwarf, he said to Sjúrður:[20] "Don't you hit any more dwarves, he wasn't in our band![21]
33. Hoyr tað, Sjúrður Sigmundarson, eg sigi tær satt ífrá: slært tú niður ein annan dvørg, tú kemur har ikki frá."	Listen, Sjúrður Sigmundarson, I'm telling you truthfully: if you knock down another dwarf, you won't leave this place."
34. Burtur hvurvu dvørgarnir, helst fyri uttan vanda, síðan mátti Sjúrður í kolmyrkri ganga.	The dwarves disappeared, probably without danger, after that Sjúrður had to walk in pitchblack darkness.
35. So reið Sjúrður Sigmundarson, frystir hans saðilgjørð, rímfrost var tá yvir fallið heidna manna jørð.	Then Sjúrður Sigmundarson rode, his girth froze,[22] then hoarfrost had fallen over heathen ground.

18 This could be rings of a byrnie, but it could also be arm rings on the dwarf.

19 *Vara* means to expect or to guess. They are making a joke saying no one would have expected Sjúrður to do this—this was, of course, entirely expected.

20 This line is in the conditional "he would have said to Sjúrður."

21 This is in the sense of "band of dwarves" and also has connotations of army or troop.

22 This is referring to the girth on his saddle.

36. Sjúrður ríður til og frá,
ongan veg kann finna,
dvørgamoyggin til hann kom,
hin vitra og hin svinna.

Sjúrður rides to and fro,
he can't find his way,
the dwarf maiden came to him,
the wise and sensible one.

37. Har kom fagra dvørgamoyggin,
skín sum sól á sjó,
hon mundi vera í gulli rend,
perlur á jørðina dró.

The fair dwarf maiden came there,
she shone like the sun on the sea,
her clothes were bordered with gold,[23]
she drew pearls on the ground after her.[24]

38. Svaraði hin ungi Sjúrður,
tungu ber hann so snjalla:
"Hoyr tað, yndig dvørgamoyggin,
flyt meg heim til halla!"

The young Sjúrður asked,
he spoke so eloquently:
"Listen, lovely dwarf maiden,
take me home to the hall!"

39. Tað var yndig dvørgamoyggin,
fylgdi honum so væl
av tí høga fjallinum
í ein djúpan dal.

It was the lovely dwarf maiden,
she led him so carefully
off the high mountain
into a deep valley.

40. Fylgdi hon honum í dalin niður
fram við eini á,
borgir sóu tey undan koma,
á pílarum stá.

She accompanied him down into the valley
along a river,
they saw castles come into view,
that stood on pillars.

41. Tá svaraði Sjúrður
av so tungari sorg:
"Hoyr tú, yndig dvørgamoyggin,
hvør býr her í borg?"

Then Sjúrður asked
grief-stricken:[25]
"Listen, lovely dwarf maiden,
who lives here in the castle?"

42. Svaraði yndig dvørgamoyggin,
øll í gulli skín:
"Hann býr her í hesi borg,
sæli faðir mín.

The lovely dwarf maiden answered,
shining with gold:
"He who lives here in this castle,
is my dear father.

43. Hoyr tað, Sjúrður Sigmundarson,
tak teg fullvæl vara,
hvat mín faðir til tín sigur,
tú skalt ei aftur svara.

Listen, Sjúrður Sigmundarson,
be very cautious,
you shall not respond to
what my father says to you.[26]

---

23 This line is actually conditional, and it says literally "she was probably bordered with gold." This must be referring to her clothes.

24 We have added "after her" to make the meaning clear. This must be referring to some kind of train.

25 Sjúrður probably wanted to be led back to his own hall.

26 The two final lines of the stanza are the other way round in the Faroese, reversed

44. Hann biður teg í smiðju við sær,
tá verður skamt til dags,
men so snart tú kemur har,
tú rennur burt sum vaks.

He will ask you to go to the smithy with him,
when the day is short,[27]
but as soon as you get there,
you will run away like wax.

45. Hann veit, at Sjúrður
Sigmundarson,
honum er ikki at eggja,
hann biður teg í smiðju við sær
stórar stengur at sleggja.

He knows that Sjúrður Sigmundarson
is easy to goad,[28]
he will ask you to go to the smithy
with him
to hammer big metal bars.[29]

46. Tá ið tú kemur í hallina inn,
legg teg niður sjúkan,
svarar tú honum eittans orð,
høvur av herðum fúka."

When you come into the hall,
lay yourself down as if ill,
if you answer him with just one word,
heads will fly off shoulders."

47. Sjúrður kom í hallina inn,
var so síðla á kvøldi,
dvørgurin var í síni smiðju,
smíddi við stórum eldi.

Sjúrður came into the hall,
it was so late in the evening,
the dwarf was in his smithy,
he forged by a large fire.

48. Dvørgurin skuldi í hallir ganga,
sum hann plagdi fyrr,
hann sær standa ein stóran hest
bundnan við hallardyr.

The dwarf was about to walk into the hall,
as he usually did,
when he sees a large horse standing
tied up by the hall door.

49. Yvrið dregur at dvørginum,
hann gerst í kinnar reyð,
setti spjót í hallargátt,
hurð av hongslum fleyg.

The dwarf became incensed,
his cheeks became red,
he drove a spear into the threshold
of the hall,
the door flew off its hinges.

50. Dvørgurin so til orða tekur,
tað var alt so brátt:
"Hvat er hetta fyri ein kempa,
her er komin í nátt?"

The dwarf then speaks,
it happened so quickly:
"What kind of warrior is this,[30]
that has come here tonight?"

---

here to preserve the sense in the translation.

27 This seems to mean when there is not much of the day left.

28 *Honum er ikki at eggja* is an idiom meaning easy to goad.

29 *Stengur* can also mean spear or lance.

30 *Kempa*, which we have translated as warrior, can also mean hero or giant.

51. Dvørgurin tók sítt gylta spjót, letst í brynju nýggja: "Skaffið fram ta miklu kempu, brádliga vil eg hann síggja!"	The dwarf took his gilded spear, and puts on new armour: "Fetch that mighty warrior, I want to see him right now!"
52. Tá svaraði dvørgamoyggin: "Lat tað nú so vera, hann er her av neyðum komin, tú skalt honum einki gera."	Then the dwarf maiden answered: "Now let it be, he has come here because of trouble, you shall do nothing to him."
53. Tað var yndig dvørgamoyggin, tekur at faðir at læra: "Kempan er bæði mikil og mødd, tú skalt hann ikki skaða."	It was the lovely dwarf maiden, she begins to instruct her father: "The warrior is both great and tired, you shall do him no harm."
54. Dvørgurin brá sín bitra brand, Sjúrða ætlar at vega, dvørgamoyggin um oddin tók: "Elva nú ongan trega!"	The dwarf brandished his sharp sword, intending to slay Sjúrður, the dwarven maiden grasped the point: "Cause no hurt now!"
55. Dvørgurin kastar gyltum brandi, allur í gulli skín: "Sjúrður, gakk at breiða borði, drekk bæði mjøð og vín!	The dwarf threw the gilded sword, shining with gold: "Sjúrður, go to the wide table, drink both mead and wine!
56. Eg veit tað, Sjúrður Sigmundarson, tær er ikki at eggja, tú skalt koma í mína smiðju stórar stengur at sleggja."	I know, Sjúrður Sigmundarson, that you are easy to goad, you shall come into my smithy to hammer big metal bars."
57. Sjúrður upp frá borði steig, skuldi í smiðju fara, mintist aftur, at dvørgamoyggin bað hann ikki svara.	Sjúrður rose up from the table, he was about to go to the smithy, he remembered that the dwarf maiden told him not to answer.
58. "Eg skal geva tær brynjuna, gjørd er av silvuri hvíta, hvar tú verður í striði staddur, hana man einki bíta.	"I shall give you armour, which is made of white silver, when you are in battle, nothing may cut it.

59. Eg skal geva tær spjót so gott,
gjørt av góðum treysti,
stikk so manniliga til,
ikki skal tað bresta."

I shall give you such a good spear,
made very strong,[31]
stab with it in a manly way,
it won't break."

60. Árla var um morgunin,
sólin skín so víða,
Sjúrður klæðist for síni song,
hann býr seg heim at ríða.

Early in the morning,
the sun shone so widely,
Sjúrður dresses himself before his bed,
he readies himself for riding home.

61. Svaraði Sjúrður Sigmundarson,
tungu ber so snjalla:
"Hoyr tú, yndig dvørgamoyggin,
flyt meg heim til halla!"

Sjúrður Sigmundarson replied,
he spoke so eloquently:
"Listen, lovely dwarf maiden,
get me home to the hall!"[32]

62. Svaraði yndig dvørgamoyggin
av so tungari sorg:
"Eg skal flyta teg so langt,
at tú sært Hjalpreks borg."

The lovely dwarf maiden answered
grief-stricken:
"I shall get you so far
that you see Hjalprek's castle."

63. Hon fylgdi honum so langt á leið
við trá og tunga sorg,
inntil, hyggi [eg], fyrst tey sóu
Hjalpreks kongins borg.

She led him so far on the journey
with grief and deep sorrow,
until, I see, that they first saw
King Hjalprek's castle.

64. Har mundu tey skiljast at
við trá og tunga treyt,
hann kysti hana so søtan koss,
at vín á vørrum fleyt.

There they were separated
with grief and great difficulty,
he kissed her so sweetly,
like wine flowed over the lips.[33]

65. Dvørgamoyggin aftur vendi,
hon feldi tár á kinn,
Sjúrður gekk til hallar heim
for Hjalprek kongin inn.

The dwarf maiden turned back,
tears fell on her cheek,
Sjúrður went home to the hall,
before King Hjalprek.

---

31 The word *treystur* has connotations of it being durable.

32 He is asking the dwarf maiden to help him get back home. He is literally asking to be conveyed or transported.

33 This likely means the kiss was sweet as wine.

THE BEAUTIFUL DWARF MAIDEN OR DWARF MAIDEN II (DVØRGAMOYGGIN FAGRA OR DVØRGAMOY II)

1. Ásmundur saðlar gangaran sín, hann ríður út av veldi: "Ei kundi eg ta jomfrú fá, higar kom á kvøldi."	Ásmundur saddles his horse, he rides out from his realm: "I could not have the maiden, that came here last night."
2. Ásmundur ríður út árla morgun við sínum fylgdarsveini, kongurin flutti moynna heim, ið dvørgurin hevði í heimi.	Ásmundur rides out early in the morning, with his companion, the king took[1] the maiden home, that the dwarf had in his home.
3. Kongurin kemur inn árla morgun, talar til dreingir fróar: "Tit skulu fara um landið út brúdleypsfólki at bjóða!	The king comes in early in the morning, and speaks to the cheerful heroes: "You shall go around the kingdom to invite the wedding guests!
4. Sjálvur eri eg manna maki, brøður eigi eg fleiri, ríðið fram á Sjúrðar fund, tí hann er á háttri meiri!	I myself am the equal of men, I have many brothers, ride to meet Sjúrður, because he is better in demeanour!
5. Kvittið fram yvir Húnaland, fornum kempum at bjóða, kenni eg Ásmund kellingarson og hansara dreingir góðar."	Hasten over Húnaland, to invite ancient heroes, I know Ásmundur kellingarson[2] and his good heroes."
6. Sveinar riðu á markir út vítt um vegir allar, riðin er Larsin dvørgakongur av skógnum heim til hallar.	The king's men rode out on the fields, far and wide on all roads, Larsin the dwarven king has riden from his forest home to the hall.
7. Dvørgurin kastar reyðum skildri, í borgum sær hann einki, burt er bæði skjøldur og svørð, og horvin brúður av beinki.	The dwarf throws down his red shield, in his castle he sees nothing, both shield and sword are gone, and the woman has disappeared from the bench.

1 Literally it says he moved or relocated her home.

2 Ásmundur's byname means "son of a hag" or "son of a woman."

8. Ásmundur ríður á bergið fram við tílíkan brandin ein: "Ætlar tú ikki moynna at hevna, ið kongurin flutti heim?"	Ásmundur rides forth to the hill with such a sword: "Are you not intending to avenge the maiden, that the king took home?"[3]
9. "Bæði snart og skundiliga leggst mær nú í minni, burt er bæði skjøldur og svørð, nái eg ikki á sinni."	"Both quick and hastily, I continue to remember it,[4] the shield and sword are both gone, I can't get at them at this time."
10. Ásmundur so til orða tekur, mælir á tungu inni: "Eg skal læna tær skjøld og svørð, betri er ikki at finna.	Ásmundur then begins to speak, saying: "I shall lend you a shield and sword, any better are not to be found.
11. Læna skal eg tær skjøldin tann og svørðið tað hitt besta, sjálvur skal eg í ferðini fara tann Húnakong at gesta."	I shall lend you the best shield and sword, I will go on the journey myself, to visit the King of the Huns."
12. Riðu teir til hallar heim fast av miklum alvi, sum kongurin og tann dvørgamoy sótu í búnum talvi.	They rode home to the hall though of mighty strength, as the king and that dwarf maiden sat playing chess.[5]
13. Ein kom maður í hallina inn, sigur øllum frá: "Eg sær fult eitt átjan hundrað at borgararmi gá."	One man came into the hall, and tells everyone: "I see a full eighteen hundred men, approaching the wing of the castle."[6]
14. Kongurin upp frá borði steig, hann studdist við skjøld og svørð: "Burt er Høgni og alt mítt lið, teir eru so leingi til ferða."	The king rose from the table, he put on his shield and sword: "Høgni and all my troops are gone, they have been travelling for so long."

3 The king (who has not been named) has abducted the maiden.

4 This is the narrator referring to the contents of the ballad.

5 This literally means they sat at a prepared chess table.

6 This could also imply fortress.

15. Kongurin sló sín hond mót borð og dregur svørð av skeiðum: "Nú vildi eg, Sjúrður og Virgar sterki vóru í borgum heima!"	The king slammed his hand against the table and draws the sword from its scabbard: "Now I wish that Sjúrður and Virgar the strong were home in the castle!"
16. Hann talar til Gislar, bróður sín: "Mítt mál kannst tú væl greina, bið hann koma í brúðarhús at drekka tann mjøðin reina!"	He speaks to Gíslar his brother: "You can explain my intention well, invite them to come to the bridal house[7] to drink the pure mead!"
17. "Standið ei longur við borgararm, loysið tær saðilreimar, býður hann tær í brúðarhús at drekka tann mjøðin reina!"	"Don't stand any longer by the wing of the castle, loosen the saddlestraps, he invites you to the bridal house to drink the pure mead!"
18. "Býður hann mær í brúðarhús at drekka tann mjøðin hvíta, her standi eg nú herklæddur so ógvuligur at líta.	"He invites me to the bridal house to drink the white mead,[8] I stand here now dressed for battle, so terrible to behold.[9]
19. Vil hann ikki farligt fljóð senda mær til handa, so skal hann brynja út alt sítt lið at verja ríki og landa."	If he does not want to hand me the dangerous woman, then he should armour all his troops to defend the kingdom and land."
20. Árla var um morgunin, sólin roðar í fjøll, leggja sínar bardagar skamt frá kongins høll.	It was early in the morning, the sun reddened the mountains, they place their battles a short distance from the king's hall.
21. Ásmundur ríður í herin fram, ætlaði sær at vinna, kongurin reið honum straks ímót, har mundu tveir reystir finnast.	Ásmundur rides to the army, intending to win, the king rode immediately against him there two brave men could be found.

---

7 The place where the bride and bridegroom receive guests.

8 This could also be a question: "Is he inviting me to the bridal house...?"

9 This is presumably the dwarf king speaking.

22. Kongurin gav so stórt eitt høgg av so góðum treysti, so sló hann til Ásmund, hann fell av sínum hesti.	The king gave such a mighty blow of such great strength, he struck Ásmundur, he fell off his horse.
23. Ásmundur stoyttist í jørðina niður, sum hann var vanur at gera, út kom kongins dýra drottning, væl kann rúnir skera.	Ásmundur plunged to the ground, as he was want to do, out came the king's dear queen, who can carve runes well.
24. Hon tók frá honum møðið alt og alt hans illsku grand, sjónligur var hann hvørjum manni, einki har hann vann.	She took all the mead from him and all his ability to do wicked harm, he was visible to everyone, he has not won anything.[10]
25. Dvørgurin spennir sín hest við spora, rætt sum fuglur í ský, legði niður liðið alt og tók tað væna vív.	The dwarf spurs his horse, just as the bird in the sky, he felled the whole army and took the beautiful woman.
26. Hann legði niður alt hans lið og tók tað væna vív, kongurin misti góðs og land, behelt sítt egið lív.	He felled his whole army and took the beautiful woman, the king lost property and land, but kept his own life.
27. Hann legði niður alt hans lið og tók tað fljóð, hann átti, eina ríður kongurin aftur at sínum slotti.	He felled his whole army and took the woman that belonged to him, the king rides alone back to his castle.
28. Ein kom maður í hallina inn, smílist undir lín: "Nú kemur Sjúrður Sigmundarson og Høgni bróðir tín."	One man came into the hall, secretly smiling: "Now comes Sjúrður Sigmundarson and your brother Høgni."
29. "Vælkomin Høgni, bróðir mín! tú hevur so drúgvant riðið, tapt er bæði land og vív og so tað valdra liðið."	"Welcome Høgni my brother! You have ridden for so long, both land and woman are lost and the army of outstanding men."

10 Ásmundur has embarrassed himself.

30. "Eg havi farið um lond og ríki, men Virgar eg ikki fann, hann reið seg at biðja moy so langt í fremmanda land."	"I have travelled around lands and kingdoms, but I haven't found Virgar, he rode to a foreign land so far away to propose to a maiden."[11]
31. Svaraði Sjúrður Sigmundarson, mælir av tungum inna: "Vit skulum ríða á bergið fram tann dvørgakong at finna."	Sjúrður Sigmundarson answered, saying: "We shall ride forth to the cliff to find that dwarf king."
32. Árla var um morgunin, sólin skein bjørt á heiði, riðu so á bergið fram fast av miklari reiði.	Early in the morning, the sun shone brightly on the heath, then they rode to the cliff though in great anger.
33. Sjúrður gekk at hellisdurum, var ikki gott at finna, unti sær ikki upp at lata, klývur tað stálið stinna.	Sjúrður walked to the doors of the cavern, it wasn't easy to find, he didn't succeed in opening the door, he split the sturdy steel.
34. Moyggin sat fyri breiða borði, dvørgur í smiðju stendur: "Ofta er best frá monnum longst, enn tit skuldu verið frændur."	The maiden sat at a wide table, the dwarf stood in the smithy: "Often it is best to be a long way from men rather than to be their friends."
35. "Frændur eru vit ikki í dag, tó lata vit tær stevna, til tess eru vit higar komnir bróður sakir at hevna.	"We aren't friends today, even though we have come to meet you, because of this we have come here to avenge our brother's affairs.[12]
36. Kongurin flutti moynna heim, tað var so mikil vandi, tú hevur vogið liðið alt og røvað tað heila landið."	The king took the maiden home, there was such great danger, you have killed all the troops and have pillaged the whole land."
37. Dvørgurin klæðir seg við stál bæði til hond og fót, riðu so frá hellisborg burt í oyðin skóg.	The dwarf clothes himself in steel, both hands and feet, he then rode away from the cavern fortress to a desolate forest.

11 The final two lines are reversed in the Faroese, and we have put them this way round to preserve sense in the English translation.

12 This must be Høgni speaking.

38. Høgni gav so stórt eitt høgg, frá man fræ ttast víða, ikki beit svørð á stáli stinna, dvørgurin hevði smíðað.	Høgni gave such a great blow, it has been told about far and wide, the sword didn't bite into the sturdy steel that the dwarf had forged.
39. Riðu saman á grønum vølli, er mær ei á tí hól, síðan stríddust kempur tvær fult í tímar tólv.	They clashed on the green field, I am not exaggerating, then the two heroes fought for a full twelve hours.
40. Dagurin tók at kvølda, fellur yvir døgg, Høgni sterki undan dreiv, eitt spring for hvørt eitt høgg.	The day turned to evening, dew was falling, the strong Høgni gave ground, one leap for every blow.
41. Høgni fell av hesti niður, møðin at honum seig, Sjúrður bindur hjálm á seg árla í sólarreið.	Høgni fell off the horse, he had become tired, Sjúrður fastens on his helmet early in the sunrise.
42. Sjúrður gav so stórt eitt høgg, frá man fræ ttast víða, ikki beit svørð á stáli stinna, dvørgurin hevði smíðað.	Sjúrður gave such a great blow, it has been told about far and wide, the sword didn't bite into the sturdy steel that the dwarf had forged.
43. Riðu saman á grønum vølli, er mær [ei] á tí hól, síðan stríddust kempur tvær fult í tímar tólv.	They clashed on the green field, I am not exaggerating, then the two heroes fought for a full twelve hours.
44. Síðan stríddust kempur tvær hendan dag til enda, tyngist svørð í Sjúrðar hondum, tekur spjótum at senda.	Then the two heroes fought to the end of this day, the sword is becoming heavy in Sjúrður's hands, he begins to throw spears.
45. Kastar hann eitt, og kastar hann tvey, og kastaði hann tað triðja. Dvørgurin tók mót øllum teim, hann kendi ei til sviða.	He throws one, and he throws two, and he threw the third. The dwarf caught all of them,[13] he didn't feel any pain.

13 This may mean that he was hit by them all.

46. Sjúrður vá upp sín bitra brand, tó hendur bóru hin seinan, feldi hann yvir dvørga høvur, einki varð honum at meini.	Sjúrður struck with his sharp sword, though he bore rather it late,[14] he let it fall over the dwarf's head, nothing caused him any injury.
47. Dvørgurin gav so stórt eitt høgg, tað hoyrdist út í Frans, høggur niður í Sjúrðar høvur hjálm av høvdi hans.	The dwarf gave such a great blow, it was heard all the way in France, strikes down on Sjúrður's head and knocks his helmet off.
48. Dvørgurin gav so stórt eitt høgg, Sjúrði ætlaði tað, spretti brynju av baki hans, so Grani fell á knæ.	The dwarf gave such a great blow, as Sjúrður's intended, he split the armour off his back,[15] so that Grani fell on his knees.
49. Sjúrður reiggjar svørðið umkring bæði av grimd og reiði, klývur av honum skjøldarnar, rivnaði brynjan breiða.	Sjúrður swings his sword around, both with ferocity and wrath,[16] he splits the shields, the large armour cracked.
50. Dvørgurin læt av skógnum standa, fingið hevði hann sár: "Hoyr tú, Sjúrður Sigmundarson, sigurin gevi eg tær!"	The dwarf stops the fight in the forest, he had received a wound: "Listen, Sjúrður Sigmundarson, I give you the victory!"
51. Riðu teir til hallar heim, Høgni og Sjúrður svein, sum hin fagra dvørgamoyggin situr í borgum ein.	They rode home to the hall, Høgni and Sjúrður svein, where the beautiful dwarf maiden sits alone in the castle.
52. Bjørt sat frú við breiða borð og sýir tað hvíta lín, Sjúrður flutti hana úr høll og so tað gull í skrín.	The fair lady sat at a wide table and sews the white linen, Sjúrður took her from the hall and the gold in the chest as well.
53. Hann setti hana upp á hests síns bak og førdi hana heim til halla, tók bæði skart og skreyt, nú man ríman falla.	He put her on the back of his horse and led her home to the hall, took her in both pomp and circumstance, now the ballad will end.

14 Sjúrður is late to the battle, since Høgni has been fighting by himself.

15 This is the dwarf splitting the armour off Sjúrður.

16 Now that Grani is on his knees, Sjúrður is at the same level as the dwarf and is able to hit him hard with his sword. This is what Sjúrður planned.

54. Hann flutti hana ikki í Júkagarð, men heim í høll til sín: "Høgni, heilsa konginum heim, at hetta er lønin mín!"	He did not take her to Júki's court, but home to his own hall:[17] "Høgni, send a greeting home to the king, tell him that this is my reward."
55. Hann setti hana blant moyggjaskara, hóast hon vildi treyð, Ásmundi dugnaði hon sára væl, tá hann var staddur í neyð.	He put her in the crowd of maidens, even though she was unwilling, she aided Ásmundur very well, when he was in peril.
56. Høgni átti ein son av sær, hann bar faðirs navn, inntil hann vá Artala kong, sum víða gongur [av] sagn.	Høgni had a son, he has his father's name, until he defeated King Artala, as tales famously tell.
57. Inntil hann vá Artala kong, sum víða gongur [av] sagn, vant hann upp síni silkisegl og sigldi so inn í havn.	Until he defeated King Artala, as tales famously tell, he hoisted his silk sail, and sailed into the harbour.
58. Hann sigldi inn á eina maka havn, har legði hann seg við frið, inntil hevndar sakir vóru, brynjaði hann sítt lið.	He sailed into a quiet harbour, there he laid in peace, until the quarrel was avenged, he armoured his troops.
59. Síðan kallaði hann Aldrias, tí honum var eingin at ráða; hann var ungur og óstiltur í sjálvsins ráði draga.	After that he was called Aldrias, because none could rule over him; he was young and impetuous following his own decisions.[18]
60. Ráddi hann fyri Húnalandi eftir Artans deyða, kallaði hann Ásmund Aldriansson, tí hann bar kinn so reyða.	He ruled over Húnaland after Artan's death, he was called Ásmundur Aldriansson, because his cheeks were so red.

17 The king would have been expecting Sjúrður to bring the maiden home to him, but Sjúrður takes her away for himself.

18 This literally means he followed his own advice.

ÁSA THE DWARF MAIDEN OR DWARF MAIDEN III (ÁSA DVØRGAMOY OR DVØRGAMOY III)

1. Árla var um morgunin,
sólin skín so víða,
Sjúrður klæðist for síni song,
hann býr seg út at ríða.

Early in the morning,
the sun shone so widely,
Sjúrður gets dressed in front of his bed,
he readies himself to ride.

2. Sjúrður reið á skógvin fram
eystur um heyggin brúna,
opnan sá hann gullsal,
og gullið læk í túni.

Sjúrður rode into the forest
east of the brown mound,
he saw a golden hall open,
and the gold spilled out into the courtyard.

3. Túnið var av marmorsteini,
hurðar av fílabeini,
hongslini vóru [av] syfrisviði,
bjálkar av sildarteini.

The courtyard was made of marble,
the doors of ivory,
the hinges were of cedarwood,[1]
the beams of strips of silver.[2]

4. Har vóru hurðar av syfrisvið,
málar við ídningshorni,
glógvar so gull í gøtum har,
sum ljómur av havrakorni.

There were doors of cederwood,
decorated with horn,[3]
gold shines on the roads there,
like the glistening of an oat grain.[4]

5. Sjúrður hugsar við sjálvum sær:
"Úti skal eg ikki standa,
antin her búgva fólk ella trøll,
her fari eg inn at ganga."

Sjúrður thinks to himself:
"I shall not stand outside,
whether people or trolls live here,
I shall go in here."

6. Sjúrður gekk í hallina inn,
skín sum fonnin hvíta,
dvørgamoyggin fyri sat,
innilig at líta.

Sjúrður walked into the hall,
shining like white snow,
the dwarf maiden sat before him
beautiful[5] to look at.

---

1 í Króki (*Sandoyarbók*, vol. 2, p. 157n3) notes that *sifrisi* should be read *syprisviði.*

2 í Króki (*Sandoyarbók*, vol. 2, p. 157n4) notes that *sildarteinur* should read *silvdarteini.*

3 According to Hammershaimb and Jakobsen, *Færøsk anthologi*, vol. 2, p. 137, this is an indeterminable type of horn.

4 The line here is *sum ljómur av havrakorni. Ljómur* in modern Faroese would mean "sound," but clearly shining gold cannot be compared to the sound of an oat grain. We have preferred to understand it as meaning something closer to the Old Norse *ljómi*, meaning "beam, ray, radiance," and this is also the interpretation found in Hammershaimb, *Sjúrðar Kvæði*, 191.

5 We have used the reading from B. Grundtvig and Bloch, *Føroya kvæði*, vol. 1, p. 287, st. 11, *unnilig*, since *inniligur* (meaning in a heartfelt way) does not make sense here.

7. Svaraði Ása dvørgamoyggj: "Tú ert ikki borin at standa," snúgvuliga úr sessi brá, bar honum stól til handa.	Ása the dwarf maiden said: "You are too highborn to stand,"[6] she rose from the seat quickly, and carried a chair to him.
8. "Mangur hevur á skógvin riðið frúur at biðja sær, higar er eingin komin tann, líknast hevur at tær."	"Many have ridden through the forest to ask for a lady's hand, none have come here that can be compared to you."
9. Hon fylgdi honum í gullsal, hildust tey um hendur: "Her kannst tú við eygum sjá, hvør vítt mín sal er rendur.	She led him to the golden hall, they held each other's hands: "Here you can see with your own eyes, how extensively my hall is edged with gold.[7]
10. Hoyr tað, Sjúrður Sigmundarson, tú ert so nýtur drongur, her kannst tú við eygum sjá, hvør vítt mín salin gongur."	Listen, Sjúrður Sigmundarson, you are such a brave hero, here you can see with your eyes, how spacious my hall is."
11. "Hoyr tú, Ása dvørgamoyggin, fagra og so fríða, hvussu eita teir garpar tveir, á henda skógvin ríða?"	"Listen, Ása dwarf maiden, so fair and beautiful, what are the two warriors named who ride in this forest?"
12. "Hálvdan og hann Eirikur her hava riðið leingi, ríða seg í Ásgarðar at royna Óðins dreingir.	"Hálvdan and Eirikur have ridden here for a long time, they are riding to Ásgarðar to test Óðin's heroes.
13. Hálvdan og hann Eirikur her hava riðið á sinni, ríða seg í Ásgarðar at hitta Óðin inni.	Hálvdan and Eirikur have ridden here before, they are riding to Ásgarðar to meet Óðin inside.

6 This line literally means "you are not born to stand," which we interpret to mean too highborn to stand.

7 That gold edges the hall here is our interpretation, as *rendur* is often used as in *rendur í gullið*.

14. Tað er so vant í tygara landi, har blæs vindur og kavi, ríður so mangur einsamallur, hann rænar tygara fæ.	It is so bad[8] in your land, where wind and snow blow,[9] so many ride alone that steal your property.[10]
15. Tað er so vant í tygara landi, har blæs veður og vindur, betri er í gullborgum ást við meg at binda."	It is so bad in your land, where weather and wind blow, it is better to fall in love with me in golden castles."[11]
16. "Hoyr tú, Ása dvørgamoyggin, tað mást tú ei stunda, eg gifti ikki óðal mítt burtur á heidnar grundir.	"Listen, Ása dwarf maiden, you must not long for that, I won't marry my ancestral property[12] away on heathen earth.
17. Hoyr tað, Ása dvørgamoyggin, tað mást tú ei vænta, eg gifti ikki óðal mítt burt á heidna landa."	Listen, Ása dwarf maiden, you must not expect that, I won't marry my ancestral property away in heathen lands."
18. Tað var Ása dvørgamoyggin, øll í gulli glæsti, hon gekk seg at gullkistu, upp við mentum læsti.	It was Asa the dwarf maiden, who shone all in gold, she went to a golden chest, and unlocked it with dexterity.
19. Hon sendi honum klæðini, glógva sum gullið reyða: "Ei man *nakar í tygara landi tílíkar mentir eiga.	She passed him the clothes, they shine as red gold: "None in your land have such skills.[13]

8 *Vant* should be *vánt* (from *vándur*), meaning bad.

9 The first two lines of the stanza are formulaic.

10 We have taken this reading from variant B of the ballad. Grundtvig and Bloch, *Føroya kvæði*, vol. 1, p. 287, st. 25. What it literally says here is "so many ride alone, he steals your property."

11 The final two lines of the stanza are the other way round in the Faroese, but we have reversed them here to preserve meaning in the English translation. These lines are also formulaic.

12 *Óðal* is allodial property.

13 This seems to mean that none would be skilled enough to make such clothes.

20. So væl mást tú tey klæði slíta,
glógva sum gullið reyða,
leingi hava ligið á kistubotni
eftir tann Dagmors deyða."

You must wear out those clothes well,[14]
they shine like red gold,
they have lain at the bottom of the chest
since Dagmor's death."

21. Svaraði Sjúrður Sigmundarson,
gull ber seg á hand:
"Eg føri ikki heiðin klæði
aftur í vára land."

Sjúrður Sigmundarson answered,
carrying gold on his arm:[15]
"I will not bring heathen clothes
back to our land."

22. Hon gav honum brynjuna,
gjørd var av silvuri hvíta:
"Tak við, Sjúrður Sigmundarson,
vita um tú mant nýta!"

She gave him the armour,
it was made of white silver:
"Take this, Sjúrður Sigmundarson,
see if you might make use of it!"

23. Svaraði Sjúrður Sigmundarson,
gull ber seg á hand:
"Eg føri ikki heidna brynju
aftur í vára land."

Sjúrður Sigmundarson answered,
carrying gold on his arm:
"I will not bring heathen armour
back to our land."

24. Svaraði Ása dvørgamoyggin,
fagra og hin fríða:
"Dvølst í nátt og ver hjá mær,
í morgin skalt tú ríða."

Ása the dwarf maiden answered,
the fair and beautiful one:
"Stay tonight and be with me,
you shall ride tomorrow."

25. "Eg dvøljist ikki longur hjá tær,
enn drekka skal moyggja minni,
skunda lati eg míni ferð,
vit hittast annað sinni."

"I will not stay any longer with you,
but shall drink to the memory of maidens,
I will hurry on my journey,
we will meet again another time."

26. Sjúrður svav í heygnum,
tað var alt so brátt,
hann gat barn við dvørgamoynni
á teirri somu nátt.

Sjúrður slept in the mound,
it was all so sudden,
he conceived a child with the dwarf maiden
on the same night.

27. Árla var um morgunin,
sólin skín so víða,
Sjúrður klæðist for síni song,
hann býr seg út at ríða.

Early in the morning,
the sun shone far and wide,
Sjúrður dressed before his bed,
he readies himself to ride.

---

14 He must wear these clothes until they are completely worn out, because they are so valuable.

15 These are arm rings.

28. "Nær skal eg bryggja, nær skal eg blanda vín, nær skal eg tín aftur vænta, Sjúrður, at vitja mín?"	"When shall I brew, when shall I mix wine, when shall I expect you, Sjúrður, to visit me?"
29. "Væl mást tú bryggja, væl mást tú mjøðin blanda, tá triði máni úti er, skalt tú meg aftur vænta."	"You must brew well, you must mix the mead well, when the third month has passed, you shall expect me."
30. Sjúrður fór av høllini út, heldur sær á gleim, tá var Grani burtur lopin, hann skuldi ríða heim.	Sjúrður went out of the hall, he was in a cheerful mood, Grani had run away, but he should ride home.
31. Sjúrður fór av høllini út, heldur sær á gleim, tá var Grani burtur lopin, hann skuldi ríða heim.	Sjúrður went out of the hall, he was in a cheerful mood, Grani had run away, but he should ride home.
32. "Eg skal læna tær hestin tann, inniligur at ríða, so loypur hann yvir dalir og fjøll, sum aðrir í grøna líða.	"I shall lend you that horse, good to ride, he leaps over valleys and mountains, as others do over green slopes.
33. Ríð honum heilur og happadrúgvur, tað er ikki vandi, sjáldan loysti faðir mín falkan tann úr bandi.	Ride him healthy and happy, there is no danger, my father seldom untied that horse[16] from its tethers.
34. Ríð honum heilur og happadrúgvur, bæði við gleði og gleim, tá tú kemur úr skógnum út, tú sært tín fola ein."	Ride him healthy and happy, both with happiness and cheerfulness, when you come out of the forest, you will see your foal."
35. Hon fylgdi honum so langt á leið, bað honum góðan dag: "Far væl, heilur og happadrúgvur, alt gangi tær væl!"	She went with him so far on the way, wished him a good day: "Fare well, be healthy and happy, may everything go well for you!"
36. Hon fylgdi honum so langt á leið, bað honum góðan frið: "Far væl, heilur og happadrúgvur, alt gangi tær við!"	She went with him so far on the way, wished him peace: "Fare well, be healthy and happy, may everything go your way!"

---

16 *Falkur* is a *heiti* used in ballads for horse. It can also mean falcon (the literal meaning) or, in ballads, ship.

37. Sjúrður reið eftir vegnum fram,
bæði við gleði og gleim,
tá hann kom úr skógnum út,
hann sá sín fola ein.

Sjúrður rode along the road
both in happiness and cheerfulness,
when he came out of the forest,
he saw his foal.

38. Tað er Sjúrður Sigmundarson,
tungu ber hann snjalla:
"Eg veit mær eingi *sviðri[17] ráð
enn ríða heim til halla."

It is Sjúrður Sigmundarson,
he is so eloquent:
"I know of no worse advice,
than to ride home to the hall."

39. Sjúrður skuldi til hallar ríða,
frá man frættast víða,
hann sær mann úr fjalli koma,
brádliga mót sær líða.

Sjúrður was going to ride to the hall,
such is told far and wide,
he sees a man come down from the
mountain,
suddenly heading towards him.

40. Har kom ein so grimmur risi,
Sjúrður ikki kendi,
hann hevði eygað eitt í heysi,
finskan boga í hendi.

There came such a gruesome giant,
Sjúrður didn't realize,
he had one eye in his head,
and a Finnish bow in his hand.

41. Sjúrður skuldi til hallar ríða,
mátti aftur venda,
risin skeyt sína stong í vøll,
tá mátti kappin standa.

Sjúrður was going to ride to the hall,
he had to turn back,
the giant shot his long spear into the field,
then the hero had to stop.

42. Svaraði Sjúrður Sigmundarson,
mælir á tungu inna:
"Lova mær til hallar heim,
vit hittast annað sinni."

Sjúrður Sigmundarson answered,
saying:
"Let me go home to the hall,
we'll meet another time."

43. Risin so til veitslu tekur,
mælir í fyrsta orði:
"Tú nært ikki til hallar heim,
og ikki av einum spori.

The giant then begins to speak,
he first speaks these words:
"You won't make it home to the hall,
and not one step further.[18]

44. Tí tú hevur sovið hjá
dvørgamoynni,
ikki sagt mær frá,
har for skalt tú, Sjúrður,
ikki til hallar ná!"

Because you have slept with the
dwarf maid,
and not told me about it before,
that's why, Sjúrður, you won't
make it to the hall!"

---

17 í Króki (*Sandoyarbók*, vol. 2, p. 159n2) states that in the manuscript this word is *sigri* and notes that CCF has *sviðri*, while the edition suggests *siðri* as the correct reading, meaning "worse" (cf. the Icelandic adjective in the comparative *síðri*).

18 This is how Hammershaimb (*Sjúrðar Kvæði*, 193) understands this line.

45. Risin gevur høggini tung, sum tey varpa grót, stundum flýddi kappin undan, stundum helt ímót.	The giant gives heavy blows, that send rocks flying, at times the hero dodged, at times he fought back.
46. Sjúrður skuldi til hallar ganga, tykist komin í treyt, tað var tann svarti fjallatussi, stongina á hann skeyt.	Sjúrður was going to go to the hall, he seemed to have got into trouble, it was the black mountain giant, he hurled his lance at him.[19]
47. Sjúrður skuldi til hallar ganga, mátti venda aftur, tá kom Grani leypandi, varð honum við tað lætt.	Sjúrður was going to go to the hall, had to turn back, then Grani came running, with that it became easy for him.
48. Tá kom Grani leypandi, jørð við hógvar tróð, gæsar uppi við høvdinum, aftur á herðar stóð.	Then Grani came running, with his hoofs he trod the ground, he tears along with his head back to his shoulders.
49. Tá kom Grani leypandi, hansara sporar ringja, snarliga vendi síðu til, Sjúrður í saðil springa.	Then Grani came running, his footsteps[20] ringing, he quickly turned side on, Sjúrður leapt into the saddle.
50. Sjúrður leyp í saðilin upp yvir leysan loga, studdi seg hvørki við skjøld ei svørð, ei við saðilbuga.	Sjúrður leapt up into the saddle over loose flame,[21] supported himself with neither shield nor sword, nor with saddle bow.
51. "Tú gert einki at brigða mær dvørgamoynna at gifta, nú skal eg, tín fjallatussi, høggum við teg skifta!"	"You do nothing by reproaching me for marrying the dwarf maid, now I shall exchange blows with you you mountain giant!"[22]

19 The giant hurled his lance at Sjúrður.

20 Here we have interpreted *sporar* to mean footsteps rather than spurs, which would be the other reading, since it seems to refer to the horse.

21 The first two lines of the stanza are formulaic and the stanza as a whole can be found in other ballads (with the name of the character replaced). "Loose flame" seems to mean flickering flames that are high.

22 These two lines are reversed in Faroese, but we have exchanged them to preserve the meaning in English translation.

52. Bardust fullar tógva dagar, hvørgin sigur fekk, inntil tann hin triðja, ið sól til viða gekk.	They fought for two full days, neither was victorious, until that third day, as the sun was setting.
53. Bardust fullar tógva dagar, hvørgin sigur vann, inntil tann hin triðja, ið sól til viða rann.	They fought for two full days, neither was victorious, until that third day, as the sun went down.
54. Risin sipar jarnstongina, tað var alt so fast, Grani kundi skáka væl, hann misti fyrsta kast.	The giant threw the iron lance, it was so hard,[23] Grani could turn and twist well, he missed the first throw.
55. Sjúrður rendi mót risanum, øllum tókti undur, høgg so tann hin grimma risa í miðjum kníggjum sundur.	Sjúrður went against the giant, everyone thought it a miracle, then he chopped that gruesome giant in two at mid-knee.
56. Tað var tann svarti fjallatussi, læt ikki á sær finna, stubbarnar setti hann niður í jørð, hann bardist ikki minna.	It was the black mountain giant, he didn't let it show, he planted the stumps on the ground, he didn't fight any worse for it.
57. Tað var Sjúrður Sigmundarson, sínum svørði brá, hann kleyv tann hin grimma risa sundur í lutir tvá.	It was Sjúrður Sigmundarson, he brandished his sword, he chopped that gruesome giant into two pieces.
58. Tað er Sjúrður Sigmundarson, heldur sær á gleim, síðani tað ríður hann aftur til hallar heim.	It was Sjúrður Sigmundarson, he was in a cheerful mood, after that he rides back home to the hall.
59. Sjúrður gekk í hallina inn, var so síðla á kvøldi, Hjalprekur fyri borði situr við sítt dreingjaveldi.	Sjúrður went into the hall, it was so late in the evening, Hjalprekur sits at the table with his group of heroes.

23 The giant threw the spear very hard.

60. Hjalprekur kongur til orða tekur við sítt dreingjaveldi: "Hoyr tað, Sjúrður Sigmundarson, hvar hevur tú verið á kvøldi?"	King Hjalprekur says with his group of heroes: "Listen, Sjúrður Sigmundarson, where have you been for the evening?"
61. Sjúrður svarar honum aftur, frá man frættast víða: "Møtti mær ein fjallatussi, hann beyð mær at stríða."	Sjúrður answers back to him, it is told far and wide: "I met a mountain giant, he challenged me to fight."
62. Sjúrður svarar honum aftur við allskyns makt og meingi: "Møtti mær ein fjallatussi, hann dvaldi meg so leingi."	Sjúrður answers back to him with all kinds of might and strength:[24] "I met a mountain giant, he delayed me for so long."
63. Árla var um morgunin, sólin skín so víða, Sjúrður klæðist for síni song, hann býr seg út at ríða.	Early in the morning, the sun shone so widely, Sjúrður dressed before his bed, he readies himself to ride.
64. Sjúrður reið á skógvin fram eystur um heyggin brúna, opnan sá hann gullsal, gullið læk í túni.	Sjúrður rode through the forest east of the brown mound, he saw the golden hall open, the gold spilled into the courtyard.
65. Sjúrður gekk í hallina inn aftur í sama heyg, tá sá hann, hvar dvørgamoyggin lá har inni deyð.	Sjúrður went into the hall, back into the same mound, then he saw where the dwarf maiden lay dead in there.
66. Gróv hann hana í heyggin niður, so er greint ífrá, mikið gull og mentarsnót legði hann henni hjá.	He buried her down in the mound, so I've been told, a fine woman, and much gold he lay by her.
67. Og so mundi hann hjá henni grava moybarnið tað hitt fríða, síðan mundi Sjúrður aftur til hallar ríða.	And by her he buried the beautiful girl-child,[25] then Sjúrður rode back to the hall.

24 We have interpreted *meingi* as likely referring to *megi*, meaning "strength." The reading of *meingi* in the sense of "multitude" makes no sense here.

25 This is Sjúrður's daughter.

THE BALLAD OF KVØRFINN OR DWARF MAIDEN V (KVØRFINNS TÁTTUR OR DVØRGAMOY V)

1. Tíðrikur situr á Brattingsborg, hann skín sum reyðargull, nú skal ríma eitt dvørgafrøði, nú gerst mín ríma full.	Tíðrikur sits in Brattingsborg, he shines like red gold, now I will compose verses on the theme of dwarves, now my ballad-composing is concluded.
2. Tíðrikur situr á Brattingsborg, hann sær seg út so víða: "Nú lystir meg á Birtingsskóg á heiðinmark at ríða."	Tíðrikur sits in Brattingsborg, he looks out far and wide: "Now I want to go to Birtingsskógur to ride to the heathen forest."
3. Svaraði Virgar Valintsson fyrsta orðið tá: "Ríður tú á Birtingsskóg, tú kemur har ikki frá."	Virgar Valintsson answered the first word then: "If you ride to Birtingsskógur, you won't escape from there."
4. Út varð loystur gangarin, Tíðrikur skuldi at ríða, heima sat Virgar Valintsson eina so lítla tíð.	The steed was untethered, Tíðrikur was going to ride, Virgar Valintsson sat at home for a short while.
5. Heima sat Virgar Valintsson eina so lítla stund, hann læt saðla Skemming tá, reið á sín harras fund.	Virgar Valintsson sat at home for a little while, then he had Skemmingur saddled, and rode to find his lord.
6. Virgar steig á Skemmings bak við Mimaring í hendi. Skemmingur stóð á grønum vølli, á Birtingsskóg hann rendi.	Virgar stepped on Skemmingur's back with Mimaring[1] in his hand, Skemmingur stood on the green field, he ran to Birtingsskógur.
7. Tað var Virgar Valintsson, á Skemmings bak hann steig, Skemming rendi á Birtingsskóg, hann kongin aftur reið.	It was Virgar Valintsson, he mounted onto Skemmingur's back, Skemmingur ran to Birtingsskógur, he caught up with the king.

1 This is the name of Virgar's sword.

8. Tað svaraði hann Tíðrikur, tá ið hann Virgar kendi: "Hvør er hesin av Tíðriks gørpum, ið meg aftur rendi?"	Tíðrikur answered with this, when he recognized Virgar: "Which of Tíðrikur's heroes is this, who caught up with me?"
9. Svaraði Virgar Valintsson, hann sá yvir skógin fríða: "Eg læt saðla mær Skemming tá, eg vildi ikki heima bíða."	Virgar Valintsson answered, he looked over the beautiful forest: "I had Skemmingur saddled, I didn't want to wait at home."
10. Ríða teir á Birtingsskóg, søgur ganga frá, Tíðrikur biður hestar hvíla: "Vit skulu á skógin gá!"	They ride to Birtingsskógur as the story relates, Tíðrikur orders the horses to rest: "We shall walk into the forest!"
11. Lógu teir á Birtingsskóg eina so lítla stund, vaknaði Virgar Valintsson, hann hoyrdi hestadund.	They lay in Birtingsskógur for a little while, Virgar Valintsson woke up, he heard the rumbling of horses.
12. Virgar leyp á Skemmings bak, einki óttast hann tá, hann sær eina so mikla kempu ríða sær skamt ífrá.	Virgar leapt on to Skemmingur's back, he feared nothing then, he sees such a mighty a giant ride not far away from him.
13. Virgar leyp á Skemmings bak, á sítt svørð hann lítur: "Nú skal taka til Mimaring, og vita, hvussu bítur."	Virgar leapt on Skemmingur's back, he trusts his sword: "Now I will take Mimaring, and see how well it bites."[2]
14. Tað var Virgar Valintsson, læt at skógum standa, møtti eina mikla kempu, fátt kundi henni granda.	It was Virgar Valintsson, he went for the forest,[3] he met a mighty giant, few could hurt it.
15. Svaraði Virgar Valintsson, hann sá tann mikla mann: "Hví ríður tú í Birtingsskóg í mín harras land?"	Virgar Valintsson said, he saw the mighty man: "Why do you ride in Birtingsskógur on my lord's land?"

2 Literally "how it bites."

3 He goes into the forest.

16. Yvrið dró at Sjúrða unga,
søgur ganga frá,
hann hevði upp sítt búgvið svørð,
hann tað í loftið brá.

Young Sjúrður became incensed,
so stories tell,
he raised his readied sword,
he swung it through the air.

17. Sjúrður brá sínum bitra brandi,
hann royndi góðar gripir,
Virgar situr á Skemmings baki
loftaði hvørja sipu.

Sjúrður brandished his sharp sword,
he uses good arms,
Virgar sits on Skemmingur's back,
he caught every blow.

18. Tá vaknaði hann Tíðrikur,
hann hoyrir brandar falla,
tekur hann til sítt góða svørð,
hann letur á Virgar kalla.

Then Tíðrikur woke up,
he heard swords falling,
he takes his good sword,
he calls on Virgar.

19. Enntá óttast Tíðrikur,
hann hoyrir brandar syngja,
burtur var Virgar Valintsson
við hesti og Mimaringi.

Even Tíðrikur is afraid,
he hears the swords sing,
Virgar Valintsson is gone
with horse and sword.

20. Sjúrður høgdi ógvuliga,
væl mundi Grammur duga,
flýgur so eldur úr Virgars brynju,
at skógurin stóð í loga.

Sjúrður hacked so terribly,
Grammur[4] was very capable,
such sparks fly from Virgar's armour,
that the forest was in flames.

21. Tíðrikur læt til hallar standa,
heim av skógnum fer,
gloymdi eftir á Birtingsskóg
bæði skjøld og svørð.

Tíðrikur went for the hall,
goes home from the forest,
in Birtingskógur he forgot
both shield and sword.

22. Sjúrður høgdi ógvuliga,
inntil hann var móður,
settist niður á grønan vøll,
men ikki vóru dreingir fróir.

Sjúrður hacked so terribly.
until he was tired,
he sat himself down on the green field,
but the heroes weren't happy.

23. Svaraði Virgar Valintsson,
í víggi hevði staðið:
"Siga skalt tú mær, mikli maður,
hvar ert tú av frænda ræði?"

Virgar Valintsson said,
he had been in battle:
"You have to tell me, mighty man,
which family are you from?"

4 This is the name of Sjúrður's sword.

24. "Sjúrða skalt tú nevna meg,
eg sigi tær satt ífrá,
næsti maður Hjalprek kongi
bæði í gulli og ráði.

"You shall call me Sjúrður,
I tell you truthfully,
the closest man[5] to King Hjalprekur,
in both gold and authority.

25. Grani eitur gangari mín,
Sjúrða skalt tú meg nevna,
næsti maður Hjalprek kongi
bæði til gulls og evna."

Grani is the name of my steed,
you shall call me Sjúrður,
the closest man to King Hjalprekur
in both gold and ability."

26. Svaraði Virgar Valintsson
av so tungum bræði:
"Hevði tú høgt við Mimaringi,
eg hevði tær ikki bestaðið."

Virgar Valintsson answered
with such heavy resentment:
"Had you cut with Mimaring,
I would not have withstood you."[6]

27. Svaraði Sjúrður Sigmundarsonur,
tá ið hann Virgar kendi:
"Hvar er sjálvur Tíðrikur,
ið teg higar sendi?"

Sjúrður Sigmundarsonur answered,
when he recognized Virgar:
"Where is Tíðrikur himself
who sent you here?"

28. Svaraði Virgar Valintsson,
hann kann væl orðum greina:
"Tíðrikur er á skógnum burtur
við allar sínar sveinar."

Virgar Valintsson answered,
he can relate words well:
"Tíðrikur is in the forest
with all of his warriors."

29. Svaraði Virgar Valintsson,
hann læt so orðum byrja:
"Nú skal ríða for Tíðrik heim,
og fleiri sømdir spyrja."

Virgar Valintsson answered,
he started his words like so:
"Now we shall ride to Tíðrikur's home,
to gain more honour."

30. Svaraði Sjúrður Sigmundarson,
hann skeyt tann leik av hendi:
"Tað er eingin á Brattingsborg,
mínum gangara torir at venda."

Sjúrður Sigmundarson answered,
he pushed that dispute to the side:
"There is no one on Brattingsborg,
that dares to turn my steed away."

31. Sjáldan skiljast leikir væl,
geri tað ei at loyna:
Sjúrður og Virgar Valintsson,
teir mundu hvør annan royna.

Disputes seldom end well,
it is not to be kept a secret:
Sjúrður and Virgar Valintsson,
they tested each other.

---

5 The man next in line in terms of power and wealth.

6 Virgar is mocking Sjúrður that he has the better sword.

32. So eru orð við ráðum greind, tó ei er um at røða: Sjúrður og Virgar Valintsson hvør mundi annan møða.	Words are expounded as advice, though there is no reason to speak about this: Sjúrður and Virgar Valintsson each tired out the other.
33. So eru orð við ráðum greind, tó ei er um at dylja, ríða dyst við ókendar menn, og sjáldan væl at skilja.	Words are expounded as advice, though there is no reason to hide it, to ride and fight with unknown men, is seldomly to be understood well.
34. Svaraði Sjúrður Sigmundarson, hann mælir á sama sinni: "Vit skulu ríða á skógi fram og fleiri roysni vinna."	Sjúrður Sigmundarson, he speaks at the same time: "We shall ride through the forest and perform more great deeds."
35. Árla var um morgunin, sólin skín so víða. Sjúrður og Virgar Valintsson á heidnar markir ríða.	Early in the morning, the sun shone far and wide. Sjúrður and Virgar Valintsson ride in heathen forests.
36. Sterkir royna stinna alva, ei man teimum bella, hestar leypa, garpar flytast, jørð um bógvar fella.	The strong test the strength of the tough,[7] they will not be injured, horses run, heroes are carried, earth is thrown about the front legs.
37. Sterkir royna stinna alva, svørð við sporum draga, hestar leypa, garpar flytast, jørð um bógvar vaða.	The strong test the strength of the tough, they draw swords as well as spurs, horses run, heroes are carried, the front legs wade through earth.
38. Hestar leypa, garpar flytast, svørð við sporum ringja, *hjálmar skína, grímur stýra, gyltir hjálmar syngja.	Horses run, heroes are carried, they let swords as well as spurs ring, helmets shine, halters steer, golden helmets sing.
39. Ríða yvir Birtingsskóg á tí sama sinni, ei var annað tílíkt lið, dreingir leggja í minni.	They ride over Birtingsskógur at the same time, there was not another company like that, heroes commit it to memory.

7 Lyngbye suggests a literal translation of "Stærke prøve store Kræfter" (the strong try great strengths) for this line. Lyngbye, *Færøiske Qvæder*, 410n35.

40. Ríða yvir Birtingsskóg yvir mark og bleyta mýri, ei var annað tílíkt lið at sita til saðla dýra.	They ride over Birtingsskógur over forest and soft meer, there was not another company like that that sit in costly saddles.
41. Ríða yvir Birtingsskóg, sum risar í homrum byggja, dvørgar klæða fríðan sal, og trøll for fótum liggja.	They ride over Birtingsskógur, as giants live in crags, dwarves adorn the beautiful hall, and trolls lie under foot.
42. Síðla var um aftanin, dagurin tók at kvølda, drekar taka at ýla hátt, og úlvar taka at gella.	Early in the evening, the day turned to evening, dragons start to howl loudly, and wolf howls start to echo.
43. Úlvar taka at ýla hátt, tað dregur at myrkum æli, sóu hvørki himmal ella jørð, og neppa stig fyri saðli.	Wolves start to howl loudly, a dark storm approaches, they saw neither sky nor earth, and hardly a step in front of the saddle.
44. Sóu hvørki himmal ella jørð, og neppa stig fyri saðli, ei høvdu fleiri tílíkir garpar verið í verri vali.	They saw neither sky nor earth, and hardly a step in front of the saddle, other such heroes had not been on a worse battlefield.
45. At syngja tók í homrum hátt, risar halgir njóta, heitan eld við fótum troða, harðar málmar at bróta.	Singing started high in the crags, giants enjoy holy days, tread hot fire with their feet, to break hard ore.
46. Harðir steinar sundur sprungu, málmur við eitri rennur, drekar hamra stórar stengur, eldur í smiðju brennur.	Hard rocks cracked apart, ore runs with poison, dragons hammer great bars,[8] fire burns in the smithy.

8 The image here is of bars of metal that are hammered in a smithy (by dragons). Lyngbye translates this to giants (*risser*) doing the hammering. Lyngbye, *Færøiske Qvæder*, p. 415, st. 45, but the Faroese clearly says dragons, as it does in Lyngbye's Faroese text.

47. Drekar hamra stórar stengur,
gyltar brandar sleggja,
óttast Virgar Valintsson,
ilt var um at eggja.

Dragons hammer great bars,
pound golden swords,[9]
Virgar Valintsson is afraid,
evil was about to be instigated.

48. Svaraði Virgar Valintsson:
"Nú er aftur at venda."
So var svørð í slíðrum heitt,
teir kundu tað ikki henda.

Virgar Valintsson answered:
"Now we should turn back."
The sword was so hot in its scabbard
that they couldn't hold it.

49. Svaraði Sjúrður Sigmundarson,
hann læt so orðum byrja:
"Latið tað ikki frættast heim,
for Tíðriks garpar spyrjast!"

Sjúrður Sigmundarson answered,
he let the words start like this:
"Don't let that get around at home,
for Tíðrikur's heroes to find out!"[10]

50. Svaraði Sjúrður Sigmundarson,
hann heldur á búnum stáli:
"Minni sigist for Tíðriks garpum,
dreingir gita við máli."

Sjúrður Sigmundarson answered,
he's grasping ornamented steel:
"Less than this can be told to
Tíðrikur's heroes,
heroes make conjectures with language."[11]

51. Svaraði Sjúrður Sigmundarson:
"Vit skulu á skógvin ríða,
hoyra fáa vit annan sang,
tá ið náttin tekur at liða."

Sjúrður Sigmundarson answered:
"We shall ride through the forest,
we will hear another song,
when the night nears it's end."

52. Ríða teir á skógvin fram,
myrkt var teimum fyri eyga,
komu at tí húsinum,
tað skín sum gullið reyða.

They ride through the forest,
it was dark before their eyes,
they came to the house,
that shone like red gold.

53. Svaraði Sjúrður Sigmundarson:
"Vit skulu hjá konum gista,
morgin skulu vit føra heim
alt tað, ið lív kann lysta!"

Sjúrður Sigmundarson answered:
"We shall stay the night with the women,
tomorrow we shall bring home
whatever we want!"

---

9 Here and below we have translated *sleggja* as pound, meaning "powerfully hammer."

10 Sjúrður is saying that it should not be known widely that Virgar wanted to turn back in st. 48 (i.e., that he was afraid).

11 Similarly to the stanza above, Sjúrður is warning Virgar that if Tíðrikur's men hear about this, they will gossip about Virgar being afraid.

54. Svaraði Sjúrður Sigmundarson: "Vit fara ikki úti at standa, vit skulu gista her í nátt, í morgin royna branda!"	Sjúrður Sigmundarson answered: "We are not going to stand outside, we shall shall stay here tonight, tomorrow we shall test the swords!"
55. Svaraði Virgar Valintsson, hann tók tá til at tala: "Nú skal leggja hjálmar av, í morgin hestar saðla!"	Virgar Valintsson answered, he started to speak then: "Now we shall take off our helmets, tomorrow we will saddle our horses!"
56. Gingu teir í húsið inn, tað skein sum gullið reyða, sóu fyri borði standa mangar brandar beygar.	They went into the house, it shone like red gold, they saw standing before the table many beautiful swords.[12]
57. Sóu fyri borði standa mangar brandar beygar, sótu fyri moyar tvær, tær skína sum gullið reyða.	They saw standing before the table many beautiful swords. Two maidens sat there before them, they shine like red gold.
58. Sótu fyri moyar tvær, klæddar í silki smá, dýrur drykkur á borði stendur, søgur ganga frá.	Two maidens sat there before them, dressed in fine silk, costly drink stands on the table, so stories tell.
59. Sjúrður tók teir dýru drykkir, hann mundi ikki mangan biðja, stillar sótu moyar tvær, tað tókti teim best at tiga.	Sjúrður took the costly drinks, he wasn't used to waiting, the two maidens sat quiet, it seemed to them best to be silent.
60. Tað var Sjúrður Sigmundarson, hann læt so orðum byrja: "Hvør ræður fyri hesi borg? tað ráði eg fyrst at spyrja."	It was Sjúrður Sigmundarson, he started speaking: "Who rules this castle? I want to ask that first."
61. Svaraði Virgar Valintsson: "Vit skulu í borgum byggja, vilja tit ikki aftur svara, tit skulu fyri brondum liggja."	Virgar Valintsson answered: "We shall stay at the castle, if you don't answer, you shall be placed before the swords."

12 See note to st. 116 of *Brynhildar táttur* (pp. 62–63n70) for the difficulties in translating *brandar beygar*.

62. Svaraði onnur dvørgamoyin,
øll í gulli skín:
"Harri ræður fyri hesi borg
er Kvørfinn, faðir mín."

One of the dwarf maidens answered,
she shone all in gold:
"The lord who rules this castle
is my father Kvørfinn."

63. Svaraði Sjurður Sigmundarson,
ei var drongur ræddur:
"Er tín faðir á skógnum burtur,
ella er hann heima staddur?"

Sjúrður Sigmundarson answered,
the hero wasn't afraid:
"Is your father away in the forest,
or is he at home?"

64. "Faðir mín er á skógnum burtur,"
moyin tekur at telja,
"hvørja nátt við risar berjist,
málm úr homrum at velja."

"My father is away in the forest,"
the maiden starts to tell,
"every night he fights with giants,
to get ore from the crags."

65. Svaraði Virgar Valintsson,
hann sló tað upp í gleim:
"Nú skulu vit taka dvørgamoyar
og føra til hallar heim!"

Virgar Valintsson answered,
he brushes this off with glee:
"Now we shall take the dwarf maidens
and take them back to the hall!"

66. Svaraði Virgar Valintsson,
hann læt síni orð so falla:
"Nú skal taka moyar tvær
og føra tær heim til halla!"

Virgar Valintsson answered,
he let his words fall like this:
"Now we shall take the two maidens
and bring them back to the hall!"

67. Virgar tók tær moyar tvær,
setti á Skemming fríða,
Sjúrður tók tað besta svørð,
sum dvørgurin hevði smíðað.

Virgar took the two maidens,
he sat them on the handsome Skemmingur,
Sjúrður took the best sword
that the dwarf had made.

68. Sjúrður tók tað besta svørð,
sum dvørgurin hevði smíðað,
síðan allar aðrar brandar
støkkir av um miðju.

Sjúrður took the best sword
that the dwarf had made,
then he takes all the other swords
and snaps them in the middle.

69. Sjúrður tók tað gull og silvur,
alt tað, ið Grani bar,
síðan skundar hann síni ferð
av dvørgaborg avstað.

Sjúrður took the gold and silver,
all that Grani could carry,
then he hurries on his journey
away from the dwarf castle.

70. Ríða teir eftir skógnum fram,
teir spara ei fljótar hestar,
tá skalv bæði himmal og jørð,
og dagurin tók at bresta.

They ride through the forest,
they don't spare the fast horses,
both sky and earth then trembled,
and the day started to break.

71. Tað lýsir yvir heidna skóg, sólin tekur at branda, drekar taka at ýla hátt, tá ið risar í hallir ganga.	It shines over the heathen forest, the sun starts to blaze, dragons start to howl loudly, when giants go into their halls.
72. Kvørfinn kom av skógnum heim, hann tykist vera komin í vanda, hann sær opnar hallisdyr fyri sær tá standa.	Kvørfinn came home from the forest, he suspected danger, he sees the hall doors standing open before him.
73. Dvørgurin gekk í hallina inn, einki ið hann sigur, hann sær liggja á breiðum borði brandar, av um miðju.	The dwarf goes into the hall, he says nothing, he sees lying on the wide table swords that are snapped in the middle.
74. Kvørfinn gekk í hallina inn, ilt var um at eggja, sá seg um til moyar tvær, hann kundi tær ikki síggja.	Kvørfinn goes into the hall, evil was about to be instigated, he looked around for the two maidens, he couldn't see them.
75. Dvørgurin leyp um hallargólv, ilt er um at eggja, kyndi eld í stóru smiðju, brandar aftur at sleggja.	The dwarf leapt over the floor of the hall, evil is about to be instigated, he kindled fire in the great smithy, to pound swords again.
76. Dvørgurin leyp um hallargólv, ilt var um at eggja: "Nú skal ganga at stóran stiðja, brandar aftur at sleggja."	The dwarf leapt over the floor of the hall, evil was about to be instigated: "Now I shall go to the great anvil, to pound swords again."
77. Dvørgurin leyp um hallargólv, ei var til góðs at bera: "Hevndar skulu moyar tvær við hørðum sømdum verða."	The dwarf leapt over the floor of the hall, it was not good to bear: "The two maidens shall be avenged with ferocious redress."
78. Sjúrður og Virgar Valintsson heim í garðin fóru, úti sjálvur Hjalprek kongur fyri teimum stóð.	Sjúrður and Virgar Valintsson went home to the court, King Hjalprek himself stood outside before them.

79. "Ver vælkomin, Sjúrður, heim av hesari ferð, tú hevur vunnið á heiðinmark gull og búgvið svørð."	"Sjúrður, welcome home from this journey, you have won gold and a decorated sword in the heathen forest."[13]
80. Tá svaraði Hjalprek kongur, mælir fyri munni á sær: "Hvat er hetta fyri mikla kempa, ið førir moyar tvær?"	Then King Hjalprek answered, saying: "What kind of mighty warrior is this, who brings two maidens?"
81. Svaraði Sjúrður Sigmundarson fyrsta orðið tá: "Hetta er Virgar Valintsson, Tíðriki kongi frá.	Sjúrður Sigmundarson answered the first word then: "This is Virgar Valintsson, from King Tíðrikur.
82. Hetta er Virgar Valintsson, ið førir moyar tvær, hann hevur verið í hesari ferð á heiðinmark við mær."	This is Virgar Valintsson, who brings two maidens, he has been on this journey to the heathen forest with me."
83. Tí svaraði Hjalprek kongur, hann mælir fyri munni sínum: "Virgar, gakk í hallina inn við dvørgamoyum tínum!"	King Hjalprek answered that, saying: "Virgar, go into the hall with your dwarf maidens!"
84. So var hann av ferðum móður, søgur ganga av, tríggjar nætur Virgar sterki hjá Hjalprek kongi svav.	He was so tired from the journey, so stories tell, Virgar the strong slept for three nights at King Hjalprek's.
85. Árla var um morgunin, sólin skein so víða, Virgar klæðist for síni song, hann favnar moyar fríðar.	Early in the morning, the sun shone so widely, Virgar dressed himself before his bed, he embraces the beautiful maidens.
86. Virgar gongur for Hjalprek kong, biður hann dugnað gera: "Læna mær skútu av landi út, moyar um sund at føra!"	Virgar goes before King Hjalprek, asks him for help: "Lend me a ship from the land, to take the maidens over the sound!"

13 The two lines are reversed in the Faroese, but we have exchanged them to preserve the sense in the English translation.

87. Tí svaraði Hjalprek kongur: "Skútu skalt tú fá, flyta yvir Singarfjørð dvørgamoyar báðar."	King Hjalprek answered to that: "You shall get a ship to take both dwarf maidens across Singarfjørður."
88. Tí svaraði Hjalprek kongur: "Skútu læni eg tær, flyta yvir Singarfjørð dvørgamoyar tvær."	King Hjalprek answered to that: "I shall lend you a ship, to take two dwarf maidens across Singarfjørður."
89. Virgar læt av lunni skura eina forgylta skeið, sigldi yvir Singarfjørð, so føgur var tann leið.	Virgar had a gilded skip, quickly run of the rollers,[14] they sailed over Singarfjørður, the journey was so lovely.
90. Tað var Virgar Valintsson, søgur ganga frá, flutti moyar á Selgjarland, har læt hann borgir slá.	It was Virgar Valintsson, so stories tell, he took the maidens to Selgjarland, where he had castles built.
91. Hann læt gyltar borgir gera, gitið man verða leingi, síðan fór Virgar Valintsson aftur for Tíðriks dreingir.	He had golden castles made, it will be told for a long time, then Virgar Valintsson went back to Tíðrikur's heroes.
92. Virgar læt á Selgjarlandi gyltar borgir gera, setti inni moyar tvær, tær skuldu silki bera.	On Selgjarland Virgar had golden castles made, he kept the two maidens there, they should wear silk.
93. Setti inni moyar tvær, tær skuldu silki virka, síðan fór Virgar Valintsson aftur for Tíðrik sterka.	He kept the two maidens there, they should weave silk, then Virgar Valintsson went back to the strong Tíðrikur.

14 Lyngbye notes that *skura av lunni* means the speed at which the ship was pulled on rollers down to the sea. Lyngbye, *Færøiske Qvæder*, 430n87.

THE GIANT OF HÓLMGARÐAR OR THE MOUND GHOST (RISIN Í HÓLMGØRÐUM OR DYSJADÓLGUR)

1. Eg veit eina rímuna,
inni hevur ligið leingi,
gjørd um Virgar Valintsson
og fleiri reystar dreingir.

I know a ballad,
it has lain inside me for a long time,
it is about Virgar Valintsson
and many courageous heroes.

Refrain *Fuglin í fjøruni hann eitur már,*
silkibleikt er húgva hans,
so knept er han[s] hár.
Fuglin í fjøruni.

The bird on the beach, it is called a seagull,[1]
his hat is pale as silk,
his hair is so short.
The bird on the beach.[2]

2. Gjørd um Virgar Valintsson,
royndur í avreksverki,
hartil Sjúrða Sigmundarson
og snarpan Nornagest.

It is about Virgar Valintsson,
who has performed many great deeds,
as well as Sjúrður Sigmundarson
and the brave Nornagestur.

3. Tríggjar eru gøturnar,
og ein víkur ífrá,
Virgar gekk á heyggin burtur,
sum hans avi lá.

There are three paths,
and one deviates from the others,
Virgar went away to the mound,
where his grandfather lay.

4. "Vakir tú í heygginum,
sæli avi mín?
Hetta er Virgar Valintsson,
fostursonur tín."

"Are you awake in the mound,
my late grandfather?
This is Virgar Valintsson,
your fosterson."

5. "Tóast tú ert mín fostursonur,
og eg tín avi betur,
um enn nú rivna dalar og fjøll,
eg fari ikki út í vetur."

"Although you are my fosterson,
and I even your grandfather,
even if valleys and mountains split,
I will not go out this winter."

6. "Vilt tú ikki Miming
higar senda mær,
við báðum mínum hondum
eg bróti upp yvir tær."

"Won't you send Miming[3]
here to me,
I am breaking up the mound above you
with both my hands."[4]

---

1 The original says *már*, which means "marten," which is not a bird. It should likely be *más*, as for example the refrain appears in *Álvur kongur* CCF variant F. See Grundtvig and Bloch, *Føroya kvæði*, vol. 1, p. 394; this is how we have chosen to translate it here.

2 Above is the refrain from variant A. Variants B and D have the *Grani bar gullið av heiði* refrain. The refrain for variant C is not recorded in CCF.

3 A sword.

4 We have exchanged the lines of the Faroese here to preserve the sense in English, and we have added "the mound" for clarity. It means that Virgar will break up the mound above the dead man to get to the sword.

7. Ikki vildi dysjadólgur heyggin lata bróta, báðum hondum um Miming treiv, hann bað sín son væl njóta.	The mound-ghost[5] didn't want the mound to be broken, with both hands grasping Miming, he told his son to enjoy it very much.
8. Mælti Virgar Valintsson, hann Miming fekk í hond: "Hvar veitst tú nú heilivágin mestan vera í land?"	Virgar Valintsson spoke, he took Miming in his hand: "Where is the best medicine that you know of in the land?"
9. Tí svaraði dysjadólgur, hevði ligið leingi: "Eg veit nógvan heilivág, men tú vinnur hann einki.	The mound-ghost answered to that, he had lain for a long time: "I know of a lot of medicine, but you won't win it.
10. Tað er eitt hús í Hólmgørðum, sum liggur til risans son, tað er nú fult av heilivág og ongum øðrum mun.	There is a house in Hólmgarðar, that is for the giant's son, it is now full of medicine and no other treasure.
11. Men kvittar tú [í] Hólmgarðar á hesum sama heysti, lat hann ikki sita, tann Fávnisbanan sterka!"	But if you leave for Hólmgarðar this same autumn, do not let him stay,[6] the strong Fávnisbani!"
12. Tað var Virgar Valintsson, settist á gangaran reyð, so reið hann á Sjúrðar fund, so snart sum fálkur fleyg.	It was Virgar Valintsson, sat himself on the red steed, then he rode to meet Sjúrður, as quickly as the falcon flies.
13. Mitt í miðjum grasagarði akslar hann sítt skinn, so gekk hann í høgaloft fyri Sjúrð hin unga inn.	Right in the middle of the garden he throws his cloak over his shoulders, then he went in to the loft room before the young Sjúrður.

5 *Føroysk-ensk orðabók* translates *dysjardólgur* to be "hill troll," but it is clearly something approaching more like an Old Norse *draugr* (an undead person with a body), so we have chosen "mound-ghost." A Tolkeinesque translation would be "barrow-wight." See *Føroysk-ensk orðabók*, s.v. "Dysjardólgur."

6 This likely means Virgar should not let Sjúrður stay at home, but rather he should go with him.

14. Kongins hall var skipað væl bæði gul og blá, næsta manni Hjalprek kongi Sjúrður situr hjá.	The king's hall was well-decorated[7] in both yellow and blue, the man sitting next to King Hjalprekur is Sjúrður.
15. "Statt upp, Sjúrður Sigmundarson, eg krevji teg fyrsta sinni, nógvan veit eg heilivág, um tú ert maður at vinna.	"Stand up, Sjúrður Sigmundarson, I make demands of you for the first time, I know of a lot of medicine, if you are man enough to win it.
16. Tá mást tú búgva teg bitrum væl og gyrða tín hest við spora, um enn tú hevði havt átjan hundrað, tað kundi honum lítið forðað.	Then you must equip yourself well with a sharp sword,[8] and girth up your horse with spurs, even if you had had eighteen hundred,[9] it would not hinder him much.
17. Har kunnu lítið svørð á bíta, ei heldur bitrir brandar, átjan alin er jarnstong hvør til allar risans gantar."	Swords can do little cutting there, and neither can sharp blades, each iron lance is eighteen ells long that all the giant's warriors[10] have."
18. Riðu so av hallini út við so fáum liði, Virgar og Sjúrður Sigmundarson og Nornagestur hin triði.	Then they rode from the hall with such a small company, Virgar and Sjúrður Sigmundarson and the third is Nornagestur.
19. Tað var Virgar Valintsson, hann heim í garðin fór, úti Vilkus risans son fyri honum stóð.	It was Virgar Valintsson, he went home to the court, Vilkus the giant's son stood outside before him.
20. Svaraði Sjúrður Sigmundarson, mælti so for seg: "Hevur tú nakran heilivág avlops selja mær?"	Sjúrður Sigmundarson answered, saying: "Do you have any surplus medicine to sell to me?"

7 Here we have translated *skipað* as decorated to account for the golden and blue in the second line of the stanza, although ordinarily the word would mean, for example, "appointed" or "organized."

8 "Sharp sword" is not in the Faroese; it simply says "sharp," so we have added "sword" for clarity.

9 We might assume here that this is eighteen hundred men.

10 The Old Norse word *ganti* means a dandy or a player, someone who is perhaps conceited and foolish. The Orðkort database acknowledges this definition but glosses *ganti* as "kiempe," meaning, "giant, warrior." See Fróðskaparsetur Føroya, Orðkort, s.v. "Ganti."

21. "Ongan havi eg heilivág avlopis hjá mær, hvaðan er hasin mikli maður, Sjúrður, ið fylgir tær?"	"I have no surplus medicine with me, where is that mighty man from who travels with you Sjúrður?"
22. "Hetta man vera maður tá, í okur tekur mun, hetta var hin, ið risan vá, tann sterki Valintsson."	"This must be the man then, that seems to us to make a difference,[11] this was the one who slew the giant, the strong Valintsson."
23. "Hav tú takk, tú segði mær, og eg tað ikki visti, nú skal brynja út liðið alt, tí eg var tann, ið misti."	"You shall have thanks that you told to me, since I didn't know of it, I shall now fit the whole company out in armour, because I was the one who lost."
24. Árla var um morgunin, sólin roðar í fjøll, tá hevði Vilkus, risans son, brynjað út hundrað øll.	Early in the morning, the sun reddens the mountains, Vilkus, the giant's son, had then fitted the whole hundred out in armour.
25. Tá hevði Vilkus, risans son, brynjað út hundrað tólv, Sjúrður og Virgar Valintsson teir riðu har tveir ímót.	Vilkus, the giant's son, had then fitted twelve hundred out in armour, Sjúrður and Virgar Valintsson, the two rode against them there.
26. Bardust fullar tógva dagar, duplur hanga við stengur, møddist Virgar Valintsson, í blóði har hann stendur.	They fought for fully two days, foam hangs from the horses' bits,[12] Virgar Valintsson got tired, as he stands there in blood.
27. Harra Gud í himmiríki, mikil er tín makt, so var Virgar í víggi staddur, opin fell hann aftur.	Lord God in heaven, your power is mighty, Virgar was in the battle like that, he fell backwards with his arms spread out.[13]

11 It is difficult to understand what this line means, and here we have therefore used the reading from variant B of the ballad *sum okkum tykir í mun*. Grundtvig and Bloch, *Føroya kvæði*, vol. 1, p. 315, st. 37. *Í* and *ið* sound the same (and *ið* and *sum* can be used synonymously), and *tekur* and *tykir* do not sound very different

12 This is the interpretation in Lyngbye, *Færøiske Qvæder*, 385n40. The horses are foaming at the mouth.

13 In Faroese it literally says he fell backwards "open," that is with his arms spread

28. Tað var hin snarpi Nornagestur,
brandin undir hann skeyt,
tók hann Virgar Valintsson,
hann bar hann burt av breyt.

It was the brave Nornagestur,
he thrust the sword under him,
he took Virgar Valintsson,
he carried him away off the path.

29. Sjúrður gjørdist í høggum tungur,
øllum tókti undur,
avleiðis gekk hann risans rekkar,
trongdi teir miðjan sundur.

Sjúrður became heavy in his blows,
everyone thought it a marvel,
he drove the giant's warriors from their path,
he pushed them apart in the middle.[14]

30. Sjúrður gjørdist í høggum tungur,
tað mundu flest øll síggja,
avleiðis gekk hann risans menn,
trongdi teir sundur í níggju.

Sjúrður became heavy in his blows,
almost everyone might see that,
he drove the giant's men from their path,
he pushed them apart into nine groups.[15]

31. Virgar liggur undir heyggjunum,
tóktist líða mein,
at hin snarpi Sjúrður
hann skuldi berjast ein.

Virgar lies by the mound,
he seemed to suffer an injury,
so that the brave Sjúrður
had to fight alone.

32. Virgar leyp undan heyggjunum,
sum skeinur hevði fingið,
báðum hondum um Miming treiv,
hann ruddi fyri sær geingi.

Virgar leapt up from the mound,
he who had received scratches,[16]
he grasped Miming with both hands,
he cut a path through the fighting throng.

33. So bardust teir frændur báðir
víðar vøllir fram,
eftir stóð Vilkus risans son
við sín triðja mann.

The two friends both fought like that
through the wide battlefields,
Vilkus the giant's son was left
with his third man.

34. Tað var Vilkus risans son,
hann kreyp undur borgarlið:
"Kæri Sjúrður Sigmundarson,
gev tú mær nú grið!"

It was Vilkus the giant's son,
he crept under the castle gate:
"Dear Sjúrður Sigmundarson,
have mercy on me now!"

---

out open, spreadeagled in a vulnerable position.

14 He is pressing the army back.

15 He is pressing the army back and splitting it up.

16 This can also mean slashes, but it does not imply a significant injury.

35. Mælti Sjúrður Sigmundarson nú so fyri seg: "Gjarna gevi eg tær grið og frið, um tú kannst skjóla teg."	Sjúrður Sigmundarson spoke like this: "I will gladly give you mercy and peace, if you can hide yourself."
36. Tað var Sjúrður Sigmundarson, hann vendi honum ífrá, tá kom Virgar Valintsson, hann hjó hann í lutir tvá.	It was Sjúrður Sigmundarson, he turned away from him, then Virgar Valintsson came, he chopped him in two pieces.
37. Mælti Sjúrður Sigmundarson, hyggi[n] fyri seg: "Eg havi vunnið tann heilivág, men takka mást tú meg!"	Sjúrður Sigmundarson spoke prudently: "I have won that medicine, but you must thank me!"
38. Mælti Virgar Valintsson, varð honum so fyri munni: "Sjúrður, tak mót heilivág, tú ert tann, hann hevur vunnið!"	Virgar Valintsson spoke, it came out of his mouth like this: "Sjúrður, accept the medicine, you are the one who has won!"
39. Virgar førdi burt heilivág á gangarum tvá, síðani hevði Sjúrður á Hólmgørðum ráð.	Virgar took away the medicine on two steeds, since then Sjúrður ruled in Hólmgarðar.
40. Virgar førdi burt heilivág á tveimum gangarum sínum, men Sjúrður ráddi fyri Hólmgørðum, tað vil eg fyri øllum tína.	Virgar took away the medicine on his two steeds, but Sjúrður ruled over Hólmgarðar I will tell everyone about it.
Refrain *Fuglin í fjøruni hann eitur már,* *silkibleikt er húgva hans,* *so knept er han[s] hár.* *Fuglin í fjøruni.*	*The bird on the beach, it is called a seagull,* *his hat is pale as silk,* *his hair is so short.* *The bird on the beach.*

THE GIANT OF LEITTRABERG (RISIN AV LEITTRABERGI)

1. Eg veit eina rímuna,
inni hevur ligið leingi,
risin liggur á Leittrabergi,
talar við sínar dreingir.

I know a ballad,
it has lain inside me for a long time,
the giant lies on Leittraberg,
and speaks with his heroes.

2. Risin talar við sínar dreingir,
gott er at taka til evna:
"Hvar vita tit mín faðirs bana?
Nú lystir meg hann at hevna."

The giant speaks with his heroes,
it's good to get started on the subject:[1]
"Do you know where my father's killer is?
Now I desire to avenge him."

3. Allir drýptu høvdið niður,
eingin tordi tala
uttan hansara høvuðsmaður,
betri hevði hann tagað.

All of them hung their heads,
no one dared to speak
except for his leader,[2]
it would have been better if he had kept silent.

4. "Hoyr tú, frægi Filkussonur,
siga skalt tú mær,
ið hvør var mín faðirs bani?
Ella havi eg høvdið av tær."

"Listen, brave Filkussonur,
you shall tell me,
who was my father's killer?
Or I will have your head."

5. Tað var frægi Filkussonur,
tá tagdi hann so leingi:
"Um enn eg sigi tín faðirs bana,
á honum vinnur tú einki."

It was the brave Filkussonur,
he was silent for so long:
"Even if I name your father's killer,
you won't win against him."

6. "Hoyr tú, frægi Filkussonur,
sig mær satt ífrá:
hvussu var hann á navni nevndur,
ið mín faðir vá?"

"Listen, brave Filkussonur,
tell me truthfully:
what is he named,
he who slew my father?"

7. Svaraði frægi Filkussonur,
tykir í tí mun:
"So er hann á navni nevndur,
Sjúrður Sigmundarson."

The brave Filkussonur answered,
he thinks there might be riches in it:
"He is named thusly:
Sjúrður Sigmundarson."

1 As in, it is good to get started on the subject of the ballad.

2 This must be the leader of the heroes.

8. Tað var risin á Leittrabergi, læt síni orð so snúgva: "Hoyr tú, frægi Filkussonur, hvar man Sjúrður búgva?"	It was the giant on Leittraberg, he began to speak: "Listen, brave Filkussonur, where does Sjúrður live?"
9. Svaraði frægi Filkussonur við trega og tungum vanda: "Hann býr sær í Hólmgørðum í Noregis landi.	The brave Filkussonur answered with sorrow and heavy grief: "He lives in Hólmgarðar in the land of Norway.
10. Hann hevur mangan risan dripið fyri sítt hvassa svørð, kemur tú fyri Hólmgarðar, tílíka rakar tú ferð."	He has killed many giants with his sharp sword, if you come to Hólmgarðar, your journey will end in the same way."
11. Tað var risin á Leittrabergi, letur á vreiði renna: "Fyri tú spottar og happar meg, tú skalt á báli brenna."	It was the giant on Leittraberg, he vented his anger: "Because you mock and harrass me, you shall burn on a bonfire."
12. "Um tú letur meg steikja, um tú letur meg brenna, Sjúrður verður ikki tín fangi, tað fært tú at kenna."	"If you will have me roasted, if you will have me burnt, Sjúrður won't be your prisoner, you will find that out."
13. Svaraði frægi Filkussonur, klæddur í brynju nýggja: "Sjúrður verður ei tín fangi, tað fært tú at síggja."	The brave Filkussonur answered, dressed in new armour: "Sjúrður will not be your prisoner, you shall see."
14. Risin fór sær haðan burtur við teirri somu ferð, so fór hann í smiðjuna at smíða sær skjøld og svørð.	The giant went from there in the same way,[3] then he went into the smithy to forge a shield and a sword for himself.
15. Risin smíðar jarnstongina, ógvuligt at líta, átjan alin var hon long, hon glógvar sum silvurið hvíta.	The giant hammers the iron lance, dreadful to see, it was eighteen ells long, it shines like white silver.

3 Literally "at the same speed."

16. So letur risin av Leittrabergi síni skipini gera, allar letur hann streingirnar av reyðargulli vera.	Then the giant of Leittraberg has his ships be made, he has all of the ropes be made of red gold.
17. So letur risin av Leittrabergi síni skipini búgva, allar letur hann streingirnar av reyðargulli snúgva.	Then the giant of Leittraberg has his ships be readied, he has all of the ropes be twisted out of red gold.
18. Risin gekk til strandar oman, fróur í huga full, hann laðar í sín forgylta knørr væl tjúgu tunnur gull.	The giant went down to the beach, happy, he loads his gilded ship with about twenty barrels of gold.
19. Risin gekk til strandar oman, búðist ei við frið, Torkil við Strond og Tórir á Grund teir fóru honum við.	The giant went down to the beach, he readied himself for battle,[4] Torkil við Strond and Tórir á Grund went with him.
20. Risin gekk til strandar oman, søgur ganga av, hann stígur í sín forgylta knørr, so stokkurin gekk í kav.	The giant went down to the beach, so stories tell, he steps into his gilded ship, so that the gunwale went under the sea.[5]
21. Vindur upp síni silkisegl, gull við ráum brann, strykar ei á bunkan niður fyrr enn við Noregis land.	He hoists his silken sails, gold shone by the yards,[6] he doesn't lower the sails[7] before they were in Norway.

4 This literally means "he readied himself not for peace," as in he is preparing for battle. It is also slightly ambiguous because it could also mean that he is not peaceful in himself, either.

5 The image here is that the giant is so heavy that when he steps on board his ship, the top of the hull goes underwater.

6 A yard is a wooden beam to which the sails are tied. In the line, it literally says that the gold "burnt," as in shined brightly.

7 This literally means that he did not strike the sails down onto the deck.

22. Vindur upp síni silkisegl,
so er greitt fyri mær,
strykar ei á bunkan niður
fyrr enn við Hólmgarð.

He hoists his silken sails,
so I've been told,
doesn't lower them
before they were by Hólmgarður.[8]

23. Smalasvein í líðini situr,
goymir at smalu og geit:
"Eg sær skip eftir havi koma,
havnir vilja leita."

The shepherd sits on the hillside,
herds the sheep and goats:
"I see ships come over the sea,
they are looking for harbours."

24. Allar rekur hann smalurnar
saman á grønan vøll,
síðan akslar hann kápu blá,
hann gár í kongins høll.

He drives all the sheep
together on a green field,
then he throws a blue cloak round his shoulders,
he goes into the king's hall.

25. Síðan akslar hann kápu blá,
hann gár í kongins høll:
"Eg eri mær av einum luti
vísari, enn tær eruð øll.

Then he throws a blue cape round his shoulders,
he goes into the king's hall:
"I'm a bit
wiser than they all are.

26. Eg eri mær av einum luti
vísari, enn tær eruð øll,
eg síggi skip eftir havi koma,
seglini hvít sum mjøll."

I'm a bit
wiser than they all are,
I see ships come over the sea,
the sails are white as snow."

27. "Sært tú skip eftir havi koma,
seglini hvít sum lín,
vera man risin á Leittrabergi,
at hevna faðir sín."

"Do you see ships come over the sea,
the sails white as linen,
of course the giant of Leittraberg
has come to avenge his father."

28. Tí svaraði smalasveinur,
fyri breiða borði stóð:
"Tykti mær, at ein grimmur risi
fram eftir bunkan fór."

To that the shepherd answered,
he stood before the wide table:
"It seemed to me that an ugly giant
walked forward across the deck."

29. Tað var Sjúrður Sigmundarson,
tók tey orð í geyma:
"Undarligt hevur fyri mær borist
hesa nátt í dreyma.

It was Sjúrður Sigmundarson,
he paid attention to those words:
"A strange thing appeared before me
last night in dreams.

8 Here "Holmgarður" is in the singular, elsewhere it is "Holmgarðar" in the plural.

30. Meg droymdi, at Grani úti saðlaður stóð, meg droymdi, at fyri honum rann so mikið blóð.	I dreamt that Grani stood saddled outside, I dreamt that so much blood ran in front of him.
31. Meg droymdi, at spjótið mítt fell frá mínum belti, meg droymdi, at mítt góða svørð á blonkum brynjum gelti.	I dreamt that my spear fell from my belt, I dreamt that my good sword rung on shining armour.
32. Meg droymdi, at hjálmurin í mínum hondum var, meg droymdi, at mítt góða svørð ígjøgnum risar skar."	I dreamt that the helmet was in my hands, I dreamt that my good sword cut through giants."
33. Føgur var tann snekkjan, hon kendi fagurt land, læt hann síni akker falla á tann hvíta sand.	That ship was beautiful, it touched the beautiful land, he had his anchor lowered down onto the white beach.
34. Læt hann síni akker falla á tann hvíta sand, fyrstur steig risin á Leittrabergi sínum fótum á land.	He lowered his anchors down onto the white sand, the giant of Leittraberg was the first to go ashore.
35. Fyrstur steig risin á Leittrabergi sínum fótum á land, og hann hin frægi Filkussonur undir hans høgru hond.	The giant of Leittraberg was the first to go ashore, and he, the brave Filkussonur, at his right hand side.
36. Gingu teir frá strondum niðan, ríkir menn og reystir, lunnar brustu, og jørðin skalv, teir drógu sín knørr í neystið.	They went up from the beach, rich and powerful men, the rollers[9] banged and the ground shook, they dragged their ship into the boathouse.
37. Sjúrður stendur í glasglugga, kann væl randir rjóða: "Nú skal ein til strandar oman, risanum frið at bjóða."	Sjúrður stands in the window, well able to redden shields: "Now one man shall go down to the beach, to offer the giant peace."[10]

9 The rollers are the rollers the ship is being moved on (despite it previously having been anchored).

10 This closing quotation mark is not in the edition and has been added by us.

38. Sig, Sjúrður býður teim øllum heim,
glaður for uttan ekka,
sita yvir tað breiða borð,
tann brúna mjøð at drekka.

Say, Sjúrður invites them all home,
happy without worry,
to sit by the wide table,
to drink the brown mead.

39. Sjúrður býður teim øllum heim,
meiri av monnum og minna,
um teir vilja halda frið
og ongar neisur vinna.

Sjúrður invites them all home,
higher and lower status men,[11]
if they will keep the peace
and do no dirty tricks.

40. "Um teir vilja halda frið
og ongar neisur vinna,
men verður oss nakað vanboðið,
so mæli eg um minna."

"If they will keep the peace[12]
and do no dirty tricks,
but if any do us an injustice,
then I will remember it."

41. Risin og allir hansara menn
ganga á hvítum sandi,
tað er hann Sjúrðar sendisvein,
ríður niður til strandar.

The giant and all his men
walk on the white sand,
it is Sjúrður's messenger,
who rides down to the beach.

42. "Sjúrður býður tykkum øllum heim,
glaðir foruttan ekka,
sita yvir hans breiða borð,
tann brúna mjøð at drekka.

"Sjúrður invites you all home,
happy without worry,
to sit by his wide table,
to drink the brown mead.[13]

43. Sjúrður býður øllum heim,
meiri av monnum og minna,
um tær vilja halda frið
og ongar neisur vinna.

Sjúrður invites everyone home,
higher and lower status men,
if they will keep the peace
and do no dirty tricks.

44. Um tær vilja halda frið
og ongar neisur vinna,
men verður oss nakað vanboðið,
so mælir hann um minna."

If they will keep the peace
and do no dirty tricks,
but if any do us an injustice,
then he'll remember it."

---

11 Lyngbye, however, translates this as "hver mand med bedre sinde" (each man with a better mind) and a footnote saying "Flere eller færre af mændene" (more or fewer of the men), so it is unclear here exactly how he interprets the line. Lyngbye, *Færøiske Qvæder*, 449.

12 The opening quotation mark is not in the edition and has been added by us.

13 This and the following stanzas recall stt. 38–40.

45. Risin gekk frá strondum niðan, niðan frá sínum liði, tekur hann Sjúrðar sendisvein, hann beit hann av um miðju.	The giant went up from the beach, up from his band, he takes Sjúrður's messenger, he bites him off at the waist.
46. Beit hann hann í miðju sundur, søgur ganga frá. Sjúrður stóð í glaslugga, fullgjølla hann tað sá.	He bit him apart at the waist, so stories tell, Sjúrður stood in the window, he saw it clearly.
47. Sjúrður býður sínar menn gyrða seg við svørð: "Tað síggi eg á risanum, at nú er ilt á ferð."	Sjúrður tells his men to gird themselves with swords: "I see it on the giant, that evil is afoot now."
48. Sjúrður biður sínar menn klæða seg í brynjur góðar, ikki óttast risans her, hóast hann sýnist stórur.	Sjúrður asks his men to dress themselves in good armour, to not fear the giant's army, even though it seems large.
49. Sjúrður biður sínar menn klæðast í brynju bjarta, standa nú so manniliga, ikki hava kálvahjarta.[14]	Sjúrður asks his men to put on bright armour, to stand like men now, to not be cowards.
50. Sjúrður bindur sítt hjálmaband, Gestur stóð honum næst, ongantíð á ævini bant hann tað so fast.	Sjúrður fastens his helmet strap, Gestur stood next to him,[15] never in his life had he fastened it so tightly.
51. Mitt í miðjum grasgarði akslar risin sítt skinn, og so búgvin gongur hann í høgar hallir inn.	In the middle of the garden the giant throws his fur cloak around his shoulders, and thus prepared he goes into the high halls.
52. Og so búgvin gongur hann í høgar hallir inn, sum Sjúrður frægi á borði situr við *manna hundrað fimm.	And thus prepared he goes into the high halls, as the brave Sjúrður sits by the table with five hundred men.

14 This literally means "don't have a calf's heart," meaning to be brave.

15 Gestur is Nornagestur.

53. "Ver vælkomin, risin, higar nú til mín, drekk nú, hvat tær betur líkar, mjøðin ella vín!"	"Giant, welcome here to my place, now drink what you like better, the mead or wine!"
54. "Lítið er mær um mjøðin tín, hálvt væl minni um vín, eg havi ongar bøtur fingið fyri sæla faðir mín."	"Little do I like your mead, and half less again I like your wine, I have received no reparations for my late father."
55. Svaraði Sjúrður Sigmundarson, fell so væl í lag: "Hevur tú ongar bøtur fingið, ongar fært tú í dag."	Sjúrður Sigmundarson answered, it turned out so well:[16] "If you have received no reparations, you will receive none today."
56. Risin gekk at borðinum, reiggjar nevan hátt, Sjúrður situr í hásæti, hann bar seg undan brátt.	The giant went to the table, swings the fist high, Sjúrður sits in the high seat, he quickly dodges it.
57. Risin gekk at breiðum borði, illsku ætlar at prøva, knýtir hann neva við miklum alvi, Sjúrða á nasar at geva.	The giant went to the wide table, intending to do evil, he clenches his fist with great strength, to give Sjúrður a punch on the nose.
58. Tekur hann hendur um Sjúrðar háls, hann eftir hári at draga, ikki vikaðist kappin reysti, heldur enn í berg hevði staðið.	He puts his hands around Sjúrður's throat, he drags him by the hair, the bold hero didn't budge anymore than if he'd been a cliff.
59. Svaraði Sjúrður Sigmundarson, her yppist ein nýggjur siður: "Tað hevur eingin roynt uttan tú, meg eftir hári at drigið."	Sjúrður Sigmundarson answered, here a new custom was established: "No one but you has tried to drag me by the hair."
60. Sjúrður leyp úr hásæti, er mær ei á tí hól, bæði borð og borðstól tað førdi hann fram á gólv.	Sjúrður leapt from the high seat, it is not boasting, both table and trestles[17] he upended onto the floor.

16 The narrator here thinks that Sjúrður's answer is clever and well put.

17 This seems to mean a type of trestle table, where the top of the table is supported by trestles. Lyngbye translates *borðstólur* as chair, and has Sjúrður tipping over tables and chairs, but *borðstólur* means table leg, not chair. Lyngbye, *Færøiske Qvæder*, 459.

61. Sjúrður brá sínum bitra brandi, eg geri tað ei at loyna, ætlaði risanum banasár, og odd í hjálmi at royna.	Sjúrður brandished his sharp sword, I do not hide it, he intended to mortally wound the giant, and to test the point of the sword in his helmet.[18]
62. Sjúrður brá sínum bitra brandi, søgur ganga frá, oddin barst í silvurbjálka, ikki beit stálið á.	Sjúrður brandished his sharp sword, so stories tell, the point struck into the silver beam, the steel didn't bite.
63. Allir sótu Sjúrðar menn, sum gyrdir vóru við svørð, vistu ikki, hvar ið teir vóru, himli ella á jørð.	All of Sjúrður's men sat, who were girded with swords, didn't know where they were, in heaven or on earth.
64. Teir høgga títt, teir líva lítt, tá var brak í høll, øvigan bardi hann risan tá út á grønan vøll.	They hew fast, they spare little, there was a crash in the hall, he then struck the giant backwards[19] out onto the green field.
65. "Eg fór mær av Leittrabergi, búðist ei við frið. Sjúrður, kom av hallini út, tú brynja út alt títt lið!"	"I came from Leittraberg, I readied myself for battle,[20] Sjúrður, come out of the hall, equip all your troops!"
66. Árla var um morgunin, sólin roðar í fjøll, tá hevði Sjúrður Sigmundarson brynjað út hundrað øll.	Early in the morning, the sun reddens the mountains, then Sjúrður Sigmundarson had equipped all one hundred of them.
67. Tá hevði Sjúrður Sigmundarson brynjað út hundrað øll, teir løgdu sínum bardøgum so skamt frá kongins høll.	Then Sjúrður Sigmundarson had equipped all one hundred of them, they had their battles so close to the king's hall.

18 This literally says "to test the point," meaning the point of the sword, i.e., to fight the giant with the sword.

19 The idea here is that he hits the giant making him go backwards.

20 This literally says he did not prepare himself for peace.

68. Teir løgdu sínum bardøgum eftir hvøssum gróti, tað var risin á Leittrabergi, hann ríður har ímóti.	They had their battles by sharp rocks, it was the giant of Leittraberg, he rides against them there.
69. Tað er risin á Leittrabergi, hann ríður har ímóti, búkar fullu á jørðina, sum teir kasta gróti.	It is the giant of Leittraberg, he rides against them there, guts fell onto the ground, as they throw rocks.[21]
70. So ríður frægi Filkussonur víðan vøllin fram, klývur hann hvønn um tvørar herðar, móti honum rann.	The brave Filkussonur then rides forth on the wide field, he splits every man crosswise through the shoulders who ran against him.
71. Sjúrður sjálvur talar tá til snarpa Nornagest: "Tú saðla mær nú Grana, mín góða gangarahest!"	Sjúrður himself then speaks to the brave Nornagestur: "Saddle Grani for me now, my good steed!"
72. Sjúrður ríður í stríðið fram, royndi góðar gripir, niður feldi hann risans menn, tíggju fyri hvørja sipan.	Sjúrður rides into the battle, uses good arms, he felled the giant's men, ten with every blow.
73. So ríður hann Filkussonur, hevur ei handahóv, klývur hann hvønn um tvørar herðar, varpar út á sjó.	Filkussonur then rides, without any skill, he splits each across their shoulders, throws them out to sea.
74. Sjúrður tokar í herin fram, av bar barnagaman, møtir honum frægur Filkussonur, nú bar báðum saman.	Sjúrður advanced through the army, with sheer childish joy, the valiant Filkussonur meets him, now they both clashed.
75. Møtir honum frægur Filkussonur, ógvuligt at líta, hann var allur í jarni klæddur, einki svørð kann bíta.	He meets the brave Filkussonur, terrible to behold, he was dressed all in iron, that no sword can bite.

21 This is ambiguous: it could also mean "as if they throw rocks."

76. Teir høgga títt, teir líva lítt, av bar barnagaman, eldur dreiv úr svørðunum, tá ið oddar bóru saman.	They chop fast and spare little, with sheer childish joy, fire sparked from the swords, when the points clashed.
77. Teir høgga títt, teir líva lítt, teir troða jørð til kálva, dvørgamál sang í hvørjum hamri, vørildin tók at skelva.	They chop often and spare little, they wade in mud up to the ankles, it echoed from every crag, the world started to shake.
78. Sjúrður høgdi ógvuliga, mangt var honum til meina, ikki beit svørð á heysi hans, heldur enn knívur á hørðum steini.	Sjúrður chopped dreadfully, much was meant to harm to him, swords didn't bite on his head, rather like a knife on hard stone.
79. Tað var Sjúrður Sigmundarson, høgdi nú til so fast, heysurin á Filkusson forinnan hjálmin brast.	It was Sjúrður Sigmundarson, he now chopped so hard, the head of Filkussonur burst within the helmet.
80. Tað var Sjúrður Sigmundarson, sínum svørði brá, hann kleyv frægan Filkusson sundur í lutir tvá.	It was Sjúrður Sigmundarson, he brandished his sword, he split the valiant Filkussonur into two pieces.
81. Tað var Sjúrður Sigmundarson, seg tilbaka sá, alt var fallið liðið hans, tað livdu ganska fá.	It was Sjúrður Sigmundarson, he looked behind himself, all of his army had fallen, very few lived.
82. Sjúrður tokar í herin fram, ei var barnagaman, møtir hann risan á Leittrabergi, nú bar báðum saman.	Sjúrður advances through the army, there was no childish joy, he meets the giant of Leittraberg, now they both clashed.
83. Sjúrður tokar í herin fram, royndi góðar gripir, niður feldi hann risans menn, tíggju fyri hvørja sipan.	Sjúrður advances through the army, he uses good arms, he felled the giant's men, ten with every blow.
84. Risin reiggjar jarnstongini ógvuliga fast, Grani skákaði undan honum, hann misti fyrsta kast.	The giant swings the iron lance very[22] hard, Grani twisted away from him, he lost the first throw.

22 *Ógvuliga* is misspelt *ógvulia* in CCF.

85. Risin reiggjar jarnstongini,
kundi væl tann list,
Grani skákaði undan honum,
tað annað slagið hann misti.

The giant swings the iron lance,
he knew that art well,
Grani twisted away from him,
he missed the second blow.

86. Risin reiggjar jarnstongini
ógvuliga fast,
stongin kom í jørðina,
í tríggjar lutir brast.

The giant swings the iron lance
very hard,
the lance hit the earth,
and broke into three pieces.

87. Tað var risin á Leittrabergi,
fór eftir grønari jørð
aftur í sítt góða skip
at søkja sær skjøld og svørð.

It was the giant of Leittraberg,
he went over green earth
back to his good ship
to seek a shield and sword for himself.

88. Tað var risin á Leittrabergi,
firrar ei sínum lívi,
átjan alin í hvørt lop
har aftur av skipi.

It was the giant of Leittraberg,
he doesn't fear for his life,
eighteen ells in every leap
back from the ship.

89. "Hoyr tú, Sjúrður Sigmundarson,
tó tú kannst væl at ríða,
nú skalt tú koma fyri tann,
ið teg skal læra at stríða."

"Listen, Sjúrður Sigmundarson,
though you know how to ride well,
now you shall come before the one
who will teach you how to fight."

90. Teir høgga títt, teir líva lítt,
dvørgamál sang í fjøllum:
"Betri var mær inni at ligið
enn berjast móti trøllum."

They chop fast and spare little,
it echoed[23] in the mountains:
"It would have been better for me to lie inside
than to fight against trolls."

91. Gestur hann stóð honum næst,
vildi ikki undan flýggja,
setir hann niður á Sjúrðar høvur
trinnar hjálmar nýggjar.

Gestur stood next to him,
he didn't want to flee,
he puts on Sjúrður's head
three new helmets.[24]

92. Tað var risin av Leittrabergi,
vildi ei undan flýggja,
høggur hann niður av Sjúrðar høvdi
trinnar hjálmar nýggjar.

It was the giant of Leittraberg,
he didn't want to flee,
he chops down from Sjúrður's head
three new helmets.

---

23 *Dvørgamál* literally means "dwarf speech" or "dwarf language," but it actually means "echo" in Faroese.

24 This is a comic moment in the ballad.

93. Sjúrður bindur upp hjálmin tann,
skein sum gullið reyða,
tann hann fekk frá dvørgamoynni
eftir tann Dagmars deyða.

Sjúrður fastens on that helmet,
that shone like red gold,
the one he got from the dwarf maiden
after Dagmar's death.

94. Gestur hann stóð honum næst,
ógvuligt á at líta:
"Høgg nú, Sjúrður Sigmundarson,
nú man einki á bíta!"

Gestur stood next to him,
it was terrible to see:
"Strike now, Sjúrður Sigmundarson,
now nothing may bite you!"

95. Teir høgga títt, teir líva lítt,
teir troða jørð til kálva,
dvørgamál sang í hvørjum hamri,
vørildin tók at skelva.

They chop often and spare little,
they wade in mud up to the ankles,
it echoed in every crag,
the world started to shake.

96. Svaraði Sjúrður Sigmundarson,
letur so orðum lúka:
"Nú er at taka upp listir tær,
ið eg havi sjáldan brúkað."

Sjúrður Sigmundarson answered,
concludes with these words:
"Now to start using those stratagems
that I have seldom used."

97. Tað var Sjúrður Sigmundarson,
kundi væl tann list,
snarliga vendi hann Grana burtur
til at ríða dyst.

It was Sjúrður Sigmundarson,
he knew that stratagem well,
quickly he turned Grani away
to ride to joust.

98. Sjúrður reið tann fyrsta dyst,
stakk hann inn at beini,
ikki beit tá svørðið á
heldur enn knívur á hørðum steini.

Sjúrður rode for the first joust,
he thrust into the bone,
the sword didn't bite then,
rather like knife on hard stone.

99. Sjúrður reið tann annan dyst,
stakk hann inn at hjarta,
eitur dreiv í himmalin upp,
tá sortnaði sólin bjarta.

Sjúrður rode for the second joust,
he thrust into his heart,
poison spurted up into the sky,
then the bright sun darkened.[25]

100. Sjúrður reið tann triðja dyst,
øllum tykti undur,
høggur hann risan á Leittrabergi
av í knígjum sundur.

Sjúrður rode for the third joust,
everyone thought it a wonder,
he chops the giant of Leittraberg
apart at the knees.

---

25 The giant's blood has blocked the sunlight.

101. Høggur hann risan á Leittrabergi av í kníggjum tá: "Ligg nú her á grønum vølli Filkussoni hjá!"	He chops the giant of Leittraberg off at the knees then: "Now lie here on the green field by Filkussonur!"
102. Sjúrður vendi Grana aftur bæði við gleði og gleim, svørji tann eið á mína trú, hann reið til hallar heim.	Sjúrður turned Grani back both with happiness and cheerfulness, I swear this oath on my faith, he rode home to the hall.
103. Sjúrður settist í hásæti glaður foruttan ekka, talar til snarpan Nornagest, hann biður hann skeinkja drekka.	Sjúrður sat down in the high seat happy without sorrow, he speaks to brave Nornagestur, he tells him to pour him a drink.
104. Tá ið hann hevði drukkið alla sína lyst, gramdi hann seg um Grana, sín góða gangarahest.	When he had drunk all he wanted, he complained about Grani, his good steed.
105. Sjúrður gekk til strandar oman fróur í huga full, har fekk hann á risans skipi tjúgu tunnur gull.	Sjúrður went down to the beach cheerful of mind, he got twenty barrels of gold on the giant's ship.
106. Eg kann ikki kvøða meir, enn sagt er í hesum tátti, Sjúrður settist í stólin tann, ið hann sjálvur átti.	I cannot sing any more than what has been said in this ballad,[26] Sjúrður sat himself in the chair, that he owned himself.
107. Eg kann ikki kvøða meir, enn kvøðið er fyri mær, Sjúrður ræður fyri Hólmgørðum líka enn sum fyrr.	I cannot sing more than has been sung to me, Sjúrður rules over Hólmgarðar even now as before.

26 A *táttur* is a section or division of a ballad, as discussed in the introductory essay.

SUMMARIES OF THE BALLADS

HELEN F. LESLIE-JACOBSEN

Regin the Smith (Regin smiður)

(1)[1] The singer opens the ballad by declaring he will sing about mighty kings. (2–3) Sigmundur and Hjørdis get married and celebrate with a feast at Christmas. (4–8) Soon, however, war descends on the land, the men go into battle and Sigmundur is fatally wounded. (9–24) Hjørdis goes to the battlefield to find him, and as Sigmundur dies, he recounts the battle and foretells she will have a boy and she is to give him the name Sjúrður. He gives her the pieces of his broken sword and tells her the boy must avenge his death and that Regin the smith must forge a new sword from the pieces. He mentions that the dragon Frænar lies on Glitrarheiði and that Regin is loyal to few. Sigmundur then finally dies. (25–26) Hjørdis leaves crying, and King Hjalprek visits her. (27–33) Hjørdis gives birth to a boy and names him Sjúrður, has him baptized, and takes great care of him. (34–35) Hjørdis then marries Hjalprek. (36–42) Sjúrður grows up with his mother in Hjalprek's kingdom (who fosters him), growing extremely fast and becomes very strong, until he was able to give heavy blows to the king's men. (43–51) He kills some of the king's men and eventually the boys tire of being beaten and tell him it would be better to avenge his father than to beat them. Sjúrður then goes to his mother and demands to know about his father and what had happened to him. She informs him that the sons of Hundingur killed Sigmundur, but she doesn't have much hope that he will manage to take revenge. (52–60) Sjúrður rebuffs his mother, saying young dogs often have sharp teeth, and Hjørdis gives him the sword pieces, showing him Sigmundur's blood-drenched clothing. She instructs him to visit Regin to get a new sword forged from the pieces, and echoes Sigmundur by mentioning the dragon Frænar on Glitrarheiði and that Regin is loyal to few again. (61–64) Sjúrður asks for his mother's help in getting a horse, and she advises him to throw a rock in the river and to pick the horse that doesn't run away. He does so and picks the horse Grani. (65–72) Sjúrður goes to find Regin and asks him to forge a sword from the two pieces from Sigmundur. (73–79) Regin only works on the sword one night, and when Sjúrður returns to try it, it breaks into two pieces. (80–87) Sjúrður threatens to kill Regin if

1 Numbers in parentheses correspond to stanzas in the ballads being referenced.

he doesn't make a better sword, and Regin says he will do so if he can have the heart of the dragon. (88–97) Regin now works on the sword for thirty nights, and when Sjúrður returns to try it, the sword is so good that when he tries it, Sjúrður splits the anvil apart and the block underneath. He calls the sword Gramm. (98–104) Regin wants to come with him to Glitrarheiði but first Sjúrður avenges his father by killing the sons of Hundingur. (105–15) After Sjúrður has ridden through the forest, an old man joins him on a beach, it is Nornagestur. Nornagestur asks who is with Sjúrður, and when Sjúrður explains it is Regin the smith, who is also the dragon's brother, Nornagestur tells Sjúrður that Regin intends for him to die by giving him poor advice on how many trenches to dig to avoid the dragon's poison, and explains how to circumvent this. (116–19) Sjúrður prepares himself and the dragon has left the gold and is lying under a waterfall. (120–28) Sjúrður attacks the dragon and the foundations of the world tremble. As the dragon dies, it converses with Sjúrður, asking who he is. Sjúrður identifies himself, the dragon asks who came with him and advises him to kill Regin, since the dragon knows he will kill Sjúrður. (129–35) Sjúrður roasts the heart of the dragon, he burns his hands, and sticks his hands in his mouth and can understand the language of birds and animals.[2] The birds tell him to eat the heart himself rather than give it to Regin, and Regin lies down to drink the dragon blood, and Sjúrður kills him. (136–41) Sjúrður gets a large amount of gold and straps twelve chests to Grani's back and mounts him (displeasing the horse). Grani leaps over a river and the buckle bursts, and Nornagestur gets the buckle. (142) The narrator ends the ballad.

The Ballad of Brynhild (Brynhildar táttur)

(1–3) The narrator begins the ballad and tells about King Buðlin, who goes into his daughter's hall. (4–13) His daughter, Brynhild, sits on Hildarfjall on her throne, combing her hair and rejecting suitors. Her father comes in and demands that she stop refusing men. (14–26) She tells her father that Sjúrður is the only man she will accept, her father points out she has never seen him and she replies that the norns have decreed this. Buðlin asks how Sjúrður is better than other men, and she lists his exploits, including slaying the dragon Frænir. (27–34) Buðlin asks how they will get Sjúrður to come to them, and Brynhild asks for a hall surrounded by a wall of fire to be conjured

2 It is not explicitly stated in the ballad, but in Old Norse tradition it is consuming the blood of the dragon by sucking his burnt hands after he prods the heart to see whether it is done that allows him to understand the speech of birds.

up by dwarves, that only Sjúrður can ride through, which is done. (35) An interjection describing how many men have lost their lives for women. (36–46) Noble men ride to Buðli's hall,[3] King Gunnar arrives and Buðli tells Brynhild she must accept him. She hurries away to Hildarheygur, her mound (on which her hall stands). Grímur and Høgnar fight. (47–60) Brynhild, sitting on her throne, draws Sjúrður to her. He rides out and the birds tell him she is expecting him. Dressed in gold gloves and gold rings, he leaves for Buðli's land, riding the unequalled horse Grani. (61–69) Sjúrður rides down by Júki's court on the way, and Grimhild, curious about where he is going, stands outside and tries to stop him, as she has a daughter who wants to marry him. He says he must keep going to the wall of fire. He gets dressed and says he has an errand to go there. (70–81) No one dares to cross the wall of fire to win Brynhild; Grímur turns back. (73–97) Sjúrður is the only one who manages to ride onto Brynhilduheygur. Grani's hooves thunder as he leaps over and the fire burns around them, they reach a golden gate and Sjúrður chops down the door with his sword. He then splits off the latch, and he sees Brynhild in bed, lying in armour, which he splits open with his sword. This wakes her, and she asks who he is, he identifies himself and she welcomes him. He says to have been shown the way to her by an eagle. Brynhild wants him to ask her father if they can marry, but Sjúrður declines to do so, saying she has waited long enough. They fall in love and conceive a child, Ása Sjúrðardóttir. He gives her twelve gold rings. (98–113) Guðrun draws Sjúrður to her. Sjúrður asks Brynhild to fetch him a saddle, bridle and armour; Brynhild's heart chills, she understands Guðrun's plan. Sjúrður declares it unlikely he would lose his love for her, but Brynhild begs him not to go. Sjúrður rides away early one morning and meets her father on the way. Her father knows what will happen and foretells he will marry Guðrun and never have Brynhild. He says Sjúrður ought to keep his promise to Brynhild, but Sjúrður once again declares it unlikely he would lose his love for her, although her father warns him that something shameful will happen and he should not ride to the court of Júki, and asks Sjúrður to remember his words. (114–37) Sjúrður rides into the woods and encounters a beast spewing fire and poison. It suddenly disappears and Grimhild is sitting in its place. She bewitches his horse so that he can not continue, and she grabs the reins. Sjúrður says this is bold of her, she asks him to stop and speak to her beautiful daughter. Sjúrður says she is not equal to Brynhild. Guðrun comes out and says it will hardly go well to covet a man another has, for which her

3 In some parts of the ballad the name is Buðlin, in some parts Buðli.

mother hits her in the mouth and tells her to hold her tongue. Guðrun mixes a drink of forgetfulness, and Sjúrður loses his memory, forgets about Brynhild, and wants to marry Guðrun. (138–42) Sjúrður goes to the bedroom to find Guðrun, Brynhild hears about it and is full of spite. The narrator says Sjúrður will lose his life. Brynhild says Guðrun will not have him, and echoes Guðrun's words that to covet a man another has will not go well. (143–54) Brynhild and Guðrun meet, one happy and one in grief. They are at a river and Guðrun will not use the water flowing downstream from Brynhild washing her hair because she married Sjúrður and thus thinks herself superior, so she goes further out into the river. Guðrun asks where Brynhild got her ring from and she answers that she was given it by Sjúrður. Guðrun wonders why King Gunnar will not marry Brynhild, but Brynhild says she will not love two kings in one hall. Guðrun says to Brynhild that Sjúrður took Brynhild's virginity and points out that now she has him. Brynhild accuses Guðrun of lying and says Sjúrður shall die. Guðrun is undeterred. (155–160) Brynhild cries and goes to sit in her hall, Gunnar comes to visit her, but she tells him he cannot expect her to love him when Sjúrður still lives. Sjúrður comes to see her, she tells him he has not been faithful, and he says his thoughts were turned from her. (161–63) As soon as she sees him, Brynhild delivers a daughter. She orders the baby to be put into the river, and she floats away. (164–69) The narrator says that Brynhild will bring about the death of Sjúrður and comments that many men have endured threats for women and that women will cause Sjúrður to die. (170–87) Brynhild, adorned with gold and her hair in a twist, is very angry and goes into the hall. Sjúrður kicks her chair which angers her. Høgnar says he will take revenge on the one who has offended her, and Brynhild says she cannot sleep while Sjúrður still lives. Høgnar says Sjúrður is his sworn brother and he cannot do anything to him, and Brynhild answers he will get no love from her while he still lives. Høgnar says fighting Sjúrður is no easy task, and she repeats he will get no love from her while Sjúrður lives. The men plan to ride to the forest, and Brynhild tells them not to return until Sjúrður has been killed. They ask why she wants to put them in mortal danger since no one can withstand him. They ask her for advice on how to kill him, and she tells them to give him salty food and no drink with it. (188–92) Sjúrður is in the hall and Brynhild cannot look at him. She says she will never turn her love from him, Sjúrður acknowledges the situation is bad and says when they return from the forest, he will be betrothed to her. She says that will not happen. (193–209) The men ride out, and Brynhild is left behind crying. Buðlin says Sjúrður should be given his helmet since he will need to drink from it, but Brynhild says it shall be left behind. Buðlin asks why she is causing his death, she says it is because he does not love her. Her father reminds her of when she drew Sjúrður to her. Buðlin walks out of the hall, Brynhild is left with her head in her hands. The narrator comments women are dangerous. Sjúrður has no idea what is afoot as Brynhild looks out at him riding in front of the men. Sjúrður's sword is also left behind. Brynhild cries in torment and says she will not see him alive again. (210–28) The men give Sjúrður salty food and no drink while Brynhild sits on Hildarstólur. Sjúrður cannot scoop up water to drink since he does not have his helmet, so he loosens his helmet, dismounts and lies down to drink.[4] Høgnar cuts his throat and Gunnar hacks at him. Sjúrður says had he known about this, he would have defeated all of them, and he knocks Gunnar off his horse and says that although Høgnar has killed him now, he has defeated him previously in Finnmark. He goes pale. (229–35) A messenger comes to tell Brynhild that Sjúrður is dead, killed by Gunnar, she faints from Hildarstólur. Gunnar comes to visit her, she is crying in bed and he sits by her bedside. Gunnar says the corpse shall be brought back to the hall. (236–45) The men change horses, but Grani will not move because he has a mind like a person, and will not move until the decapitated Sjúrður is put on him. Sjúrður is taken home to the hall and laid by Guðrun. Brynhild is in great distress on seeing the dead man being carried in. (246–56) Brynhild dies of grief. The narrator emphasizes many men have died due to women and gives the examples of Hósin's daughter, Ingigerð, Delilah, Ásla Sjúrðardóttir and Guðrun Júkadóttir. (257–65) The dead Sjúrður is laid in Guðrun's lap and she wakes covered in blood. She knows Gunnar has been involved in this, and she kisses Sjúrður, swears to take revenge on Gunnar and runs to her loft. (266–70) It is mentioned again that Brynhild dies of sorrow. Guðrun receives gold, property and rings. A brother and her mother mentions King Artala has a lot of gold. Guðrun replies she will avenge Sjúrður's death. (271) The narrator ends the ballad.

The Ballad of Høgni (Høgna táttur)

(1–7) Artala is married to Guðrun. He announces to his men this shall be so, and he rides through the forest. Guðrun is stood before him, they are married and he takes her back to Húnaland. Guðrun plots to avenge Sjúrður. (8–11) Artala invites Júki's people (Guðrun's family) to drink at their home, and Guðrun's invites her brothers. She has wine mixed. (12–20) Høgnar says

---

4 As noted in the translation, it is emphasized and important for the plot that Sjúrður does not have a helmet with him. However, in st. 215 it is explicitly stated that he loosens his helmet straps.

he wants to go to Húnaland, but Grimhild warns if he goes, neither he nor the others will return. She wants Gíslar and Jarnar to stay at home, but they go. (21–28) Høgnar meets a mermaid on the beach, and asks her whether he will return safely from Húnaland. She says he will not and he chops her in two pieces and throws her head and body into the sea. Høgnar meets a merman, and asks him whether he will return safely from Húnaland. The merman says he will. (29–34) Høgnar launches a ship. Grimhild, crying, turns back to the court and says she will not see him alive again since she knows Guðrun will harm him. Høgnar tells Gunnar they are setting sail for the sea. (35–44) A man sees the ship and says it must be Høgnar on his way to visit his sister. Guðrun carves runes and send them out to sea. The wind picks up and the weather becomes severe. Høgnar is steering and Gunnar goes pale. The ship creaks and the oars break apart in Høgnar's hands. They land in Húnaland, the ships still making a lot of noise. (45–51) Høgnar steps on to land with Gíslar, Jarnar, and Gunnar and they go to the castle's garden. As they enter the castle, Høgnar can see evil on Guðrun's face. (52–65) Guðrun offers to store their weapons. Høgnar refuses to give his up. Guðrun asks if they remember anything about Sjúrður, who they laid bloody in her lap. Guðrun relates how Sjúrður was a better man. Høgnar thinks to himself that Guðrun is not in a good mood if she is taking up that topic. The table is set with beer. Guðrun once more asks them to discard their weapons, and Høgnar refuses. They drink mead and wine, but Guðrun is unhappy there is no conflict. (66–75) Guðrun coaxes her young son to silence Høgnar's laughter and promises him gold. He punches Høgnar on the nose, even though he initially refused to do so. Blood runs from Høgnar's nose and mouth, and he says he doesn't thank the mother who raised the child like that. He runs his sword through the child, killing him, and throws the head on the floor so King Artala can see it. (76–95) Guðrun informs Artala that Høgnar has killed their child and that she will not rule Húnaland with him any longer if he doesn't take revenge. Artala refuses since Høgnar is her brother and also points out that Gíslar and Jarnar had nothing to do with the death of Sjúrður. Guðrun wants them both to pay for the death anyway and declares she will have them killed. Artala says it is not easy to kill Høgnar and asks her for a plot to kill her brothers. Guðrun tells him to take three skins and smear them with blood, then to attack her brothers (the implication being when they fall on the skins). She informs her brothers they shall walk on the skins. Høgnar tries to send Gíslar and Jarnar back to their mother, saying that he and Gunnar were responsible for slaying Sjúrður. (96–107) Gíslar and Jarnar walked on the skins, and no one saw them get up (they have been killed). Gunnar walks on the skins and does not rise. Guðrun tells Høgnar she is avenging Sjúrður. Høgnar walks on the skins carrying his sword in the air and he doesn't fall. (108–15) Guðrun is angry because Høgnar is unharmed, and Høgnar says that before evening, they will be drinking blood like wine. Guðrun has 1200 men armoured, and Høgnar rides against them all, killing many of them. (116–28) In the morning, Guðrun comes out and finds Høgnar unharmed. She sends him into the forest to see wonders he slew in the past, and he does so. He sees a giant horse Guðrun has conjured up by witchcraft, bearing Sjúrður. The apparition of Sjúrður speaks to him and says that Høgnar did evil when he betrayed him, that both Brynhild and Guðrun had loved him, and therefore he had lost his life. Sjúrður gives Høgnar a runic belt he got from the dead dwarf maiden and says he will now ride to the heathen forest. (130–36) Early in the morning, Guðrun has armoured 1200 men and Høgnar rides against them all, killing many of them, commenting that however many he kills, Guðrun brings them back to life during the night. (137–58) Guðrun has Tíðrikur Tatlarason brought to her and she says if he took Høgnar's life it would be a manly deed. He asks how he should fight against someone who no weapons can hurt, and that no one is Høgnar's equal now that Sjúrður is dead. He states he will not win against Høgnar, and the queen goes grey. Guðrun promises to reward him with gold and property if he rides against him, and Tíðrikur responds that he will fly through the sky and see how it goes, turning into a dragon. Høgnar, who is fighting, sees the dragon flying above him. He throws his sword into the sky and it runs through Tíðrikur, who has the sword in his heart. The dragon spews down poison onto Høgnar, which burns him severely. The poison flows towards his heart, and he goes pale and is forced back to the walls of the hall. (159–77) Guðrun comes out early in the morning and is angry to see Høgnar, apparently standing unharmed leaning on the hall walls. Høgnar asks her if he can sleep during the night with Helvík the jarl's daughter, claiming he has not received a wound. Guðrun says he will be allowed this since he will be dead soon. Høgnar lies with Helvík and they conceive a son. Høgnar carves runes and they are read immediately. He says Helvík will have a son, she should call him Høgnar and that he will give him his sword, inherited from his father. The boy should also avenge his death. He also advises her on how to thwart Guðrun's plan to kill the baby by swapping him with Guðrun's baby. After twelve years, the child will recognize her. He gives her the runic belt and dies. They dress his corpse for burial, and he is buried in a mound.

The Second Ballad of Høgni or The Ballad of Aldrias (Annar Høgna táttur or Aldrias táttur)

(1–13) Guðrun and Helvík both give birth to boys. Helvík has the boy baptized as Høgnar, and Guðrun has her son called Sveinur. They sit inside for some days and then go out, Guðrun asking Helvík to go first. Helvík declines, saying she must go out first. Helvík switches their babies. Guðrun takes what she believes to be Helvík's child and cuts its throat. (14–15) Høgnar grows rapidly, and is fostered by the king of Húnaland. (16–28) Helvík rides to Lindará and meets her son there, and tells him she is his mother. He says she is lying, and at her invitation cuts her with a knife. This causes him such pain he believes that she is his mother, and she tells him he must avenge his father. She gives him a runestick that Høgnar gave him. In the runestick, he could see his father's death. She gives him the rune belt she got from Høgnar. She tells him that when he gets to the hall, no one must find him. (29–38) Early in the morning Høgnar wants to ride to the hall and he goes inside. The flame from a light burns through his foot, King Artala points out to him that his foot is burning and asks what he is thinking about. Høgnar answers that he is thinking that even though Artala possesses great riches, at some point in his life he may have to beg for water and bread. Artala says this will not happen. (39–51) Early in the morning, Høgnar invites Artala to ride to the forest, and they do so. They go to the gold cliff to examine the riches. Artala tells Sveinur (Høgnar) that he should go in first, but he says that since Artala is wearing a higher crown, he should go in first. Artala looks around the door, and Sveinur slams it shut, trapping him inside. He asks Artala whether he wants to beg for bread and water, and Artala does so. Høgnar gets a lot of gold and doesn't return until the king shrivels up and dies. (52–53) Høgnar stays the night with his mother and then rides to the king of Denmark. The narrator ends by saying many the woman is wretched, and Guðrun walks around the world holding Grani's reigns.

The Ballad of Gestur or The Ballad of Ásla (Gests ríma or Áslu ríma)

(1–3) Gestur goes to the river and finds a harp. He carries the harp on his back and stays the night at a farm where a maiden/hag lives. (4–6) The maiden/hag invites Gestur to stay with her for the night, saying Haki will be back from the forest soon, and since Gestur couldn't do anything else, he puts the harp by the fire. Haki comes back from the forest shortly afterwards. (7–9) The hag says to Haki that they shall kill Gestur that night, but Haki refuses saying he has no issue with him. She says she will kill him herself. (10–11) The hag goes up and kills Gestur. (12–14) The hag breaks up the harp and finds a maiden dressed in red. The hag says the maiden shall have an easy life, be called Kráka and be her daughter. The maiden says she is not named Kráka. (15–23) Ragnar lands and his men go into Haki's courtyard with bread to be baked. A maiden comes in and out of the courtyard and they stare at her while the bread burns. The hag pours a brewing vessel over Kráka and tells her where to sit, Kráka refuses and the hag hits her. The men ask why she hits such a beautiful woman, and she replies she has killed people in the past. (24–34) The men tear out a piece of Kráka's hair and carry it to the ship. Ragnar asks why the food is spoiled, and they say they saw a very beautiful maiden, more beautiful than Tóra. Ragnar replies that if they are mocking him, they will all be going to the gallows. They show him the hair and he says to go and tell her that Ragnar wants to see her, which they do. (35–37) Ása is out walking and calls to her a little young dog.

The Ballad of Nornagestur (Nornagests ríma)

(1) The narrator announces that this is a ballad about Nornagestur. (2–6) Twelve oxen were led to a market and then to a castle, where they were killed by the king with a great blow that everyone praised. A lot of blood flowed. (7–8) The king asks the old man (Nornagestur) why he did not praise his blow, and the man replies that the king's blow was angry and he has seen more graceful ones in the past. (9–15) The king asks if he can tell the story of Sjúrður. Nornagestur replies that he can, no one has seen such a man, leaf and grove shook when he chopped the dragon apart. Høgni was an honourable man although ugly. Gunnar was strong, powerful, wise and kind like Grimhild and it will be a long time before another like him is born. (16–19) Gunnar, Høgni and Sjúrður rode home round the marsh, Gunnar and Høgni's horses both jumped over, but Grani (Sjúrður's horse) got stuck in the fen. Nornagestur comments he has often trodden in the marsh himself. (20–25) All dismounted, and all pulled on their horses, Sjúrður the most. He orders Nornagestur to clean his horse. They rode by a river and couldn't see each other. Nornagestur cleans the horse and Sjúrður takes him as his squire. (26–28) They ride to Fávnir's lair where there is shining gold. The hair in the horse's tail is extremely long and sparkles like silver. (29–31) The king gave him weapons and a ship and told him the way. Nornagestur says that he spent his life scouting lands, and he has travelled extensively. (32–33) The courteous man dives down to lead,[5] and Kørnar the priest baptizes Nornagestur, who dies as the candle burns out.

---

5 This seems to be a lead lantern at the bottom of the sea, in which his candle is kept.

Ísmal the Brave Hero (Ísmal fræga kempa)

(1–4) Ísmal tells Hermundur that they shall ride to the king's court to ask for his daughter. He throws a cloak on and walks into the halls where Hjalprek sits at the table with five hundred men. (5–8) Ísmal stands on the hall floor with a silk-buttoned hat, red cheeks and blue eyes. He asks for the king's daughter, and the king thinks about how he should give a mocking reply, saying that if Sjúrður were to stand by Ísmal, he would be his equal. (9–12) Svanhild walks in and falls in love with Ísmal. The king thinks about how he should give a friendly reply. He tells Ísmal he will give him his daughter and a wedding feast as well. Svanhild and Ísmal are betrothed, he leaves then is sent for by the king. (13–23) Ísmal asks who will invite Sjúrður to the wedding, the king tells him to invite him himself. Ísmal rides into the forest and meets Sjúrður, who is not happy. Ísmal invites him to the wedding, and Sjúrður asks him who he is betrothed to. Ísmal tells him it is his sister and Sjúrður says that if he has been betrothed to her without his having been asked, he will beat him with clubs. Ísmal offers him another option, and Sjúrður says Ísmal will have to complete some hard tasks. (24–30) Ísmal asks what the first task is, and Sjúrður says in the forest there are dragons and Ísmal shall kill all of them before he can be married. Ísmal asks how big they are and Sjúrður tells him, then Ísmal says he is not afraid. He kills all the dragons but has poison breathed on to him and doesn't manage to leave. (31–37) Sjúrður goes back to the court and Svanhild is waiting outside. He sits in the highseat and the castle shakes. He tells his father he wishes his neck was broken since he wasn't asked about the betrothal. Svanhild asks whether he has contrived a plot that Ísmal should perform deeds. He tells her to leave since it wouldn't be seemly to kill a woman. Svanhild begins to cry and Sjúrður tells her to get out of his sight, although admits Ísmal was not a lesser man than he was. (38–41) Sjúrður mounts his horse and goes back to the forest for his sister's sake. Ísmal, lying on the field in danger from the dragons, is relieved to hear Grani approaching. Sjúrður takes him into the saddle and, dreading his wounds, finds ointment to put on him. (42–46) Sjúrður takes Ísmal home and gives him to Svanhild to heal. When he is healed, they have the wedding prepared and many people are invited, including the king of France. (47–50) Ísmal's bridesmen are King Hjalprek and Gunnar. Svanhild's bridesmaids include Gunnhild, Grimhild, Brynhild and Guðrun. Ørvaroddur played the harp and Hjálmar supported the maidens. (51–53) There are abundant newly made silver dishes, Sjúrður stands on the hall floor and tells tales of bold heroes. Sjúrður is upset by Brynhild's conversation and breaks a mead cup on the table. (54–58) Everyone was happy and the lady was escorted with candles and lanterns and an organ playing in the garden to sleep on the first night. Ísmal and his wife enter the same bed. (59–60) After a long wedding celebration with as many courtiers in attendance as there are feathers in a bird's wing, everyone went home. (61) The narrator ends the ballad.

Sjúrður and the Dwarf Maiden or Dwarf Maiden I (Sjúrður og Dvørgamoy or Dvørgamoy I)

(1–5) The narrator tells that he has known of a ballad for a long time. Hjalprekur rules a kingdom and of his many heroes, the foremost one is Sjúrður. The narrator says he will now compose verses about Sjúrður's first expedition when he rode out for the first time. (6–10) Early in the morning, Sjúrður dresses himself and the horse, adorned in scarlet, is untied. Sjúrður puts on his new armour and says that he wants to go into the forest and see marvels. (11–33) Sjúrður rode into the forest for three days, unable to see or hear anything. On the fourth day, he sees a great fleet, and as he goes towards it, he sees a whole ring of dwarves in front of him. The dwarves ask if he has come to play and he doesn't dare to answer. The dwarves are annoyed, and he thinks to himself that he doesn't want to be killed and that they can choose the terms. The dwarves attack, and Sjúrður gets punched in the nose so the blood flows down his armour. This incenses him and he kills a dwarf. Another dwarf exclaims that particular dwarf wasn't in their band and that if he takes down another, he will not be leaving. (34–38) The dwarves disappear and Sjúrður walks in the dark. It is frosty and he is lost. The dwarf maiden, wise and sensible, comes to him, wearing clothes bordered with gold. He asks her to take him home to the hall. (39–46) She leads him to a castle on pillars, and he asks who lives there. She replies that it is her father's castle and that he should not respond to what her father says to him. Nor should he go into the smithy with him, because the father knows Sjúrður is easy to goad. He should lie down on the floor in the hall; if he answers, he will lose his head. (47–59) Sjúrður comes into the hall late in the evening, the dwarf is in his smithy. The dwarf sees a large horse tied up by the hall door, which incenses him. He asks what kind of warrior has arrived. The dwarf puts on his armour and gets his spear and asks for the guest to be brought in; his daughter explains Sjúrður is in trouble and tired, and should not be harmed. The dwarf tells Sjúrður to drink mead and wine and tells him to come into his smithy. As Sjúrður rises to go, he remembers the dwarf maiden has told him not to answer. The dwarf says he will give him armour and a spear. (60–65) Early in the morning Sjúrður dresses to ride home. He tells the dwarf maiden to get him home to the hall. She is grief-stricken but says she will get him far enough to see Hjalprekur's castle. They part sorrowfully and kiss. The dwarf maiden turns back crying, and Sjúrður goes home to King Hjalprekur.

The Beautiful Dwarf Maiden or Dwarf Maiden II (Dvørgamoyggin fagra or Dvørgamoy II)

(1–5) Ásmundur says he could not have the maiden that came here last night. Ásmundur rides out early in the morning. A king[6] takes the dwarf maiden home with him and tells his men to invite guests to the wedding. They are to ride to Sjúrður. The king comments he knows Ásmundur and his men. (6–11) The king's men ride out and Larsin the dwarf king arrives back to his hall, finding that sword, shield and the woman have all disappeared. Ásmundur asks him if he is not intending to take revenge on the king who has taken the maiden. The dwarf king says both his sword and shield are gone, and then Ásmundur says he will lend a sword and shield to the dwarf, and that he will also go on the journey himself to visit the king of the Huns. (12–19) They ride to the hall and find the king and the dwarf maiden playing chess. A man comes into the hall and tells him that an army is approaching the castle. The king arms himself and comments that Høgni and his troops are a long way away and that Sjúrður and Virgar are not home. He asks his brother Gíslar to explain his intentions to the dwarf king and Ásmundur and to invite them to drink mead. He does so, and the dwarf king replies that he is dressed for battle and if the king does not hand the woman back, then he will have to defend himself. (20–27) Early in the morning they start their battles near the king's hall. Ásmundur rides to the army and the king comes towards him, strikes him and he falls off his horse. This was caused by the king's queen carving runes. Everyone sees him fall off and lose. The dwarf kills the whole army and takes the woman back. The king loses land but survives. (28–31) A man comes into the hall to tell the king that his brother Høgni and Sjúrður are here. He welcomes Høgni by telling him that the army, land and the woman are all lost. Høgni replies he has been unable to find Virgar, who went to a foreign land to propose to a maiden. Sjúrður answers they will ride to the cliff and find the dwarf king. (32–50) They ride to the cliff and Sjúrður opens the door of the cavern with difficulty. The maiden sits at a table, the dwarf is in the smithy. The dwarf comments that often

---

6 Although the king this ballad features is not named, it must be King Gunnar, since Gíslar and Høgni are his brothers.

it is best to be a long way from men than to be their friends. Høgni replies that they are not friends and have come to avenge the damage inflicted on their brother. The dwarf arms himself and rides to a forest. Høgni lands a great blow on him but it didn't pierce his armour. They fought for twelve hours and Høgni begins to get tired and give ground, eventually falling off his horse. Early in the morning, Sjúrður fastens his helmet on and gives a great blow, that also doesn't pierce the dwarf's armour. They fight for twelve hours, Sjúrður begins to get tired, and the sword gets too heavy, so he throws three spears, none of which injure the dwarf. He hits the dwarf over the head with his sword, which also does not injure the dwarf. The dwarf hits Sjúrður so hard it knocks his helmet off. Then the dwarf gives him such a blow that Sjúrður's armour splits and Grani falls to his knees. Sjúrður has planned this and now is able to split the shields and armour of the dwarf. Wounded, the dwarf gives Sjúrður the victory. (51–53) Sjúrður and Høgni ride to the dwarf's castle, where the maiden is alone sewing white linen. They take her and the gold. Sjúrður puts her on the back of his horse and takes her back to the hall, the narrator says that now the ballad will end. (54–55) Sjúrður does not take the maiden back to the king, but back to his own hall, telling Høgni to tell the king that the maiden is his reward. The maiden joins the women at his hall but doesn't want to. She had aided Ásmundur well when he needed it. (56–60) Høgni had a son with the same name, until he defeated Artala. He sailed into a harbour and lay there until the quarrel was avenged. After this, he was called Aldrias. Ásmundur Aldriansson ruled over Húnaland after Artan's death.

Ása the Dwarf Maiden or Dwarf Maiden III (Ása Dvørgamoy or Dvørgamoy III)

(1–8) Early in the morning, Sjúrður dresses himself and gets ready to ride. He rides into the forest where he sees a golden hall open and the gold spills out. The hall is made of precious materials. Sjúrður thinks to himself he shall go inside. He walks into the hall and a beautiful dwarf maiden is sitting before him. She says he is too highborn to stand and fetches him a chair. She says that many have asked for a lady's hand, but none can be compared to him. (9–10) She leads him into her hall, and says that he can see it is edged with gold and is spacious. (11–23) Sjúrður wants to know who the two warriors are that ride in the forest, she says they are called Hálvdan and Eirikur, who are riding to Ásgarðar to test Óðin's heroes. She says the weather is bad in her land and it is better to fall in love with her in golden castles. Sjúrður replies that he will not marry his property away on heathen lands. Ása the dwarf maiden unlocks a chest and hands him clothes that none in his land have the skills to make. Sjúrður says he will not bring heathen clothes back to his land. She gives him armour, and he says he will not bring heathen armour to his land. (24–26) She answers he should stay with her for the night and leave tomorrow. He says that he will not stay longer and will hurry on his way. He stays the night and conceives a child with the dwarf maiden. (27–37) Early in the morning Sjúrður dresses himself and gets ready to ride. She asks when she can expect him to visit her. He promises to come in three months. Sjúrður leaves the hall cheerful, but Grani has run away. He goes back into the mound, she lends him a horse and goes on the way with him. Sjúrður is cheerful and finds Grani just outside the forest. (38–57) Sjúrður was going to ride to the hall when a giant suddenly came down from the mountains. Sjúrður has to turn back after the giant throws his spear into the field. Sjúrður asks to go home, and they should meet another time. The giant says Sjúrður won't make it one step further because he has slept with the dwarf maiden and not told him about it. The giant deals out heavy blows, sometimes Sjúrður dodges and sometimes fights back. Grani comes running and things start to go better. Sjúrður leaps into the saddle and says he shall now fight the mountain giant. They fight for two days and on the third day as the sun goes down, Sjúrður chops the giant in two at the knee. The giant plants the stumps on the ground and continues fighting. Sjúrður chops the giant in half again. (58–62) Sjúrður is cheerful and rides home to the hall. Hjalprekur asks him where he has been for the evening and Sjúrður says he fought a mountain giant. (63–67) Early in the morning, Sjúrður dresses himself and gets ready to ride. He rides into the forest and sees the golden hall. He goes into the same mound as previously, and finds the dwarf maiden dead. He buried her in the mound and lays much gold with her. He also buries the beautiful baby girl. Then he rides back to the hall.

The Ballad of Kvørfinn or Dwarf Maiden V (Kvørfinns táttur or Dvørgamoy V)

(1–9) Tíðrikur sits in Brattingsborg, and the narrator says he will compose verses on the theme of dwarves. Tíðrikur wants to ride to the heathen forest and Virgar says he if goes, he will not come back. Tíðrikur's horse is untied while Virgar remains at home, until eventually he rides out to find Tíðrikur and catches up with him. (10–21) Tíðrikur orders that the horses shall rest and they shall walk into the forest. They sleep there and Virgar wakes to the sound of horses. He leaps on his horse's back, takes his sword and sees a might giant, who asks him why he rides in Birtingsskógur, his lord's land.

The giant is Sjúrður, and he aims blows with his sword at Virgar and lands each one. Tíðrikur wakes, hears the swords and is afraid when Virgar is gone. Sjúrður hacks with his sword Grammur so that sparks fly from Virgar's armour. Tíðrikur goes home, leaving his shield and sword behind. (22–34) Sjúrður hacks until he is tired and sits on the field, both he and Virgar are unhappy. Virgar asks him what family he is from, and he says he is Sjúrður and closest to King Hjalprekur in terms of gold, authority and ability. Virgar says that if Sjúrður had had his sword, Mimaring, he would not have been able to withstand him. Sjúrður recognizes Virgar and asks where Tíðrikur is. Virgar says that Tíðrikur is in the forest, and that they shall ride to Tíðrikur's home to gain more honour. Sjúrður says no one dares to turn his horse away. The narrator says such arguments rarely end well. Sjúrður says they shall ride through the forest and perform more great deeds. (35–41) Early in the morning, Sjúrður and Virgar ride in heathen forests. (42–51) Dragons and wolves start to howl and a storm approaches. The riding conditions are bad. Giants are singing. Virgar becomes afraid and suggests they turn back. Sjúrður advises him that that suggestion ought not to be known about at home. Sjúrður says they shall ride through the forest. (52–66) They come to a house and Sjúrður says they shall stay with the women there and continue the next day. Inside the house there are many beautiful swords and two maidens sitting at the table. Costly drink is on the table which Sjúrður takes. Sjúrður asks who rules the castle, and Virgar says if they don't answer they will be placed before swords. A dwarf maiden answers it is her father Kvørfinn who rules the castle and that he is away in the forest fighting giants to get ore from the crags. Virgar says they shall take the dwarf maidens back to the hall with them. (67–71) Virgar takes the two maidens on his horse and Sjúrður takes the best sword the dwarf had made and snaps all the others. He takes as much gold and silver as the horse can carry and they depart. (72–77) Kvørfinn comes home and sees the swords and maidens are gone. He makes a new sword and swears to avenge the maidens. (78–84) Sjúrður and Virgar go home and are greeted by Hjalprek outside the court. He asks who Virgar with the two maidens is, and he is identified by Sjúrður. Hjalprek tells Virgar to go into the hall with his maidens. Virgar was tired and slept for three nights at Hjalprek's. (85–93) Early in the morning, Virgar dresses himself and embraces the maidens. He asks Hjalprek to lend him a ship to take the maidens over the sound and Hjalprek agrees. They sail, and Virgar has castles built in which to keep the two maidens. They should sit there and weave silk. Virgar went back to Tíðrikur.

The Giant of Hólmgarðar or The Mound Ghost (Risin í Hólmgørðum or Dysjadólgur)

(1–2) The narrator knows a ballad about Virgar, Sjúrður and Nornagestur. (3–11) There are three paths, and one deviates from the others. Virgar goes to the mound where his grandfather lies. He asks his grandfather if he is awake and identifies himself. The grandfather refuses to leave the mound. Virgar asks him for Miming (a sword) and says he is breaking up the mound with his hands to get to it. The occupant within the mound (the mound-ghost) doesn't want the mound to be broken up so sends up the sword. Virgar asks him where medicines can be found. The mound-ghost says he knows of a lot of medicines, but that Virgar will not win them. He tells him about a house in Hólmgarðar full of medicine and says that he ought not leave Sjúrður behind if he goes on the trip. (12–17) Virgar mounts his horse and goes to meet Sjúrður. In the garden, he dons his cloak and goes before Sjúrður, who is sitting next to Hjalprekur. Virgar tells Sjúrður he knows of a lot of medicine if he is man enough to win it, and that he must equip himself. (18–23) Virgar and Sjúrður ride from the hall with Nornagestur. They go to the hall, Vilkus the giant's son is standing outside and Sjúrður asks if he has any medicine spare to sell him. The giant says he does not and asks who he is travelling with. Virgar is identified as the one who slew the giant. The giant thanks him for telling him and says he shall arm his company since he was the one who lost. (24–33) Early in the morning the giant had armoured his troops and Sjúrður and Virgar ride against them. They fought for two full days and Virgar got tired, he fell backwards spreadeagled. Nornagestur saves him and takes him away. Sjúrður fights heavily and splits the giant's army. Virgar is injured but gets up and continues to fight. They fight together until just the giant and one of his men are left. (34–36) The giant creeps to the castle gate and begs Sjúrður for mercy. Sjúrður says he can have mercy if he can hide himself. Virgar arrives and chops the giant in two. (37–40) Sjúrður says he has won the medicine and Virgar should thank him. Virgar says Sjúrður has won and should accept the medicine. Virgar takes the medicine away on two steeds and Sjúrður ruled in Holmgarðar.

The Giant of Leittraberg (Risin av Leittrabergi)

(1–13) The narrator knows a ballad. There is a giant on Leittraberg that speaks with his heroes, wanting to know where his father's killer is, since he wants to avenge him. The leader of the men, Filkussonur, says he will not win against his father's killer. He is asked again and Filkussonur says it was Sjúrður. The giant of Leittraberg asks where Sjúrður lives and is told he lives in Hólmgarðar in Norway. It is told he has killed many giants and that if the giant goes to Hólmgarðar, he will end up dead. The giant threatens to have Filkussonur burnt on a bonfire, who replies that if he does so he will never take Sjúrður prisoner. Filkussonur dresses in new armour and says Sjúrður will not be his prisoner. (14–22) The giant leaves and goes to forge himself a shield and sword. He has ships made and readied, with ropes made out of gold. He loads his ship with twenty barrels of gold. When he steps on his ship it goes under the water slightly, they set sail and don't stop before Norway. (23–32) A shepherd sitting on a hill sees the ships coming and goes into the king's hall, thinking he is wiser than they are. He tells that the giant of Leittraberg is coming to avenge his father and that he has seen a giant walking across the deck. Sjúrður says that in his dream the night before that Grani stood saddled with a lot of blood before him, that his spear fell from his belt and that his sword rang out on armour. (33–40) The giant has the anchor lowered and is the first to go ashore, Filkussonur with him. They drag their ship ashore. Sjúrður sends a man down to the beach to offer the giant peace, to sit at the table and drink mead, as long as they do no dirty tricks. (41–50) The messenger walks down to the beach to offer this, and the giant bites him in half at the waist. This is seen by Sjúrður from the window, and he tells his men to arm themselves and not to fear the giant's large army. He fastens his helmet on tightly. (51–65) The giant puts his cloak on and goes into the hall where Sjúrður sits by the table. Sjúrður welcomes the giant and invites him to drink, but the giant refuses, saying he has received no reparations for his father. Sjúrður says he will not be receiving any. The giant takes a swing at Sjúrður, who dodges. The giant drags Sjúrður by the hair, and Sjúrður says no one has ever done that before. Sjúrður leaps up, upends the tables, and brandishes his sword. There is chaos in the hall and Sjúrður strikes the giant so he falls backwards out of the hall onto the field. The giant says he has come from Leittraberg and tells Sjúrður to arm his troops and come out of the hall. (66–101) Early in the morning, Sjúrður has equipped them and they battle close to the hall. Filkussonur kills every man who goes against him. Sjúrður then tells Nornagestur to saddle Grani and he rides into battle felling the giant's men. He clashes with Filkussonur. Nothing harms Sjúrður, but he hits Filkussonur so hard his head bursts in his helmet and he cuts him in two. Sjúrður sees almost all of his army has been killed and it diminishes his former joy in the battle. He clashes with the giant of Leittraberg. The weapons of the giant break, and he goes back to his ship to get a shield and a sword. He can cover eighteen ells in one step on his way back from the ship, and he says to Sjúrður that he will teach him how to fight. Sjúrður says it would have been better to be inside than fight with trolls. Nornagestur puts three new helmets on Sjúrður's head, and the giant chops them off. Sjúrður puts on a helmet he got from a dwarf maiden and now nothing can hurt him. They fight and Sjúrður decides to use stratagems that he has seldom used. He turns and jousts. The giant is not injured on the first joust, but on the second he pierces the giant's heart and poison spurts into the sky and blocks out the sun. On the third joust he chops the giant apart at the knees. (102–7) Sjúrður, now happy and cheerful, rides Grani back to the hall and tells Nornagestur to pour him a drink. After drinking, he complains about Grani, his horse. He goes down to the beach and gets twenty barrels of gold from the giant's ship. The narrator says he cannot sing more than what has been said in the ballad. Sjúrður sits down in a chair and rules over Hólmgarðar now as before.

BIBLIOGRAPHY

Andersen-Vindlandicus, Peter Hvilshøj. "Origin and Age of Sjúrðar kvæði According to Rational Philology." In *Ballads: New Approaches / Kvæði: nýggj sjónarmið*, edited by Malan Marnersdóttir, Eyðun Andreassen, Sanna A. Dahl, Tina K. Jakobsen, and Erling Isholm, 101–33. Annales Societatis Scientiarum Færoensis Supplementum 69. Tórshavn: Fróðskapur, 2018.

Andersson, Theodore M. *The Legend of Brynhild*. Islandica 43. Ithaca: Cornell University Press, 1980.

Andreassen, Eyðun. "Jesus á Glitrarheiði." In *Fólkaleikur: Heiðursrit til Jóan Paula Joensen*, edited by Andreas Mortensen, 28–37. Tórshavn: Føroya Fróðskaparfelag, 2005.

——. "Sjúrðar kvæði: muntlige middelalderballader eller romantisk diktning fra 1800-tallet." In *Ballads: New Approaches / Kvæði: Nýggj Sjónarmið*, edited by Malan Marnersdóttir, Eyðun Andreassen, Sanna A. Dahl, Tina K. Jakobsen, and Erling Isholm, 134–53. Annales Societatis Scientiarum Færoensis Supplementum 69. Tórshavn: Fróðskapur, 2018.

Árnadóttir, Tóta. "Chain Dancing." In *Handbook of Pre-Modern Nordic Memory Studies: Interdisciplinary Approaches*, edited by Jürg Glauser, Pernille Hermann, and Stephen A. Mitchell, vol. 1, 716–26. Berlin: De Gruyter, 2018.

——. "Den flyvende bejler: Historie og sammenheng." In *Ballads: New Approaches / Kvæði: nýggj sjónarmið*, edited by Malan Marnersdóttir, Eyðun Andreassen, Sanna A. Dahl, Tina K. Jakobsen, and Erling Isholm, 261–92. Annales Societatis Scientiarum Færoensis Supplementum 69. Tórshavn: Fróðskapur, 2018.

Benati, Chiara. "Jens Christian Svabo's Glossary: The Oral Tradition at the Beginning of Faroese Lexicography." In *Broadening Perspectives in the History of Dictionaries and Word Studies*, edited by Hans Van de Velde and Fredric T. Dolezal, 76–91. Newcastle upon Tyne: Cambridge Scholars, 2021.

Blindheim, Martin. *Sigurds saga i middelalderens billedkunst*. Oslo: Universitetets Oldsaksamling, 1972.

Boor, Helmut de. *Die Färöischen Lieder des Nibelungenzyklus*. Heidelberg: Winter, 1918.

Bryan, Eric Shane. "Indirect Aggression: A Pragmatic Analysis of the Quarrel of the Queens in Völsungasaga, Þiðreks Saga, and Das Nibelungenlied." *Neophilologus* 97 (2013): 349–65.

Chesnutt, Michael, and Kaj Larsen. "Descriptive and Analytical Catalogue of the Manuscripts of Faroese Ballads." In *History, Manuscripts, Indexes*, vol. 7 in *Føroya kvæði: Corpus Carminum Færoensium*, edited by Michael Chesnutt and Kaj Grundtvig Larsen, 51–123. Universitetsjubilæets danske Samfund 540. Copenhagen: Reitzel, 1996.

——, eds. *History, Manuscripts, Indexes*. Vol. 7 of *Føroya kvæði: Corpus Carminum Færoensium*. Universitetsjubilæets danske Samfund 540. Copenhagen: Reitzel, 1996.

Christensen, Annika. "'Kvæði í føroyskari samtíð': Exploring Ballads as Popular Culture and Heritage in Contemporary Faroese Culture." PhD Thesis, University of Leeds, 2020.

Clausen, Marianne. *Andlig vísuløg í Føroyum upptikin 1902–2002 / Spiritual Songs in the Faroes Melodies Recorded 1902–2002*. Hoyvík: Stiðin, 2006.

——. *Hundredesyv-visebogen: Danske folkeviser og andre viser på dansk med færøske melodier; indsamlet på Færøerne 1988–1994*. Tórshavn: Jacobsen, 1995.

——, ed. *Løgini / Melodies*. Vol. 8 of *Føroya kvæði: Corpus Carminum Færoensium*. Universitetsjubilæets danske Samfund 559. Hoyvík: Stiðin, 2003.

——. "Melodies to Faroese Kvæði." In *Løgini / Melodies*, vol. 8 of *Føroya kvæði: Corpus Carminum Færoensium*, edited by Marianne Clausen, 34–99. Universitetsjubilæets danske Samfund 559. Hoyvík: Stiðin, 2003.

——. *Vísuløg í Føroyum: upptikin 1902–2004 / Danish Folk Ballads in the Faroes: Melodies Recorded 1902–2004*. Hoyvík: Stiðin, 2010.

Clunies Ross, Margaret. *The Cambridge Introduction to the Old Norse-Icelandic Saga*. Cambridge Introductions to Literature. Cambridge: Cambridge University Press, 2010.

Colbert, David. *The Birth of the Ballad: The Scandinavian Medieval Genre*. Skrifter utgivna av svenskt visarkiv 10. Stockholm: Svenskt visarkiv, 1989.

Conroy, Patricia. "Ballad Composition in Faroese Heroic Tradition: The Case of 'Hernilds Kvæði.'" *Fróðskaparrit* 27 (1979): 75–101.

——. "Faroese Literature: The Preliterary Period: 800–1850." In *A History of Danish Literature*, edited by Sven H. Rossel, 545–49. A History of Scandinavian Literatures 1. Lincoln: University of Nebraska Press, 1992.

——. "'Sandoyarbók': A Faroese Ballad Collection, Its Collector and the Community." *Fróðskaparrit* 34 (1986): 23–41.

——. "Sniolvs Kvæði: The Growth of a Ballad Cycle." *Fróðskaparrit* 26 (1978): 33–53.

Dahl, Árni. *Bókmentasøga I: Frá landnámi til Hammershaimb*. Tórshavn: Fannir, 1980.

Dalsgaard, Valdemar. "Remarks on the Refrains." In *Løgini / Melodies*, vol. 8 of *Føroya kvæði: Corpus Carminum Færoensium*, edited by Marianne Clausen, 30–33. Universitets-Jubilæets danske Samfunds Skriftserie 559. Hoyvík: Stiðin, 2003.

Einar Ól. Sveinsson, ed. *Laxdœla saga*. Íslenzk fornrit 5. Reykjavík: Hið Íslenzka fornritafélag, 1934.

Espeland, Velle, Liv Kreken, Børge Nordbø, Elin Prøysen, Astrid Nora Ressem, Olav Solberg, and Ellen Nessheim Wiger, eds. *Norske mellomalderballadar*. 8 vols. Oslo: Nasjonalbiblioteket/bokselskap.no, 2015–2016. https://www.bokselskap.no/boker?sjanger=ballader.

Finch, R. G., ed. *Vǫlsunga Saga: The Saga of the Volsungs*. Icelandic Texts. New York: Nelson, 1965.

Frank, Roberta. "Germanic Legend in Old English Literature." In *The Cambridge Companion to Old English Literature*, edited by Malcolm Godden and Michael Lapidge, 88–106. Cambridge: Cambridge University Press, 1991.

Fuss, Klaus. *Die faröischen Lieder der Nibelungensage: Text, Lesarten und Übersetzung*. 3 vols. Göppinger Arbeiten zur Germanistik 427, 428, 429. Göppingen: Kümmerle, 1985–1987.

Føroyamálsdeild, Fróðskaparsetur Føroya. Bandasavn. https://bandasavn.setur.fo/.

Føroysk-ensk orðabók. Accessed January 24, 2025. https://sprotin.fo/dictionaries?_SearchFor=&_SearchInflections=0&_SearchDescriptions=0&_DictionaryPage=1&_DictionaryId=2&_Group=.

Føroysk-ensk orðabók / Faroese-English Dictionary: With Faroese Folk-Lore and Proverbs and a Section by Professor W. B. Lockwood on Faroese Pronunciation, s.v. "Yppa." Peel: Mansk-Svenska, 1985.

Føroysk-føroysk orðabók, s.v. "Forða." https://sprotin.fo/dictionaries?_SearchInflections=0&_SearchDescriptions=0&_DictionaryPage=1&_DictionaryId=1&_SearchFor=.

Galbraith, Daniel. "Meter, Prosody and Performance: Evidence from the Faroese Ballads." *Nordic Journal of Linguistics* 42 (2019): 227–61.

Galvin, Seán Carroll. "The Many Faces of Satiric Ballads in the Faroe Islands: Identity Formation, National Pride and Charter for Everyday Life." PhD Thesis, Indiana University, 1989.

Glauser, Jürg. "What Is Dated, and Why? Saga Dating in the Histories of Old Norse-Icelandic Literature." In *Dating the Sagas: Reviews and Revisions*, edited by Else Mundal, 9–30. Copenhagen: Museum Tusculanum Press, 2013.

González Campo, Mariano. *Baladas épicas feroesas*. Tórshavn: Fróðskapur, 2008.

Grundtvig, Svend, ed. *Danmarks gamle Folkeviser*. 12 vols. Copenhagen: Selskabet til den danske Literaturs Fremme, 1853–1976.

Grundtvig, Svend, and Jørgen Bloch, eds. "Bragdar Tættir." In *Føroya kvæði: Corpus Carminum Færoensium*, vol. 5, 136–56. Universitetsjubilæets danske Samfund 427. Copenhagen: Akademisk forlag, 1968.

——, eds. *Føroya kvæði: Corpus Carminum Færoensium*. Vols. 1–6. Copenhagen: Munksgaard, 1941–1972.

Hammershaimb, V. U. "Færøisk sproglære." *Annaler for nordisk oldkyndighed og historie* (1854): 233–316.

——. *Færöiske Kvæder*. Vol. 2. Copenhagen: Berlings, 1855.

——. *Færøsk anthologi: Tekst samt historisk og grammatisk indledning*. Vol. 1. Copenhagen: Møllers, 1891.

——. *Sjúrðar Kvæði*. Copenhagen: Det nordiske Literatur-Samfund, 1851.

Hammershaimb, V. U., and Jakob Jakobsen. *Færøsk anthologi: Ordsamling og register*. Vol. 2. Samfund til udgivelse af gammel nordisk litteratur. Copenhagen: Møller, 1891.

Hansen, Sólfinn. *Endurreisn Kvæðanna*. Tórshavn: Faroe University Press, 2006.

Heggstad, L., and H. Grüner Nielsen, eds. *Utsyn yver gamall norsk folkevisedikting*. Kristiania [Oslo]: Norli, 1912.

Home Rule Act of the Faroe Islands, Pub. L. No. 137 (1948). https://www.government.fo/en/the-government/the-home-rule-act.

Isaksen, Jógvan. "Kvadene." In *Færøsk litteraturs historie 1298–1950: Fra middelalderen til det 21. århundrede*, vol. 1, 19–44. Copenhagen: Marselius, 2017.

Jacobsen, Jørgen-Frantz. *Tekster til den færøske folkevise-dans*. Copenhagen: Gyldendalske boghandel, 1927.

Jacobsen, M. A. *Úr bókmentasögu okkara*. Tórshavn: Færø Amtstidende, 1921.

Jonsson, Bengt R. "Oral Literature, Written Literature: The Ballad and Old Norse Genres." In *The Ballad and Oral Literature*, edited by Joseph Harris, 139–70. Cambridge: Harvard University Press, 1991.

Jonsson, Bengt R., Svale Solheim, and Eva Danielson, eds. *The Types of the Scandinavian Medieval Ballad: A Descriptive Catalogue*. Skrifter utgivna av svenskt visarkiv 5. Stockholm: Svenskt visarkiv, 1978.

Jonsson, Bengt R., Margareta Jersild, and Sven-Bertil Jansson, eds. *Sveriges medeltida ballader*. Stockholm: Svenskt visarkiv, 1983–2001.

Kamban, Brynhild. *Kenn mær einki um: Kyn, frásagnarviðurskifti og frábrigdi í Sjúrðarkvæðunum*. Setursrit 11. Tórshavn: Fróðskapur, 2020.

Kjær, Ivar. "Jørgen Bloch: Philologist and Record Scholar." In *History, Manuscripts, Indexes*, vol. 7 in *Føroya kvæði: Corpus Carminum Færoensium*, edited by Michael Chesnutt and Kaj Grundtvig Larsen, 3–9. Universitetsjubilæets danske Samfund 540. Copenhagen: Reitzel, 1996.

Kleiner, Yuri, and Dmitry Piotrovsky. "From Epic to Ballad: The Faroese 'Sjúrður Cycle.'" *Scandinavian Philology* 17 (2019): 134–45.

Korecká, Lucie. "Óðin Stoyttist í Jørðina Niður: Magic and Myth in the Faroese Ballads." In *Ballads: New Approaches / Kvæði: nýggj sjónarmið*, edited by Malan Marnersdóttir, Eyðun Andreassen, Sanna A. Dahl, Tina K. Jakobsen, and Erling Isholm, 327–54. Annales Societatis Scientiarum Færoensis Supplementum 69. Tórshavn: Fróðskapur, 2018.

Kringvarp Føroya. "Dansival: Kvæðasending í útvarpinum." https://kvf.fo/dansival?sid=171404.

í Króki, Jóannes. *Sandoyarbók*. Edited by Rikard Long. Vols. 1–2. Tórshavn: Mentunargrunnur Føroya Løgtings, 1968–1982.

Landstad, M. B., ed. *Norske folkeviser*. Christiania [Oslo]: Tönsbergs, 1853.

Larsen, Kaj. "Index of Informants." In *History, Manuscripts, Indexes*, vol. 7 of *Føroya kvæði: Corpus Carminum Færoensium*, edited by Michael Chesnutt and Kaj Larsen, 151–58. Universitetsjubilæets danske Samfund 540. Copenhagen: Reitzel, 1996.

Lassen, Annette, ed. *Det norrøne og det nationale: Studier i brugen af Islands gamle litteratur i nationale sammenhænge i Norge, Sverige, Island, Storbritannien, Tyskland og Danmark*. Reykjavík: Stofnun Vigdísar Finnbogadóttur í erlendum tungumálum, 2008.

Lockwood, W. N. *Die färöischen Sigurdlieder nach der 'Sandoyarbók': Mit Grammatik und Glossar*. Tórshavn: Føroya Fróðskaparfelag, 1983.

Lyngbye, Hans Christian, ed. *Færøiske Qvæder om Sigurd Fofnersbane og hans Æt: Med et Anhang*. Randers, 1822.

Margeson, Sue. "The Vǫlsung Legend in Medieval Art." In *Medieval Iconography and Narrative: A Symposium*, edited by Flemming G. Andersen, Esther Nyholm, Marianne Powell, and Flemming Talbo Stubkjær, 183–211. Odense: Odense University Press, 1980.

Marnersdóttir, Malan. "From Oral Poetry to Rap in the Faroes." In *From Oral Tradition to Rap: Literatures of the Polar North*, edited by Karen Langgård and Kirsten Thisted, 39–62. Nuuk: Ilisimatusarfik/Atuagkat, 2011.

———. "Women and Ballads: The Representation of Women in Faroese Ballad Tradition." *Scandinavica* 49 (2010): 27–48.

Marnersdóttir, Malan, and Turið Sigurðardóttir. *Føroysk bókmentasøga*. 2 vols. Tórshavn: Nám, 2011–2023.

Matras, Chr. *Føroysk bókmentasøga*. Copenhagen: Føroya málfelag, 1935.

Matras, Christian, ed. *J. H. Schrøters optegnelser af Sjúrðar kvæði: Ny kgl. Samling 345, 8°*. Færoensia: Textus et investigationes 3. Copenhagen: Munksgaard, 1951.

McKinnell, John. "The Sigmundr/Sigurðr Story in an Anglo-Saxon and Anglo-Norse Context." In *Medieval Nordic Literature in Its European Context*, edited by Else Mundal, 50–77. Oslo: Dreyer, 2015.

Ney, Agneta. *Bland ormar och drakar: Hjältemyt och manligt ideal i berättertraditioner om Sigurd Fafnesbane*. Lund: Nordic Academic, 2017.

Nolsøe, Mortan. "The Faroese Balladry." In *Kvæðagreinir*, edited by Eyðun Andreassen, 63–67. Tórhavn: Føroyamálsdeildin, 1988.

——. "Faroese Balladry." In *Løgini / Melodies*, vol. 8 of *Føroya kvæði: Corpus Carminum Færoensium*, edited by Marianne Clausen, 17–29. Universitetsjubilæets danske Samfund 559. Hoyvík: Stiðin, 2003.

——. "The Faroese Heroic Ballad and Its Relations to Other Genres." In *Kvæðagreinir*, edited by Eyðun Andreassen, 68–73. Tórhavn: Føroyamálsdeildin, 1988.

——. "The Heroic Ballad in Faroese Tradition." In *Kvæðagreinir*, edited by Eyðun Andreassen, 102–119. Tórhavn: Føroyamálsdeildin, 1988.

——. "Noen betraktninger om forholdet mellom ballade och sagaforelegg." In *Kvæðagreinir*, edited by Eyðun Andreassen, 54–62. Tórhavn: Føroyamálsdeildin, 1988.

——. "Some Problems Concerning the Development of the Faroese Heroic Ballad." *Jahrbuch für Volksliedforschung* 17 (1972): 87–93.

Novotná, Marie. "Role of the Body: Scandinavian Ballads vs. Old Norse Literature." In *Ballads: New Approaches / Kvæði: nýggj sjónarmið*, edited by Malan Marnersdóttir, Eyðun Andreassen, Sanna A. Dahl, Tina K. Jakobsen, and Erling Isholm, 293–305. Annales Societatis Scientiarum Færoensis Supplementum 69. Tórshavn: Fróðskapur, 2018.

Fróðskaparsetur Føroya. Orðkort. Accessed January 24, 2025. https://sedlasavn.setur.fo/.

O'Neil, Wayne A. "The Oral-Formulaic Structure of the Faroese *Kvæði*." *Fróðskaparrit* 18 (1970): 59–68.

Opielka, Andrea Susanne. "'At få dansen under foden': udfordringer og chancer ved balladens tolkning i dansen." In *Ballads: New Approaches / Kvæði: nýggj sjónarmið*, edited by Malan Marnersdóttir, Eyðun Andreassen, Sanna A. Dahl, Tina K. Jakobsen, and Erling Isholm, 27–48. Annales Societatis Scientiarum Færoensis Supplementum 69. Tórshavn: Fróðskapur, 2018.

——. *Danse- og sanglege på Færøerne: Oprindelse – udbredelse – nutidig tradition*. Translated by Kirsten Brix. Annales Societatis Scientiarum Færoensis, supplementum 53. Tórshavn: Fróðskapur, 2011.

——. "Færøerne og den færøske dans: en rejse gennem tiden." In *I fråst och i kålle: Texter från nordiskt balladmöte, Växjö*, edited by Karen Eriksson. Växjö: Växjö universitet, 2008. Accessed January 24, 2025. https://www.diva-portal.org/smash/get/diva2:208884/FULLTEXT02.pdf.

——. "Tanzspiele als wichtiger Bestandteil der färöischen Tanztradition." *European Journal of Scandinavian Studies* 41 (2011): 152–72.

Patursson, Jóannes. *Föroysk kvæði: Um brögd norðmanna ættarinnar úti og heima*. Oslo: Noregs Ungdomslag, 1925.

——. *Kvæðabók I–V*. Tórshavn: Kostað og útgivið hevur Føroya løgting, 1922.

Simonsen, Kim. "Literature, Imagining and Memory in the Formation of the Nation: Travel Writing, Canonisation and the Formation of a National Self-Image in the Faroe Islands." PhD Thesis, Roskilde University, 2012.

Skårup, Povl. "Kilderne til de færøske viser om Karl den Store." *Fróðskaparrit* 15 (1966): 31–69.

Smith-Dampier, E. M., ed. *Sigurd the Dragon-Slayer: A Faroese Ballad Cycle*. Oxford: Blackwell, 1934.

Solberg, Olav. "Editionen von Balladen und Volksliedern im Norden." In *Geschichte der Edition in Skandinavien*, edited by Paula Henriksson and Christian Jauss, 97–123. Bausteine zur Geschichte der Edition 4. Berlin: De Gruyter, 2013.

Svabo, Jens Chr. *Svabos færøske visehaandskrifter*. Edited by Chr. Matras. Vol. 1. Samfund til udgivelse af gammel nordisk litteratur 59. Copenhagen: Bianco Lunos, 1939.

——. *Svabos glossar til færøske visehaandskrifter*. Edited by Chr. Matras. Vol. 2. Samfund til udgivelse af gammel nordisk litteratur 60. Copenhagen: Bianco Lunos, 1943.

Syndergaard, Larry E. *English Translations of the Scandinavian Medieval Ballads: An Analytical Guide and Bibliography*. NIF Publications 30. Turku: The Nordic Institute of Folklore, 1995.

Ţăranu, Cătălin. "The Elusive Nature of Germanic Heroic Poetry: A Rhizomatic Model." *Networks and Neighbours* 1 (2013): 44–66.

Vedel, Anders Sørensen. "It Hundrede vduaalde Danske Viser, Om allehaande Merckelige Krigs Bedrifft, oc anden seldsom Euentyr, som sig her vdi Riget, ved Gamle Kemper, Naffnkundige Konger oc ellers forneme Personer begiffuet haffuer, aff arilds tid indtil denne neruærendis Dag." Early European Books: Printed Sources to 1700. Ribben: Brun, Hans, 1591. https://www-proquest-com.pva.uib.no/eeb/docview/2090326277?&imgSeq=10.

Vedel, Anders Sørensen, and Peder Syv. *Et hundrede udvalde Danske Viser om allehaande merkelige Krigs-Bedrivt, oc anden selsom Eventyr, som sig her udi Riget ved gamle Kæmper, navnkundige Konger, og ellers fornemme Personer begivet haver, af Arilds Tid til denne Nærværende Dag: Forøgede Med*. Copenhagen: Bockenhoffer, 1695.

De Vries, Jan. *Studien over Færøsche balladen*. Haarlem: Tjeenk Willink, 1915.

Weyhe, Eivind. *Hentzasavn: Kvæðasavnið hjá Jóannesi í Króki frá 1819*. Tórshavn: Faroe University Press, 2011.

Wikman, K. R. V. "Bröllop." In *Kulturhistorisk leksikon for nordisk middelalder*, vol. 2, 306–17. Helsingfors: Örn, 1957.

Wylie, Jonathan. *The Faroe Islands: Interpretations of History*. Lexington: University Press of Kentucky, 1987.